UNBOTHERED

BREAK DOWN THE BOULDERS BETWEEN YOU AND YOUR TRUE POTENTIAL

ANGELA RUMMANS

Unbothered: Break down the boulders between you and your true potential.

Note to readers:
I have tried to recreate events, locales, and conversations from my memories. In order to maintain their anonymity, in some instances I have changed the names of individuals, places, and some identifying characteristics and details such as physical properties, occupations, and places of residence.

The contents of this book are not intended to replace the advice of a trained and licensed psychological professional. For those seeking any type of treatment, I strongly advise my readers to consult a qualified professional.

Although the author and publisher have made every effort to ensure that the information in this book was correct at press time, the author and publisher do not assume and hereby disclaim any liability to any party for any loss, damage, or disruption caused by errors or omissions, whether such errors or omissions result from negligence, accident, or any other cause.

ISBN 978-1-7331611-2-1 (print)
ISBN 978-1-7331611-1-4 (e-book)

First edition.

Cover design by Tara Berg @tarabergdesign
Cover photography by Jenn Ashley Photography www.JennAshley.com
Cover photo hair by Bradley Leake @hairbybradleyleake
Cover photo makeup by Jared Lipscomb @jaredlips
Editing and book layout by Rooted in Writing www.RootedinWriting.com

Subjects: Biography and Autobiography. Personal Memoirs. Self-Help and Self Development. Family and Relationships. Sports Psychology. Personal Growth. Love and Romance. Happiness.

For the strongest woman I will ever know, my grandmother, Dot Rummans. And for my guardian angels, Laura Rummans and Sarah Creech.

To my family for encouraging me to chase after even my wildest dreams.

And finally, to my world, TRC.

A special thank you to the producers and casting directors for changing my life forever. I cannot express in words how grateful I am for you. Thank you for believing in me: RM, AG, RK, and Fly on the Wall Entertainment.

If this book does anything at all, I hope that it inspires you and shows you that anything in life is possible.

You have to be brave with your life so that others can be brave with theirs.

— KATHERINE CENTER

CONTENTS

1

UNBOTHERED PART ONE

J une twenty-something, 2018 was the day everything changed. I, along with fifteen other complete strangers, would soon become known to a whole new audience on a national level.

Eight of us were lined up in two rows of four on a stage in front of a live audience.

We were eight very confused and anxious strangers from every walk of life. Strangers then, we would become a sort of dysfunctional family that I'll be stuck with for the rest of my life. For better or for worse.

We knew nothing about one another. We hadn't seen each other until that very moment, and we weren't allowed to speak to each other just yet. There would be plenty of time for that over the next three months.

Though I could feel the anxiety, excitement, and tension of the others around me, inside I was—for the most part—numb. Picture an EKG. If emotions could be tracked like a heartbeat, mine were flatlining. When most would be going sporadic and some probably off the charts, mine were a flat-lined, deafening *beep*.

In front of us sat a lively audience. Rows and rows of

familiar faces, the past seasons' greats. We stood shoulder to shoulder in our two lines of four. Naturally, because of the four-inch heels I was wearing in addition to my 5'10" frame, I was placed in the back row.

I heard someone in the audience mutter, "She ate a grape today."

Oh, how I love backhanded compliments, I thought. If only in that moment, I knew what I had coming, the ruthless scrutiny that would soon follow me . . . forever. Life always seems to have its way of subtly foreshadowing our futures. At least my own life has.

To our left, a doorway confirmed it. This was it.

We were moments away from our first filming and moving into our new home for the summer—completely isolated from the outside world with zero communication from anyone apart from the other houseguests.

If you're already a fan of the show, you'll know that Haleigh never forgot to compliment the host on her striking beauty. It wasn't an eviction ceremony without at least some sort of acknowledgment. And Haleigh wasn't exaggerating. Julie might be gorgeous on television, but she's even more stunning and flawless in person. Breathtaking, to say the least.

Julie walked onstage to greet the audience in her black dress and heels, and I immediately felt way underdressed in my ripped-up Adriano Goldschmied jeans and white linen crop top.

"Good evening," Julie began, instantly quieting the crowd. "Welcome to the two-night premiere event. When . . ."

As she went on, my mind wandered off to an earlier time, to what would be the most important, life-changing audition of my entire life.

* * *

Instantly, the oxygen in the air seemed like it had been sucked out of the room—or perhaps my lungs hadn't been conditioned for the long, steady exhale I needed to clear out the subconscious chatter and relax my mind. It was a skill I learned in yoga that I constantly had to remind myself to use: just breathe, in through the nose and out through the mouth.

In Los Angeles, the smog-filled, oxygen-deprived air always had a way of adding a little something extra to the already high-strung Hollywood pressure. Chasing fame and fortune around aimlessly, mixed with the tainted air, causes not only a lack of oxygen to the brain, but a lack of sense of purpose too. It's enough to drive even the best of them—us—completely batshit crazy.

I see it every day, the life being sucked out of humans inhabiting this city of "angels." Angels? No. I'd say more like strung-out zombies, teetering on the fence that separates rehab from their next big role or gig. At least for those who don't have a yoga instructor personally up their asses four times a week, chanting, "In through the nose, out through the mouth."

Surely some of these Hollywood folk know a bit about the so-called added pressure to "make it" in Hollywood. I can promise you, though, that all of them think they have the gold medal when it comes to handling this pressure.

As for me, I can say with a pretty good level of certainty that I know all too much about pressure. If I close my eyes and take a deep breath, those memories come flooding into my mind like a tidal wave slamming into the coastline. Just like they had on the day of that unbeknownst life-changing audition.

The odd part, however, is that I can still so vividly remember how I handled that pressure during this life-changing moment; it was by not feeling "it," or really anything at all. As *big* as this moment was, I was emotionally, mentally, and somewhat physically numb. Unfortunately, I have to admit that more times than not, when it came time for me to perform under pressure, numbness was the familiar.

Sitting down to this audition, it began like any other.

"So, Angela, you're twenty-six and you're from, let's see here, Hilton Head Island, South Carolina! I hear it's absolutely wonderful there. My parents have a vacation home in Shipyard, I think it's called? So, are people in the south really as nice as they say?"

Suddenly, I felt something churning in the pit of my stomach. I thought for a moment it was the venti cold brew with an added double shot about go right through me, or maybe it was the scar tissue shifting around in my abdomen from a tear in the muscles I'd acquired as a young gymnast.

Either way, with my fists clenched and my nails dug into my palms, I forced out the fake smile I'd perfected over the years. The words snuck out.

"Yeah. Mm-hmm, real, *real* nice."

The memories of Frank came rolling in like one of South Carolina's afternoon summertime storms.

F-ing Frank . . .

* * *

Julie turned to us. "The first four houseguests may enter the house. Head on in," she said with her timeless smile.

As I was left standing in front of the audience, waiting to enter the house, there was a moment there that felt so familiar, it was practically déjà vu.

It was the summer of 2012, and I was at the pole vault Olympic Trials finals. I remember standing on the runway, pole in hand. There was no adrenaline. No butterflies. Absolutely nothing but a cold numbness in the pit of my stomach during that moment. I remember staring down the bar sitting at 13'11" (4.25 meters), the opening height of the competition. An easy height I had cleared numerous times.

I looked up at my coach and my mom, sitting side by side in the packed stadium of historic Hayward Field. All I could remember thinking was that I couldn't let them down.

"That leaves JC, Angela . . ." Her voice trailed off. "The house is yours! Head on in!"

Cheers all around. I grabbed my black duffel bag with all the belongings I'd have for the rest of the summer.

Deep breath. Refocus.

At the Olympic Trials, all I had to do was relax, drive out of the back, stand up, and jump.

Nine, eight, seven, six, five, four, three, two, one, and jump!

The double doors to the house shut behind me.

There was no turning back now.

FIRST IMPRESSIONS

"Angela! Please go to the diary room!" A voice came over the loudspeaker, echoing the words into every corner of every room in our house.

We had only been in the house a matter of hours at this point. I sat still, not moving a muscle. I wasn't used to this robotic voice, which for some reason got the name "Bob" later down the road.

I shot a confused look at my newest friend and ally, Rachel Swindler. My mind temporarily escaped me. For a split second I could have sworn it sounded like that persisting voice that would emerge inside my head from time to time.

"Are you gonna go, or . . . ?" Rachel said in one of her character voices. She looked back at me, equally confused as to why I hadn't bothered making any attempt to get up off the bed.

"Oh yep, I gotta go to the diary room, duh," I said as my mind refocused back to the present.

I exited the blue room, making my way to the diary room door. The voice on the loudspeaker, Bob, sounded so strangely familiar, like the little voice that shouted a much-needed warning at me every so often. I thought about the last time I had heard that little obscure voice in my head and how grateful I was to have heard it and listened to it.

* * *

It was only a few months back, a couple weeks before my twenty-sixth birthday. I was sitting in the waiting room of the dentist's office, filling out the new patient paperwork. Name: Angela Rummans. DOB: March 23, 1992. I scribbled as fast as my hand could write, annoyed at this packet of useless busy work I had to do for a simple teeth-whitening appointment. I reached the blank asking for my address.

"Skip it. Don't write it," that tiny voice chimed in, unannounced and out of nowhere.

I still don't know why, but for once in my life, thank God, I listened. I scribbled down an inaccurate home address as a dark unsettledness washed over me. It was an address I had lived in a few leases back.

A matter of moments later, I was startled when the dentist stepped out from behind the doorway and peered into the bleak waiting room. I sat still, legs crossed; I didn't move or say a word. His eyes closely examined me from under the dental headpiece he wore. He began scanning me up and down, analyzing every inch of me. His gaze moved slowly from my face down to my chest, hips, legs, all the way to the floor where my Fendi purse sat at my feet. Then slowly all the way back up to meet my eyes.

This moment of silence lasted far beyond my level of comfort. I sat, still frozen and now on edge. I stared back at Dr. U. as my stomach turned over on itself. Uneasily, I watched as the corners of his lips slowly rose.

"I'll call you back in just a minute," he finally spoke as he turned away, disappearing into one of the rooms.

* * *

I pressed the circular silver metal button to the diary room door. It lit up green, granting me access to the sacred BB diary room. I walked down the short hallway, through another door, and sat down on the black, crushed-velvet chair. The set lights shone brightly in my face.

The chair didn't recline horizontally like the one in the dentist office that Friday afternoon. There was nothing pinning my head down in here. I was safe, but I was alone in this room, the same way I was that day. Despite my safety, the lights in the diary room still evoked the terror that ensued as I stared helplessly into that solitary overhead dental light.

Both the laughing gas and the teeth-whitening machine held my head down to the headrest, pinning me there while restricting almost all movement. I felt myself slipping under. I couldn't fight the anesthesia any longer. I had given it everything I had.

I told myself over and over, *Stay with it. Stay here, Ang. Just hold on. Be brave.* It wasn't enough.

The nurses had all left for the day. The dentist and I were the only two people left in the entire dental office. A shadow appeared in my peripheral vision as the dentist entered the room. He flipped each switch one by one, turning out every ceiling light. The only light left was the dental light overhead, illuminating my face. I smelled the cigar on his breath as he leaned over me. His hand moved from his shoulder down to my chest, slipping underneath my shirt.

He started to say something . . .

* * *

I brought myself back to the present, saying out loud, "That's right, first impressions, my first impression of the houseguests. Um . . ."

I looked into the camera lens and tried to refocus on my first diary room session.

"Back to what I was saying. Uh, well," I uttered, trying to recall any of the names of the houseguests.

I was blanking. I could hardly recall a single name.

"There are quite a few *big* personalities. But everyone seems pretty cool so far," I said, bluffing.

First impressions, first impressions. I rewound as far as I could back through the live feeds of my life.

My very first, first impression . . .

Way before this show, way before modeling, way before I became known as a pole vaulter, I was just a little girl. I think we forget that we were all just children at one point. A blank canvas. That we all had to learn and work to get to where we are today.

It's our journey that sculpts us, but it is not to be confused with what defines us. It shapes us into the person we are by the life lessons it instills in us. Before we can become great, we must learn. The hardships, the heartbreaks, the successes, the failures—we learn from them and we grow.

For me, my journey began with a sport.

Gymnastics: my sport, my identity, and soon, my world.

It's a sport that, if you allow it, *will* become your identity. Sure enough, I let it, and it did. I was just a youngster, naive and vulnerable.

It's a true blessing I was able to learn this lesson at a relatively young age: We are not defined by our successes or our failures. We are not defined by what we do, whether it's our sport or our occupation.

We are who we are, and ultimately, we are what we love. Who we are and what we love is ever changing and evolving, just like you and me. Change, while it can be scary as hell, signifies both learning and growth. Regardless of your aspirations, no matter what you desire to be great at, change is essential on the journey to become great at whatever that may be.

At age four, I aspired to be a great gymnast one day.

I believe it was fate that put me in the Hilton Head Island Gymnastics Academy when I was only four years old. Well, actually my brother's seventh birthday party did, but it felt like fate.

It was an insulated steel warehouse with no air-conditioning, located on the north end of the island. The floors were freshly painted a shiny, vivid yellow. The bright, royal-blue mats were all brand new. The place smelled like a combination of fresh paint, rubber, and new leather.

In my eyes, the gym was a giant playground—my dreamland. There were bars, beams, the floor, and multiple vaults! I wanted to swing from the highest bars and dig down to the bottom of the massive foam pits full of pink, yellow, and light blue cubes.

I was fearless as a child and constantly pushed the limits. I climbed on top of the highest balance beam and dove head-first into the foam pits.

It was love.

3

MORE THAN MEETS THE EYE

They say takes a mere seven seconds to make a first impression. But who the hell is "they" and what gives them this all-authoritative title?

It is not me, because I would say from personal experience that it's taken about half that time before someone's labeled me as the "approachable bitch."

Sixteen of us, including myself, sat shoulder to shoulder around the semicircular, orange-and-green couch in the living room. The first and last place I would sit during my stay on season 20.

I'm what I like to call an observer. Others often use the term "standoffish bitch," with an occasional "entitled" thrown in there more often than not. I wasn't the loudest in the room or even remotely close. That was never me. I made sure I wasn't the quietest either.

Coming from a family that's extremely non-expressive, I consider the four of us—my mom, dad, brother, and yours truly—to be bilingual. English isn't our first language. Body language is. We have never been the type to express ourselves verbally or even talk about our emotions for that matter. I'm not sure if us Rummans are even physically capable.

We express ourselves through facial expressions, body movements, the tone and volume of our voices, and even our posture. Why talk about our emotions when we can just make each other figure them out, right? *Wrong.*

I used to be able to take one look at my mom, sitting way up in bleachers watching my gymnastics practice, and tell whether or not she was happy with me at any given moment. Arms crossed, lips pursed: she was either irritable or on edge. Hands clasped, sitting forward: she was anxious.

One by one, we introduced ourselves to the others in the house. I sat quietly, still observing, gathering insight into what the others might be thinking or feeling in this moment.

Steve hadn't stopped sweating. JC's foot tapped incessantly, possibly from nerves.

Amid our introductions, no one knew it, but the first competition of the season had already begun: who could be the absolute loudest in the house. Needless to say, I didn't feel like participating in this one.

I continued to sit back and quietly watch, my ears eager and my eyes peeled in the most nonchalant way. I focused on the way each houseguest held themselves, their attitudes when they addressed the others. The way the guys fidgeted with their necklines and the girls flipped and stroked their hair.

There were several houseguests I pinpointed right off the bat. They sat scattered around the circular couch. What we had in common was a similar energy. I had gathered all I needed to be able to align myself with all the right ones.

I'll be the first to admit that there have been a few times my first impression analysis totally missed the mark.

There was one in particular: fucking Frank.

* * *

Other than my father, Coach Frank—a former Marine and gymnastics coach—was the first authoritative male to enter my life. I was nine. He made an impeccable first impression with the gym moms, to say the least. With his olive skin, dark hair, and charismatic demeanor, he knew *all* the right things to say.

I couldn't help but notice the spectator attendance at practices from all the mothers seemed to grow exponentially during his reign. I had never seen the bleachers more populated. At any given time, the attention all seemed to fixate in a certain area of the gym, which ironically also happened to be where Frank was located.

"Mrs. Kingsley, your daughter's not on vault." I wish I had the balls back then to say it.

He was a conversationalist. Engaging and courteous when he needed to be, he knew when to turn on the charm. The gym moms seemed delighted to have something so visually pleasing to entertain their eyes while their kids practiced cartwheels. What they didn't know was there was much more there than met the eye.

Through the perception of a young and malleable mind, Frank seemed like he knew what he was doing. He ran a tight ship, and he was extremely knowledgeable about the sport.

We all thought he was the perfect fit at first. If only perfection resembled a square peg in a round hole.

Frank's coaching style was nothing short of intense. Our practices were structured for the first time in my life. Playtime, or "open gym" we called it, was a thing of the past. He meant business.

The former Marine adamantly demanded respect. Underneath his army-green USMC T-shirts and his jet-black hair, it wasn't long before his true colors began to show.

Inside the gym, away from the parentals, his personality varied greatly.

Bipolar? Split personality? Schizophrenic? Not to be insensitive to these unfortunate and very real personality disorders, all of which were quite possible in his case and fit the bill perfectly.

The moment he stepped into the gym, far away enough from the parents, he became Frank the Marine, like a switch had flipped.

His filter faded, and his rude and sarcastic sense of humor came out. Nine times out of ten, us children didn't find being the butt of the joke all too humorous. But he did.

Frank's music of choice: Metallica, played at full volume to a gym full of children. A bit off-putting, in my nine-year-old opinion.

As a young gymnast around nine years old, there were quite a few firsts here for me. It was the first time I was subjected to verbal abuse, the first time I felt emotional abuse, and the first time I had to endure physical abuse. The worst part about it all was not only did we all think we deserved what we got, but in my mind, he ultimately became the representation of male authority.

Frank had a daughter named Sadie, who was often present at practices, especially during the summer months. She was younger than us, maybe by a couple of years. With her olive skin and black hair, she was like a fun-sized Pocahontas.

Unlike Pocahontas, she seemed fragile and almost *too* skinny. And though Pocahontas had no problems diving off large cliffs and tumbling down hills, Sadie didn't seem to want to have anything to do with tumbling or jumping off anything at all.

It was blatantly obvious to a bunch of eight- and nine-year-olds that Frank had forced gymnastics on her. He didn't seem to care that she was terrified of the sport or that it was torture for her. We all felt sorry for her as we witnessed Frank force her to try new skills all the time; despite her fear, she would usually comply. At even the first sign of unwillingness, he would lock her in the un-air-conditioned bathroom and turn off all the lights. We could hear her screams and cries. It was painful.

That was only the beginning with Frank.

4

THE METALLIC PINK CAMEL TOE

At some point while competing in the first real competition of season twenty, when full-sized doors and chopping blocks the size of JC's body were flying straight at me trying to knock me off the foam surfboard I was standing on ten feet off the ground, I realized I might have made a mistake.

I stood there on that surfboard in pretty much a three-point stance, wearing a metallic-pink unitard, wondering (a) how bad my camel toe was right now and (b) if I even *wanted* to win this competition.

It wasn't that long ago at all that the competitive side of me *still* felt I had something to prove. Despite everything I had accomplished in my athletic career, for me it had never been enough. It's like a sickness, a disease, that I had caught early on in my gymnastics career. The inability to find satiety and the incessant craving for validation. No amount of accolades could ever feed the hunger I felt from needing to prove myself.

I'm not there *yet.* This thought stemmed from a deep-rooted belief that I was not enough.

They say the truth sets you free. And the truth was that what had motivated that intense drive to achieve was rooted deep in my childhood. Years went by, almost twenty, and I still felt like there was a thirst that could only be quenched by either accomplishments or the validation of none other than my parents. This burning desire became the forefront of every decision I made and orchestrated my life for so long.

Gymnastics was the seed of this deep-rooted problem. At its essence, gymnastics is a validation-based sport. After every routine or performance, we either look to our coaches, hoping for a "not bad" or a "nice" (if we're lucky), or look to the judges to give us a numerical evaluation. I confused this evaluation with my self-worth. When a judge held up the sign with 9.25 out of 10, the perfectionist I grew to be said, "I wasn't enough. It wasn't perfect." Tenth by tenth, as my score dropped with each deduction below the perfect ten, my self-esteem dropped as well, until it became my way of measuring my self-worth.

Years later, around my mid-twenties, I spent my time and even my own hard-earned dollars digging into my subconscious with the guidance of a licensed therapist to get to the root of some of my problems. It didn't surface easily; this was no pimple ready to pop.

I had to dig this one out to gain the self-awareness I needed to rationalize these thoughts. When I did finally come to this realization, I was finally able put the idea that I needed to prove myself to gain validation to rest for good. Just like that, with this acknowledgement I was able to move past it.

All I was left with in that moment were my thoughts and memories. As I stood digging my toes into that damn surfboard—my legs, quads, and ass *en fuego*—I didn't need to prove anything to anyone. Success or failure, I was enough, and I was doing this for no one other than myself.

I came here to win this game, and this time I was here to compete for Angela Rummans. The pain inflicted by this never-ending three-point stance was agonizing. *My quads, my calves, my ass*, I thought.

I wanted to give up, but the competitor in me *never* gave up. I figured out almost twenty years ago that our bodies can hang on long after our minds are ready to give up. I knew the place where I could send my mind, where I could get away from the discomfort of all kinds of pain—physical, emotional, mental. It was a place I discovered as a young gymnast. I was Alice, and I called this place "Wonderland."

I repeated the words in my head: *Mind over matter. Don't let go.* These words triggered a memory . . . Fucking Frank.

The memories flooded in. I was nine years old again, and it was our team picture day on a hot summer afternoon.

Before we knew what was going on, he grabbed us one at a time and hung each of our four-foot, fifty-pound bodies from the metal, single-rail bar that sat about nine feet above the ground.

If we fell, we would fall onto a thin, hard four-inch mat. One of those mats might've been sufficient padding on the wall of a gymnasium with a bunch of kids running around and playing dodgeball, but it wasn't enough cushion for a little person to fall on, especially if that person was an nine-year-old child suspended nine feet in the air.

It was like hanging off of a slippery cliff. I was afraid to look down. The only option was to hold on for dear life.

"If any of you spoiled, ungrateful little brats falls before your hands rip and the blood runs down your little arms, you'll have to run laps around this fucking gym until practice is over. Do you hear me?" Frank barked.

"Yes!" we said with a whimper.

Without a delay, Frank exclaimed, "Yes what?"

"Yes sir!" we said in unison, fighting back the tears.

The bar I gripped was cold. The chill was soon replaced with a burning sensation as the tears pricked the corners of my eyes. I looked around at my teammates; not a single one of us had a dry eye now.

It wasn't long before the burning sensation in my hands

turned into a roaring blaze. I could feel my skin beginning to tear from my palms. Blood was beginning to seep from these rips. My arms trembled, my grip beginning to fail me. I heard nothing but sniffles all around me. Though the injuries were superficial, the wounds that were imposed upon us would scar us for the rest of our lives.

Despite the pain and fear, I told myself I would *not* be the first one to fall. I closed my eyes and willed my body to endure. Mind over matter—something else that Frank instilled in me.

There was so much more that Frank was able to ingrain in our "ungrateful little minds," such as the term "spoiled little brats," Frank's favorite three words to call us. This phrase will forever be burned into my memory thanks to Frank.

Let's rewind the tape. Back to the origination of this lovely little phrase on that hot summer afternoon during our team picture day. All my teammates and I were sitting around waiting for our turn to have our pictures done. We sat impatiently, dressed in our long-sleeved, bedazzled competition leotards. Our hair was slicked back and hardened with copious amounts of hairspray. Looking for a way to entertain ourselves while we waited, one of the girls on my team happened to find a whiteboard and a dry-erase marker to go with it.

This quickly became the object of attention. After we had exhausted the usual games of tic-tac-toe and hangman, one of my teammates jokingly wrote "Frank stinks." Just as quickly as the words were written, they were erased. We laughed. And though the joke was fleeting, the memory of what was about to happen is permanently etched into my mind, never to disappear like those two little words had so easily.

We didn't know it, but Frank had been watching us from afar. He had seen those two words written. He had seen them erased. He had heard us laugh at his expense. Though no trace of the words were left on the whiteboard, they might as well have been engraved in large letters into one of the balance beams or written in white chalk across the gym floor.

Frank the Marine loomed over us. This time he was a very different Frank than the one we had been used to. A switch flipped inside of him, and his temper soared. Frank the drill sergeant emerged with all his fury.

Spit flew out of his mouth as he screamed, "Ungrateful brats!"

A slew of derogatory names and vocabulary followed.

Before, we would endure his verbally abusive, not-so-funny jokes at our expense. You know the old saying "sticks and stones may break my bones, but words will never hurt me"? His words did kind of hurt. His words made you feel like shit, but we could always bring ourselves back from it. Somehow, someway, someone would make light of the situation later and make his words sting a little less.

Words weren't enough this time. This time, it was as if he really wanted to break our bones. Or maybe he wanted to break our spirit.

Like laundry out to dry, he hung us from that metal, single-rail bar. One by one. A single row of terrified eight- and nine-year-olds.

The drill sergeant barked, "If any of you spoiled, ungrateful little brats falls before your hands rip and the blood runs down your little arms, you'll have to run laps around this fucking gym until practice is over. Do you hear me?"

At this point, we were incapable of forming words. A mixture of snot and tears streamed down our faces.

I heard the first girl drop. I opened my eyes to see Kara crumpled on the floor. Another girl soon joined her. And then another. It was as if Kara's fall had given the rest of us permission to let go. We were all breathless and shaken, and though there was a small bit of hope in each of us that our punishment was over, Frank loomed over us once again.

"What are you spoiled brats doing? Did I give you permission to let go?"

We looked away from him, fearful to make eye contact with him.

"I *said*, did I give you permission to let go?"

"N-no, sir," a few of us mumbled.

"I can't hear you!"

"*No, sir!*" we all exclaimed at once.

He walked around us, like a shark circling its victims. He examined us. We were a mixture of blood, sweat, and tears.

And then he stood motionless, with his hands clasped behind his back.

"You ungrateful brats need to be taught a lesson. Do you know how lucky you are to have me? I came all the way from Hardeeville just to teach you ungrateful brats some proper gymnastics. Did I have to leave my hometown to coach you all? No. But your mommies insisted that their brats needed a coach like me. A *great* coach.

"Spoiled! All of you! But by the time we're done here, maybe some of you brats will be more appreciative of your coach. Now run around this gym in a single straight line until I tell you to stop. Go! Get up now!" Frank yelled.

Somehow, we managed to get up and run in a single line. We were his little soldiers, for better or for worse.

On any typical summer afternoon, the gym was sweltering. Normally it would reach around ninety-five degrees, but it wasn't uncommon for it climb to over one hundred degrees during the summertime. I don't remember how many laps we managed, but I do remember feeling like I would collapse at any given moment. A trail of little girls had long reached their breaking points; our beet-red faces were covered with a concoction of snot and tears.

Collapse we did, like dominoes. We were spent.

Frank stood before us, his face as red as ours but not from the heat. From pure fury.

"Get up, you little brats! If you weren't so spoiled, you would've lasted longer. Stand against the wall and do a wall sit, now! Go!"

With whatever strength we had left, one by one, we got up and managed to sit with our backs up against the wall and hold it there. My legs burned equally as bad as being on that surfboard. It was a different sparkly leotard I wore, but the same excruciating pain.

My little legs shook. My entire body was in the most pain I had ever felt.

By the time we were allowed to leave practice, everybody was quiet. There was no laughter or smiles or high-fives or well wishes. We were numb physically and emotionally. Pure silence as we walked out. I kept my eyes down. I think everybody just wanted to get home as soon as possible.

When I got home that night, I didn't tell anyone what had happened. They saw my hands. They saw my disheveled hair. They saw my face. They inquired about it, but I just shook my head and retreated to my room. My mom washed my hair in the sink for me that night because the hot water and soap burned my hands too much to touch. She kept asking, but I kept my mouth shut until eventually she stopped.

I didn't tell on Frank because I thought I deserved what I got. I was ashamed of my punishment.

All the fun and joy I felt about gymnastics—gone. For now, this was Frank's rule and gymnastics was scary as hell.

With my palms bound, I went to school the very next day. It was my first day as a third grader.

5

THE GOOD, THE BAD, AND THE UGLY

While my third-grade classmates were meeting their developmental milestones, improving their motor skills and their attention spans, I was training twenty hours a week, and it wasn't long until I began commuting fifteen hours on top of that. As gymnasts, even at nine years old, we're expected to have the maturity and laser-like focus of an eighteen-year-old.

I had reached a level in my gymnastics career that the small gymnastics facility on Hilton Head wasn't able to accommodate, which left me with really only two options. One, switch sports. Or two, join a gym capable of training gymnasts beyond the compulsory levels. The closest one was located in Savannah, GA.

While I couldn't have been more ecstatic to say good fucking riddance to Frank, there was one minor drawback. This new gym was an hour-and-a-half drive from my home in Sea Pines, each way, five times per week. Needless to say, we put a few miles on my mom's Ford Expedition over the next decade.

These next ten years, while competing on various teams at various gyms around Savannah, I had well over twenty—that's right, two-zero—gymnastics coaches. That's twenty-something potential role models I could have had in my life. Wouldn't that have been a lovely little uplifting twist to my story.

Unfortunately for me, I had close to ten to fifteen verbally degrading men and women who told me that I would never be good enough, that I would never amount to anything, that I was too "thick" and needed to slim down or, my personal favorite, that I "suct."

Among these coaches, there were a handful of what I considered good ones mixed in with the bad and the ugly. I'll start with the good—actually the best—and we'll save the worst for last.

The Good

"We cannot know the light without experiencing the darkness."

I was spiraling, sinking downward into the depths of my depression. I was a young teenager in my darkest of hours. Call me dramatic, but to this day it's difficult for me to reminisce about this mentally destructive time in my life. My head was filled with the most toxic thoughts that I sometimes couldn't put out of my mind.

Imagine someone tied your spirit to an anchor and threw it off a ship into a bottomless ocean. Deeper and deeper, you endlessly sink into the depths where no light can penetrate. That's what it felt like. It was like drowning in perpetual darkness.

More than a life raft or a rescue buoy, I needed a person who understood what I was going through. Marie did. Marie was the light that appeared amid the darkness.

Without me having to say a word, she seemed to already know what was going on the inside. She opened up to me about the horrifying coaching situations she had to endure when she had been a gymnast.

She told me stories of training in conditions that were

nothing short of torture. Sneaking out of a certain camp searching for food because she and her teammates were physically starving. Eating toothpaste to dull the hunger pains.

She saved my gymnastics career for the time being and brought me a sense of hope and happiness when I was going through some of the darkest, most miserable moments in my life as a gymnast. She was so much more than just a coach to me. She was a role model and also a friend, and to this day, I follow her on social media. Marie has a beautiful family and a happy life, and she deserves the world and will always have a special place in my heart.

The Bad

Inter arma enim silent leges. In times of war, the law falls silent.

I stuck my landing on what I thought was the *perfect* bar routine.

"Not bad," Nina remarked as she shifted her focus to another one of my teammates.

Not bad! I thought. *That was fucking perfect, you psycho bitch.* I hit all my handstands, stuck my dismount. *What more do you want, lady?*

I stood beside the chalk bucket, sulking. I grabbed the biggest piece of chalk I could find and violently rubbed it against my Reisport grip until it disappeared to dusty smithereens.

If that was not bad, what do you call this, Nina? I thought as I hopped back up on the bars and performed another routine that was far from what *I* considered perfection.

First, I slammed my feet on the ground in my release move, an automatic five-tenth deduction. I missed all four handstands and took not one, but two steps on my dismount.

I looked up at Nina to find her face twisted into a look of disgust. It was the most satisfying thing I had seen all day.

"What in the *hell* was that? Slop!" she shouted. "Do you

really think you're going to qualify for nationals this season? You won't even make it to the state meet with a routine like that! You don't deserve . . ."

I tuned her out as she rambled on with the typical verbal abuse. This time the insults gave me the instant gratification I was searching for.

The only thing I disliked more than Nina was the balance beam. With Nina coaching me on the balance beam, you have yourself a fucking shit show. I'll be the first to admit, I couldn't stay on that damn thing if my life depended on it. Often the life of my uterus did.

Allow me to define a term we often use in gymnastics: "straddling the beam," or its euphemistic counterpart, "splitting the beam."

For those of you that may be unfamiliar, imagine you are performing a skill—a flip, so to say—on the balance beam. Both of your feet leave the beam in unison, and instead of your two feet landing back on the beam, one foot goes to the left side of the beam and the other foot to the right. But guess what does land on the beam? You guessed it! Your crotch, vagina, labia—whatever you want to call it—gets smashed on the beam. Even without balls, it's excruciating.

My acroseries on beam had always been the culprit of this painful phenomenon. "Acro" meaning topmost and "series" meaning a combination of gymnastics skills.

My acroseries consisted of a back-handspring straight into a back-layout step out. It was the most arduous and terrifying skill I had to perform in all my gymnastics career.

I searched, and there really isn't a synonym of the word *hatred* that exists to fully embody the level of resentment I had toward this skill in my beam routine. It was often the first agonizing thought the moment I opened my eyes each morning, and my vagina and I regularly spent all day, every day dreading this stupid skill.

It was any ordinary day at practice, our last event of the

evening. I stood staring down at the beam beneath my feet, contemplating how much longer I could stand here before Nina yelled aloud in her piercing voice to remind me, and everyone else within a fifty-foot radius, that a "hesitation" before my acroseries was a deduction.

"Two tenths," she yelled.

Everything was a damn deduction. If I picked my wedgie or breathed too heavily, it would probably also cause a deduction.

After a subtle eye roll, I closed both eyes and visualized myself performing the skill perfectly. It took everything in me to muster up the courage to throw this damned skill.

I jumped backwards, flipping my body upside down as my hands hit the beam. I stepped down perfectly squared-up, ready to transition into the next part of the skill. So far, so good.

Without hesitation, I began to jump backwards, flipping upside down once again into the layout. This time my hands would not touch the beam—a layout is a complete flip.

As my feet left the ground for the second time, I felt an excruciating pain in my ab. Like someone chucked a throwing knife at me mid-skill and it had sunk into the middle left side of my abdomen. I balked midair as my body crumbled into a tangled mess on the ground beneath the beam. I didn't "split the beam" this time; instead, I tore my ab muscle.

As I laid there, I felt the right side of my abdomen pulsating. I could hardly take a full breath in. Nina began bitching as I slowly began to pick myself off the ground. Every muscle I moved, I felt this invisible knife sinking deeper and deeper into my stomach. I thought I was going to throw up, the pain was so intense. I stood all the way up for a split second and almost immediately doubled back over with pain. I leaned over, placing a hand on each knee, trying to take a full breath in, trying to hold in the tears.

Right when I thought the pain couldn't get any worse in this moment, Nina's screeching voice penetrated my ears.

"What in the hell was that? Why can't you stay on the balance beam? You fall off every routine. What is wrong with you?"

I continued to stand there with my hands planted firmly on my knees, trying to remove any strain in my abdominal region. Still, I couldn't make words.

"Get back up on the beam and finish!" Nina yelled.

I felt every eye in the gym on me. Still doing a damn good job of holding in the tears, somehow, someway, through the pain, I climbed back up on the beam and began again.

I stood at the end of the beam. The next skill in my routine was a switch leap to a shushunova. If you're a gymnast, you'll understand that this skill felt like I was about to attempt actual suicide. A shushunova is essentially a straddle jump, landing on your stomach perpendicular to the beam. I literally had to jump as high as I could in the air, straddle my legs, and land on top of this pulsating pain.

The emotions welled up inside of me. Tears filled my eyes, blinding me. I didn't dare wipe my eyes, letting on that I had broken down. The beam beneath my feet was a wet blur. I took a deep breath and gave it everything I had in me. Mind over matter . . . mind over matter.

Somehow, I finished that routine and made it through the rest of the practice. It was excruciating and scarring, both physically and mentally.

Inter arma enim silent leges, in layman's terms, means to win at all costs. During the short time I spent training under Nina, I performed better than any other time in my gymnastics career. It was the closest I had come to reaching that perfect 10.0. I won almost every meet I competed in, and while I was happy to win, there was no compensation for the mental torture and the verbal abuse we were subjected to as adolescents.

A first-place ribbon wasn't going to heal the scar tissue in the ab I'd torn practically in half. It's still there; to this day, I can feel it, the physical scar tissue that's hardened. The emotional scarring too, it's all just memories now.

This toxic mentality is not uncommon in young athletes, because for many of us, it has been ingrained in us since the very beginning of our athletic careers. To win at all possible costs despite our happiness or our health.

It laid the groundwork of my misery. In the end, nothing is more important than our mental health and our happiness, not a single gold medal or college scholarship.

The Ugly

When I use the term ugly, I am absolutely not referring to a person's physical appearance being aesthetically displeasing. Beauty to me embodies so much more than facial symmetry or whatever today's pop culture finds attractive, a full set of lips or a small waist-to-ass ratio.

Romi was a former Bulgarian gymnast herself and encompassed all of those things, but through my eyes, she was the furthest thing from a beautiful person. She was cold and she was heartless.

It was the first day back to the grind after the Georgia State gymnastics meet, most likely a Monday. Any tension left over from the built-up anticipation seemed to melt away as my teammates and I sat in a circle in the center of the gym floor, casually stretching and chatting with one another.

At promptly four o'clock, the double doors slammed shut as Romi emerged in her shiny purple spandex that she wore three, maybe four out of the five days a week we practiced. This was long before wearing spandex leggings was a thing or counted as socially acceptable pants. Her wiry hair, which closely resembles a brown Brillo pad, bounced as she marched her way straight to the center of the floor before us.

Her hands were planted firmly on her hips, and her nose was so high in the air I could see straight up her nostrils. The judgmental look on her face soon turned to disgust as she began to speak.

"You all suct!" she scoffed looking down upon us.

I often had a hard time understanding Romi due to her thick Bulgarian accent.

I turned to one on my teammates. "D-did she just say we suck?" Without a response, the look on Hannah's face confirmed my question.

"You embarrassed me." There was a long pause. "Each and every one of you. You're all an embarrassment."

Her upper lip curled in disdain. I felt every ounce of happiness being "suct" out of my body.

"I cannot stand to vatch your fat asses perform another sloppy routine."

She looked us up and down and pointed out which of us had thighs too thick and whose butt was too big.

I felt the sharp sting of humiliation. Like prey bitten by a venomous snake, her words infected us with harmful toxins, causing poisonous thoughts to seep into our malleable minds. These thoughts bred lifelong complications and were the origin of my negative and distorted body image. Romi had planted the seeds to what would one day, years down the road, become a full-blown eating disorder.

All it took was that one coach ripping off the blindfold to reveal my own self-awareness. My eyes were wide open to everything, all the negativity and distorted perceptions of myself.

I saw nothing but my flaws and all the things I wanted to change about myself. For the first time in my life, I began to scrutinize myself with critical, dissatisfied eyes.

I pinched the sides of my narrow, size-double-zero hips to measure the thickness of my "love handles." I was disgusted by my lack of a thigh gap and the way my thighs would ever-so-slightly brush against each other when I walked. The appearance of my legs pressed flat against the front seat of my mom's car became more than I could handle.

In my newfound awareness, I recognized the look on my mother's face when she would stand in our front hallway examining herself in our full-length mirror, tugging at her jeans. It was the same critical look Romi had wiped across her face when she would examine us.

"I need to lose five pounds. Just five," my mother would say to herself.

I thought she was crazy. My mom was the most beautiful person in the world to me. She had that effortless, natural Jennifer Aniston type of beauty. But, like a sponge, I absorbed these thoughts as my own.

"If I lost five pounds, would my skills be easier to perform? I think I need to lose five pounds too." As I questioned my body image, I became aware of each calorie I consumed daily.

6

ANYBODY WANT SOME EGGS?

Ten o'clock struck. "Wakey wakey, houseguests!" Bob came over the loudspeaker with the same persuasive tone in his voice. Simultaneously, each of the houseguests pulled the covers over our faces to protect our eyes from the blinding set lights that followed this announcement.

It didn't take long before we all fell into a sort of robotic routine.

"Anybody want some eggs?" Tyler asked aloud, like clock-work, every morning.

I was the only reply. "Not unless it's egg whites," I said, politely declining his offer.

It didn't take long before this question became rhetorical.

"Sorry, babes, yolks today," Tyler replied.

I rolled my eyes sarcastically, trying to force a convincing look of disapproval through my smitten grin.

Same pan, same spatula, same lifeguard standing shirtless, scrambling eggs. Discreetly watching his morning routine became my favorite part of my morning routine. I sat in the same middle swivel chair, observing him while ignoring others.

The only thing that differed this morning was the color of the bandana tied around his forehead holding in the few flyaways from his sun-bleached bun. I sat staring, enjoying this shirtless view probably a bit too much. I spun myself in several circles as the smell of eggs filled the kitchen, masking the smell of coffee. The same way it had yesterday, and the day before yesterday, and the day before that. Every. Damn. Day.

Routines were something I was all too familiar with. The monotony brought it all back, just as clear as day.

Once upon a time, my life was reduced down to one big routine in order to perform the perfect routine, the perfect 10.0. While we strive for that perfect score, perfectionism becomes ingrained in us, and soon our self-worth assimilates to that same ten-point scale.

Gymnastics is one of the few sports that takes points away from us. Each deduction, tenth by tenth, my score slowly dropped, as did my self-esteem.

Over the years, this "routine to perform the perfect routine" had become my prison and slowly my hell. I was trapped in a sort of purgatory between two worlds: wanting to become the gymnast my parents told me I could be and longing to just be *fucking* normal.

When I talk about the bigger routine, I don't mean the minute-and-a-half floor routine or the sixty-second beam routine my poor uterus so dreaded. I'm talking about the weekly routine, the purgatory, that repeated itself fifty-two times a year.

As each mechanical fifty-two-week year passed and I climbed from Level 7 all the way up to Level 10, the weekly routine only got worse. The twenty hours I spent weekly in the gym and fifteen hours in the car increased, as did the hours of schoolwork when I began taking college-credit classes in high school.

Tenth grade rolled around and before I knew it, in addition to the same miserable commute and my demanding Level 10 training regiment, AP classes added an extra five to six hours of homework a night.

Let's do a little basic math problem here. School lasted seven hours. The commute to and from practice was three hours. Practice, a miserable four to five hours. Homework, let's round down to five hours. That left me with around four hours to sleep, eat, shower, and hate my life.

On any given school night, around 2:30 a.m., it sounded like a combination of a garbage truck and a shop-vac. This familiar sound was the early morning street sweeper. Like one of Pavlov's dogs, it began to trigger an emotional response. As soon as I heard this sound, my conditioned response became that all-too familiar thickening of my throat.

I was either up late cramming before an exam or bullshitting my way through an essay. Right around 2:30 a.m. was when they would make their rounds through the streets of Sea Pines.

A few short hours later, my morning would begin with the usual. "I'm not going to school today! I didn't sleep last night! *You can't make me!*" I would yell facedown in a pillow. It had also become part of the routine.

I was the epitome of a difficult fifteen-year-old. A *real* bitch. I was going through some of the darkest years of my life to date. I woke up every morning into a recurring nightmare with a ruthless vocabulary directed at whichever parent was trying to get me out of bed.

It wasn't long before almost all communication stopped. My disrespectful attitude and resentment toward everyone around me—parents, peers, coaches—reached its unbearable peak. I began to become withdrawn. I held everything inside: my words, my feelings, my depression. I bottled these feelings and stuffed them down until there was nothing to be felt at all.

* * *

Five nights a week, practice let out at eight on the dot, as always. My mom sat waiting in the car. I didn't waste a minute. I grabbed my gym bag and ran barefoot out to the car, avoiding all possible conversation with parents and coaches.

I slammed the door behind me, not saying a word.

"I picked up chicken teriyaki for dinner from the mall," my mom said as she reached into the backseat and handed me a white to-go box.

I opened the box. "It's swimming in grease. Gross," I said ungratefully.

My mom shook her head in disapproval. The conversation ended there.

The whole way home, we sat in total silence. I switched on the overhead interior light, illuminating my side of the car. In the dim light, I strained my eyes to makes sense of my notes. Among the drool stains and massive ink spots from falling asleep with a pen in my hand mid-word, it was impossible. I took a deep breath as the feeling of defeat and frustration washed over me. All I wanted to do was roll down the window and chuck my notebook as hard and as far as I possibly could.

Instead, I switched off the overhead light and continued to sit there quietly. I stared straight ahead as a silent tear rolled down my face, joining the other stains on the pages of my spiral notebook. The light blue lines of my college-rule notebook were the only thing that bled for me.

I thought for so long that I would be trapped in this purgatory indefinitely. I couldn't escape or quit for so many reasons.

The *q* word is the worst four-letter word in the gymnastics language. Not "shit," not "damn," not even the one I repeated the most inside my head: "fuck you."

Who would I be if I didn't do gymnastics anymore? I thought. *A failure. With a capital F.*

Gymnastics had become my identity. It had become what satisfied the hunger of needing to prove myself. It provided me with the validation I needed to feel like *I* was enough. And if I was to quit, I couldn't possibly repay my parents for the time and money they spent on my gymnastics career.

The guilt would crush me. I simply could not allow myself to quit. It didn't matter how miserable I was. I cared more about trying to make my family proud of me than I cared about my own personal happiness. I would rather suffer than let them down.

This routine lasted exactly twelve unhappy years before I put an end to it once and for all. Over the course of my journey, I've even had to learn this lesson three separate times before it *really* sunk in. I reached this ever-so-important realization once when I quit gymnastics, once when I gave up pole vaulting, and the final time, day eighty-something in the *Big Brother* house: there is *nothing* more important than your own personal happiness.

7

WONDERLAND

We stepped out into some sort of enchanted forest. A row of pine trees stood before us, each tree designated to a single houseguest. We climbed up our trunk, held on tight, and waited anxiously for the competition to begin. The sky opened up and down came the frigid rain, like a running faucet overhead.

"Good night, houseguests," Julie Chen signed off.

The live show was over. This meant we no longer had to censor our filthy mouths.

"Fuck!" Somewhere down the line to my left, I heard the unmistakable voice of JC.

I laughed out loud and glanced upwards. To my dismay, a stream of thick, viscous yellow goo wiped the smile right off my face. This foul goo managed to find its way into my mouth. Ironically, it was warm and slightly sweet. *Honey*, I thought. The leaves in the forest began to rustle as they danced around us, clinging to the sticky substance we were now covered in.

We stood like soldiers at attention. A solitary row of shivering bodies quickly fatiguing. The moans and groans from the rest of the cast evolved into an extensive list of four-letter words, music to my ears. This competition was made for me. I'd had some practice hanging on to things much longer than I needed to—twelve years of practice.

The bitter rain and honey goo seeped between my back the tree trunk, sending goosebumps down my spine. It ran all the way down to our fingertips, the only thing connecting us to the slimy trunks. Seven or so feet separated us from the ground below. The first few houseguests had already taken the fall.

I held tight as each tree in the forest simultaneously swayed back and forth, trying to shake us from its branches. My forearms ached from fatigue. I forced my mind into the same happy place I had created and hid in when I was a child, inspired by a favorite childhood movie of mine, *Alice in Wonderland*.

It was my own sort of Wonderland, my safe haven where I could escape from pain, where nothing could touch me, and where no words could hurt me.

I closed my eyes and it all came back, as vivid as ever. There was a moment of peace as the rain washed away the suffering, and I wandered aimlessly through Wonderland. As usual, time seemed to come to a crashing halt.

I slipped into what seemed like another realm. *Where am I?* Time made no sense.

In the book *Alice's Adventures in Wonderland*, Alice is asked a question by the Caterpillar:

> *"Who are you?" said the Caterpillar.*
>
> *This was not an encouraging opening for a conversation. Alice replied, rather shyly, "I—I hardly know, sir, just at present—at least I know who I was when I got up this morning, but I think I must have been changed several times since then."*
>
> *"What do you mean by that?" said the Caterpillar, sternly. "Explain yourself!"*

"I can't explain myself, I'm afraid, sir," said Alice, *"because I am not myself, you see."*

Time sat still, silent on his black throne in the castle of eternity, next to the Caterpillar. I felt so small, maybe invisible, but mustered up the courage to speak.

"I'm sorry," I said.

"For what are you sorry, child?" Time replied.

"Forgive me, please, sir, for I have wasted so many years of you."

His eyes softened. "My child, though the time you possess has a definitive limit, by no means have you squandered me away.

"It's the way you spent me. That, my dear, is what really matters. The way you spent me defines the person you are. Who you have become. Don't you see? Come, dear, for I will show you . . ."

The present began to dissolve around me. I could make nothing out. Everything around me melted to a colorful blur. Everything except Time. Time stood still, before me, clear as day.

He looked at me sternly. "Listen, we don't have too long. When we arrive, no need to speak, my darling. Simply observe."

* * *

A room appeared from the blurry abyss. I was standing in the lobby of Hilton Head Island Gymnastics Academy. I spotted my unmistakable six-year-old self from afar. Low ponytail, middle part, wearing my favorite leotard with the fish on it. The yellow gym floors were even more vivid than I remembered.

I had just gotten a new skill: my roundoff back handspring

backflip. I saw the joy in my face as I celebrated with my teammates.

I saw my mom enter the lobby. My younger self ran to greet her. "Mommy!" she screeched as she sprinted toward our mother. My child-self wrapped her arms around Mom's waist.

"What is it, sweetie?" My mother picked my body up and situated me on the side of her hip.

"I got my back tuck! Wanna see it?"

Before she even had the chance to answer, little me had already run back out on the floor and was halfway through demonstrating her newest, most rewarding skill. She stuck the landing with the biggest grin on her face and looked straight to Mom for gratification.

I stood there watching my mother. She clapped and smiled with the most fulfilling expression I'd ever witnessed. It was everything I needed and more.

Through my closure, I realized there was never a set goal that I had to reach in order to call myself or my gymnastics career successful or to gain my mother's approval. It was successful. I was successful, because it shaped the person who I have become today in the very best ways.

I felt a pang of guilt that I hadn't expressed enough gratitude for all my mother had done for me. She saw my talent early on and encouraged it, giving me all of herself to provide me with the best opportunities to excel. The countless hours she spent driving me to practices, waiting for hours, and chauffeuring me home. I had by no means spent the past twelve years wasting away in a gymnastics gym making my parents throw their money at a career that would never see fruition.

And I hadn't remembered this memory until just now. With my eyes beginning to tear, I wanted to run to my mom and hug her the same way my younger self just had.

Gymnastics had sown all the right seeds for me to cultivate

each of my somewhat-unconventional future endeavors. This sport, though brutal at times, had taught me a number of invaluable life lessons I was so fortunate to learn so young. It set my awareness, taught me inner strength, and showed me that, in these fast-paced times, not everything can be obtained instantly. You have to invest the time and be able to dedicate yourself to your dreams in order to be truly great at something.

It taught me both physical and mental strength. That I'm capable of achieving anything that I put my mind to and that there's no battle too great or obstacle too tall for me to conquer. I do not believe those qualities are innate or natural; it's like a muscle you have to train, and I was lucky enough to have spent twelve years strengthening that muscle.

I heard a voice come from behind me, "Now, was it all a waste, all twelve of my years?"

Startled, I turned around to see Time standing behind me.

"I wouldn't change a single thing." I smiled as the room faded again into a haze.

Something white and wet splattered across my face and chest. Feathers began to fly at me.

Was that bird shit? It was, and I was back up on the tree again hanging on by just the tips of my fingers.

Steve Maraboli once said, "Sometimes letting go is simply changing the labels you place on an event. Looking at the same event with fresh eyes."

It was time to let go. This time I let go for no other reason than to experience the thrill of falling. For those precious seconds I was suspended in the air, Time evaporated into itself, formless as each raindrop.

8

BEHIND THE BOULDERS

The moment my floor music ended, I knew it was over. The instrumental version of Fort Minor's song "Remember the Name" orchestrated the choreography of my routine during my final season of gymnastics.

I stood balancing on one foot, breathless in the center of the floor at the Level 10 state gymnastics meet, holding the last pose of the last routine of the last event of my last meet. Ever.

As gymnasts, we long for a fourth down, a third strike, or even one single second chance. But that's not how it works in our world. We have one shot. One opportunity. I alone held the fate of my gymnastics career in my hands, and in this moment, I let it all slip.

I closed my eyes and gave my last and final salute to the judges before limping my way off the floor over to my coach, who sat in one of the chairs that lined the apparatus.

Instead of sitting anxiously, waiting for the judge to reveal my score, I began ripping the white athletic tape off my ankle, not caring about anyone's subjective opinion of me. I knew whatever it was, it wasn't going to be enough. I thought about all the things I would have given in that moment to have one more chance to rewind time and do it all over again.

I pulled the last few pieces of pre-wrap off, revealing a severely swollen and purple ankle. I stared at my bare ankle as the lump in my throat began to swell.

"Are you OK, Ang?" my coach asked after a long silence.

"Yep," I mumbled, but inside my head I ranted. *No. Nothing is OK. I'm not OK. My ankle is obviously not OK, and clearly my future is far from being OK! It's over. I'm not going to regionals. No college will ever want me on their team now. It's. Over.*

Red letters flashed across screen above the judges. "A. Rummans . . ." My heart skipped a beat. I already knew my fate.

A score of 8.05 was all I could manage, tumbling on a severely sprained ankle. I was only a few tenths shy of the qualifying score I needed to go to regionals, but that didn't matter. It wasn't enough this time. My cruel and relentless inner critic read these letters as "A. Rummans, you are not enough."

A red flashing number had become what determined my self-worth for so many years. It had been ingrained in me since the very beginning, as far back as I can recall. It measured much more than my performance. It measured my happiness, my self-esteem, my confidence, and even my pride. A little red number accounted for all of that.

* * *

"That was it? Just like that you were done with gymnastics?" Tyler asked.

"Pretty much. I mean, that's basically how it ended. Shitty, huh? I fucked up and landed short on a vault right before my state meet. Sprained my ankle, tried to push through the pain —didn't work," I said, nonchalantly picking at my fingernails. I looked up at Tyler to see if he was still listening.

Since I'd known him, he was never the type to say a whole lot, at least not to me. In this moment, he said nothing. He didn't need to. His eyes spoke while his heart listened. Those light green eyes I often got lost in said it all. I saw the empathy in his expression and an unmistakable familiarity that put my mind at ease. For a second, I even felt a bit guilty thinking that he wasn't still listening.

Without a word, I could tell he understood me. There was an undeniable connection, a likeness, that I struggled to make sense of. I thought maybe he shared a similar experience. I couldn't put my finger on it, but whatever it was, something about it made me smile.

And in the same way that he understood me, I understood the language his eyes spoke. An understanding so evident that it felt as if our souls had known each other in some other life and had just met again.

I could only allow myself to look into his eyes for a few seconds at a time, in fear of becoming totally lost in them. A few seconds is all it took for his eyes to tell me his story.

He was an old soul with a past. I saw there was pain in his eyes. There were hardships he had hidden, though through his suffering, there was a resilience and an overwhelming amount of compassion, an endearing honesty, and a gentleness about him.

His compassion bred a quiet calmness; there was a sort of peace within the stillness that existed between the two of us. His energy was no different than mine. In this strange house, so far removed from normality, he felt like home.

That was all it took. My once impenetrable boulders began to chip away, piece by piece. It brought to me a sense of trust I didn't believe existed and a feeling of safety, that I needed to allow myself to be vulnerable and reveal my flaws and imperfections to him without the fear of judgment or being seen as weak.

I went on. "Well, I did keep training a few months after

until I realized it was time to move on. Sometimes good things fall apart so better things can come together. Kind of like the saying 'one door closes and another opens,' you know?" I smiled again for no apparent reason at all.

"I want to know everything. Tell me your life story," Tyler asked.

The FedEx plane had just flown over the backyard of the house, the sound of its engines drowning out any and all the noise. I knew the time was exactly 7:23 p.m., the usual time of its scheduled departure. Just like the cargo plane, there was a sense of weightlessness for a minute, like I was going to float right out of the hammock and fly away. For the first time in a long time, I trusted whatever this feeling was. I felt fully awake and alive, something I hadn't remembered feeling since my childhood. A feeling of being totally present in the moment. Even for a few seconds, I forgot all about the cameras, the filming; *we* were all that existed. Tyler and me.

There wasn't a single soul in the world that knew *everything*. Not my parents, brother, or even closest friends. Not Katherine, Ali, Natalie, or Jenn. They knew bits and pieces at most, and of course whatever dots they connected to form their own presumptions. That was all I was ever able to share. I never thought my past could make an impact or matter in the present.

I never liked to hear myself talk or thought anyone *really* cared to know absolutely everything. To understand my background, where I came from, and what I believe in. What exactly was the composition of the cloth I was cut from? What makes me tick and what I stand for. What fuels me, what my passions are, what I live for. All the fine print. My quirks, my flaws, all that makes me, well, me. Why would anyone care to know all these things?

Regardless of what I say or do, those on the outside seem to make their own assumptions and generalizations anyway. They seem to think I'm an easy book to judge by its cover.

Whether their judgements are true or false, it really doesn't make any difference because our perceptions are our reality.

In my reality, I was about to share every bit of myself with a person I had only met a little over a month ago. The cameras, the filming, and the fact that millions of people were watching the live feeds didn't matter to me. Everything in this moment felt right.

The voice inside of us that doesn't use words—our gut, we tend to call it—told me I was safe with him. In a world where we only expose our "best life," he had given me the courage to be vulnerable and to expose what lies behind those boulders. I listened to my gut and spoke through my heart.

That warm summer night in the hammock, without knowing it, I shared with Tyler so much more than just my life story. With it came a tiny piece of my heart. Here, he entered my life and became a part of the story.

9

PAIN FLOATS

"JC! We're gonna tip!" Tyler screamed.

"*JC!*" I chimed in, grabbing onto the sides of the hammock with both hands.

The most mischievous houseguest, JC, had gotten a hold of the hammock we were lying in and violently swung us back and forth like a ship getting tossed around at sea, giving his best effort to dump us out on the Astroturf below.

"We're gonna tip!" Tyler shouted as both sides of the base of the hammock began to lift off the ground.

It only took a few moments before JC had gotten all the entertainment he needed. "Bom bom bom bom-bodum bom bom bom," he babbled as he skipped away to find his next victims.

I mumbled under my breath jokingly, "You little shit."

The hammock returned to its calmer waters. Now that JC was gone, it was smooth sailing from here. As we situated ourselves, balancing our weight, Tyler yelled back to JC.

"Hey, throw me that pillow!"

The pillow returned as requested, smacking Tyler across the face.

I laughed and rolled my eyes. Part of me was surprised

that JC actually did something he was told to do; the other part was not at all surprised at the delivery.

The smile on my face had yet to fade from the excitement of our close capsize. When the dust eventually settled, the quiet calmness resumed.

"You were in my dream last night," Tyler casually mentioned, making very little eye contact.

My smile grew bigger. I couldn't help it. "Really? What was it?"

"I don't remember it, though." He went on about how he often hears me talking in my sleep.

My eyes narrowed. I *needed* to know. Finally managing to catch his eyes, I tuned back into what he was saying.

"You mumble. Sometimes I'll hear it and wake up . . ." *Blah blah blah.* I zoned out again.

My curiosity was killing me. I wanted to shout at him, "What was your dream about?", but I couldn't. It would be too obvious. *I must continue to act uninterested,* I told myself.

The conversation got back on track. All right, my life story. "Do you want the SparkNotes version, the CliffsNotes, or the unabridged version?"

"Gimme whatever version you want," he replied.

I took a deep breathe in and exhaled. *Lord, where do I start?*

"There's a lot I haven't shared with anyone here in this house. I think most everyone already knows that I was a gymnast, but I've kind of downplayed my gymnastics career quite a bit. So, why don't I start with a sort of gymnastics synopsis, and then we'll go from there? See how many times we get interrupted.

"At five years old, my parents put me in gymnastics. I was a reckless little tomboy doing flips off the couch. I think my mom and dad thought putting me in this sport might help prevent me from breaking my neck. Little five-year-old Angie started competing pretty much right away. I was in front of audiences and judges doing, like, little routines and stuff."

"Were you scared?" Tyler asked as he adjusted the pillow behind his head.

"No, I was fearless as a little kid—thought I was invincible. Still do."

I envisioned my younger self running around barefoot in my brother's hand-me-down PE uniforms. My unruly dirty blonde hair an untamable mess. Each of my ten cuticles encrusted with a ring of black dirt leftover from digging holes in the backyard.

"I think that's why I got good so fast. I had no apprehension," I added.

I thought for a moment. What if we all had the ability to stay in that place of audacity, away from corruption and all the negative external stimulus and the need to please? It's such a beautiful thing to witness a child's success when it isn't driven by the need to earn approval or praise. Simply for the love of whatever it is.

Those were the days, before my people-pleasing, perfectionist life. Failure didn't exist. The need to be praised for my achievements didn't exist. My success and growth came from a place of love from within me.

"I got to a level where I couldn't be coached at our gym on Hilton Head, so my mom had to drive me from Hilton Head to Savannah, five days a week. It was an hour-and-a-half drive each way. Starting from when I was around nine years old, I was training twenty hours a week, commuting fifteen hours, and competing on the weekends—all while going to school. I had no childhood and no life, really.

"It made me kind of a sad little kid." I paused for a second to reflect.

"You were just sad all the time?" Tyler asked. There was something about the way he asked this question that I knew without a shadow of a doubt he could relate.

A feeling of guilt came with his question, as one of my only regrets crept into mind. The guilt sat heavy on my chest.

I wished I could have explained it all to my younger self at the time and given myself the ability to rationalize what was going on, but I was far too young to understand.

I wished I could have turned back time and said thank you every damn day my mom dropped me off at practice. I wish I would've told her how grateful and how lucky I was to have her as *my* mom. She gave all of herself to me, but as a child and on into my young adulthood, I was ever so ungrateful.

I often went back to a specific time my mom picked me up from school. I was just a sixth grader, a moody little pre-teen. She had handed me a plastic baggie with my name written with black Sharpie on it in cursive. Inside it was a foil-wrapped egg salad sandwich. I opened the bag and unwrapped a corner of the foil.

"Ew, this smells awful," I complained as I took the bag and threw it down on the center console between us. "I don't want it."

"That's fine," my mother said.

I reclined the seat back and closed my eyes to take a nap. I was dreading the drive, dreading the four-hour practice ahead of me, and thinking about all the assignments I had due that week. We sat in silence. The only audible noise was the hiss of oncoming traffic.

I thought a lot about how ungrateful I was for everything my mother did for me. At the time, I was too young to see the bigger picture. All the effort and love she put into every little thing she did for me, every single day of my childhood. I hated this memory. It had become unbearable for me to reminisce, but it would always surface so easily. The pain always seemed to float to the top.

I thought about the care she took boiling the eggs before peeling and mashing them. Adding the mayo and the mustard and making sure to season it to perfection. Toasting the bread, spreading it on, and then wrapping it all up in foil and placing it into a bag, hand-lettered with my name. All the care that went into this labor of love. All for me, so I would take one look at it and throw it down.

I couldn't bear to think about that memory any longer. I looked up at Tyler as I forced these thoughts out of my mind. I continued again with my story.

"I didn't understand why I had to go through all the gymnastics stuff, because I didn't like it. So I kind of had this resentment toward my mom, which now breaks my heart to think about it." It was all I could bring myself to say, although the pain went so much deeper.

"My brother didn't get to see my mom because she was always with me in Savannah, and my dad was always with my brother at home. So I wasn't able to see my dad that much, and my brother barely got to see my mom.

"I always felt like there was sort of an animosity from my brother, like I was some sort of golden child, being taken to all these competitions every weekend and kind of like becoming the center of attention. I didn't want to be the center of attention, but it's just how it happened. I was being pushed through gymnastics. My coaches and parents were telling me I was going to do this in college and that this is how I'd pay for college."

Even though most of the time I didn't think I had a choice whether or not this was the life I wanted, I still felt the immense guilt. Everything seemed to revolve around me and my gymnastics. I had always blamed myself for our family not being as close. It was my gymnastics, which in my head meant that I was to blame for this rift in our family, splitting us into two separate orbits.

I thought back on the countless hours spent in the car with my mom, all the strain that it put on our relationship and on our family. I could hardly remember a time we had a sit-down family dinner. Every meal I ate was out of a to-go box in transit to and from a practice.

I went on. "My life was miserable. Woke up at 6:00 a.m.

Went to school. When school got out, went straight to practice. Practiced for four hours. Got home at 9:30 or 10:00 p.m.,
then did homework till 3:00 a.m."

His eyes widened. "Every day?" Tyler asked in
amazement.

I nodded. "Every night. I would sit there and hear the
street sweepers come by at 2:30 a.m. each night."

If I closed my eyes at any given time, in even the most
ominous quiet, that familiar noise still reverberated in my
mind, so clearly my skin crawled.

I watched as he unclasped his hands from on his chest. My
eyes followed his hands as they made their way past his
perfectly structured features, past his black bandana, to adjust
his bun. My eyes stopped when they met his. His compas-
sionate gold-flecked green eyes conveyed a buried pain. I
looked up at the black bandana tied around his forehead and
down to the black band tattooed around his wrist, a symbol I
was familiar with. I couldn't help but wonder.

I felt sorry for continuing to go on and on about my struggles and my pain. I knew that no matter how hard I had it,
someone else out there had it worse. If we threw all of our
struggles in a bunch like a pile of old used shoes, more times
than not we'd grab our pair right back out.

As a child, I often compared my life to those of my friends.
I looked at Katherine's life and was envious that she got to go
home after school, hang out with her brother, and swim in the
pool in her backyard. I looked at my friend Alexis's life and
wished I got to have family dinners at home on school nights
the way her Italian family did. I regularly thought about my
friend Sarah, who was homeschooled at the time, and
wondered if that would have made my life any easier. I knew
so many gymnasts that had been homeschooled to focus on
their sport. I'd miss my friends, but maybe this option was
better.

There has always been, and will always be, two ways to see

a situation. There will always be a give and a take. It's easy to think that the grass is greener elsewhere. It's even easier to lament on the negatives because, like I said, the pain floats. It surfaces before any of the good can rise to the top. For me, that was my gymnastics career. It's the pain that floats to the surface when I think about my younger years.

My soul chose gymnastics for reasons beyond me, out of my control. Not for the good, not for the bad, but for the growth it provided me. I needed this sport in my life to develop certain qualities because they were necessary to what lay ahead of me on my journey.

Life isn't all about what has happened to you. It's about how you react to it. It took years for me to realize that the thing that brought me so much unhappiness gave me so much strength, and for that I will forever be grateful.

Gymnastics will always be a piece of the definition of myself. It is the essence of my discipline, mental and physical prowess, time management, respect, dedication, bravery, and courage. It laid the groundwork for the development of my most influential quality that has led me down the path to success in most everything I've tried my hand in. This is the unwavering faith and belief in myself that I can accomplish anything I put my whole heart into.

I truly believe we attract the things and the people in our lives that we need. Some people help us by providing us with an opportunity to grow as souls. Some of these people we are destined to love and some destined to hate. The true purpose of these relationships can be as minor as learning from certain behaviors in order to surpass former behavioral habits or gaining the awareness to be able to overcome a weakness of our own. And sometimes, without even realizing it, these people will show us a tiny glimmer of light, a rendition in the form of a shining beacon, that shows us a glimpse into the meaning of the bigger picture while offering us insight into what our purpose is in this world.

Giving up doesn't mean you're weak; it often means that you are strong enough to let go. At seventeen years old, I slammed the door behind me, putting an end to all those depressing days and miserable late nights. Tyler already knew the painful ending to my gymnastics career, so I skipped ahead to the next chapter.

10

WHAT DID I GET MYSELF INTO?

"Have a seat and we'll get you miked up." A heavy-set bearded man dressed in all black handed me a tiny black microphone.

I stared down at this device, squeezing the clip to open and close it. "This tiny little thingy is a microphone? It looks like something I'd possibly clip in my hair."

"You're going to just feed that up through your shirt and clip it to your collar, a little to the left side, please."

"Testing, testing." He leaned in and spoke into my mike, breaching my personal space without hesitation. "OK, she's all set," he announced to the group.

The room seemed jammed full of people. I stared quietly at them, and they stared back at me.

Time was moving at a glacial pace. Seconds felt like minutes. The rustling of papers was the only detectable noise.

My thoughts whirled inside my head. *Am I supposed to say something? Should I just start talking? Do I introduce myself?* "Uh, hi, my name is Angela, and well—I'm not really sure what I'm getting myself into here." Yeah, nope, I decided to just continue sitting there quietly and smiling awkwardly, while trying not to hold eye contact with any one person too long.

A man in the room finally spoke. He looked down at the stack of papers in his lap as he read my name. "Angela, hi. It's nice to meet you. Happy you're here."

Sitting down to this audition, it began like any other.

"So, Angela, you're twenty-six and you're from, let's see here, Hilton Head Island, South Carolina! I hear it's absolutely wonderful there. My parents have a vacation home in Shipyard, I think it's called? So, are people in the south really as nice as they say?"

"Yeah." I clenched my hands together in my lap, digging my nails into my palms. "Sure, *real* nice."

"Why don't you tell us a story?" he asked politely, with a subtle smile on his face.

Momentarily, I had been relieved that someone had finally broken the silence, but the last thing I was prepared for was telling a story.

This was a hell of a lot different from all the other casting calls I'd ever attended. I was accustomed to no introduction. "Look straight into camera, chin up a little." Click. "Turn to your left." Click. "Turn to your right." Click. "OK, thank you. You can take your comp card," a model's version of a business card, "we don't need it."

I was taken aback when I realized the people in the room with me genuinely wanted to know who I was and not at all in a corporate, interrogative type of way. I felt human. For once I was a person, not just a body, a face, or a number. This feeling of worth melted away the apprehension. I flipped through my mental Rolodex of stories—I had a million. Many of them so deeply buried in my subconscious that digging them up in this moment would be a feat in itself.

I'd had some practice having to think on my feet twenty hours a week—twelve years of it, to be exact. There had been countless occasions of being on the spot and having to come up with a legitimate excuse while delivering it within a compelling story to one of my coaches. I'd say I had gotten pretty good at it.

The last thing I wanted to do was suck the life out of this room and walk out leaving these kind casting people depressed and feeling sorry for me, so I skipped over the story that had first surfaced at the forefront of my memory: fucking Frank. I picked up right where gymnastics had left off. I knew this story would leave a lasting impression. I was never the type to play the victim card anyhow.

I sat tapping the left heel of my black suede Stuart Weitzman stilettos.

"Well, there was this one time that I tried out for the varsity football team my senior year in high school." Probably the last thing they expected to come out my mouth. "It was actually the beginning of what eventually lead to my career as a professional pole vaulter."

The situational irony had everyone's full attention in the room.

The woman sitting to my right blurted out, "You were a professional pole vaulter?"

"I sure was. Random, huh?"

Before anyone had the opportunity ask any further questions or incorrectly demonstrate with both arms their idea of what a pole vault looked like, I did them all a favor and provided a demonstrative gesture.

"Why yes, that's the one with the long pole. You run as fast as you can, stick the tip of the pole in the box with the goal of flinging yourself up over a bar that's set at your peak climax," I said, hoping that no one picked up on the absurd amount of sexual innuendos that had just come out of my mouth.

"So, what made you want to try out for the football team?" someone from the left side of the room asked, captivated by the level of absurdity.

I thought back to that time.

It was just another muggy afternoon on Hilton Head

Island, probably mid-May sometime during my junior year. One hundred percent humidity and temperatures in the nineties, a typical summer day on the island. There wasn't a single cloud in the sky blocking the sun from pouring out its blistering afternoon rays over the practice fields. Jason, Craig, Kev, and I made our way to the locker rooms.

Jason could hardly contain his excitement. "Dude, I'm stoked! I can't wait to see the look on Coach Stapleton's face."

Anything out of the ordinary that could possibly spice up the usual mundane tryout process was enough for this crowd to get "stoked" about.

What am I getting myself into this time? I thought. *My mother is going to actually murder me.*

Having just recently given up a potential athletic college scholarship by quitting gymnastics, I was already on her shit list. The way I saw it, I had nothing to lose and football sounded fun.

Earlier that day in Spanish class, I'd been sitting backwards on top of my desk with both feet up on the back of the chair. I'd been staring out the window, thinking about what I was going to do with myself after school now that I didn't have twenty-plus hours of gymnastics practice a week.

With all this extra free time, I had all the time in the world to do some soul searching. Really excavating the depths of those dark trenches in my mind. Somewhere during one of my deep meditative mind explorations, mid-AP Spanish class, I had sort of an epiphany, so to say.

I came to this realization that I'd been living in sort of a comfort zone, and this comfort zone I had been dwelling in was not a place of growth. This comfort zone was merely a mirage of my complacency, a mythical land filled with my false contentment. This mirage disguised itself as sort of an oasis, my own personal refuge, where I could hide to avoid all possible danger. I thought about how so many of us never leave this comfy oasis, but personal growth lies just beyond its walls among the unsettledness and feelings of uncertainty.

Meanwhile, amid all this free time I had, I adopted a new mindset. I chose to perceive this uncomfortable feeling of uncertainty as a positive place to reside and see it as my place of growth. I made that feeling my best buddy. As I began to get really comfy with being uncomfortable, I decided I would no longer force things in my life. What flows would flow. I embraced this feeling, and it ultimately allowed me to begin to let go of the death grip that I had on my life. I was ready to say yes to whatever life threw my way.

I only had room in my life for the things that shared the frequency of my energy; that which were meant for me. The more I remained present and stayed in the now, the more I was able to keep myself open to all things. I let go of the steering wheel and everything was just fine.

So, as I sat on one of the classroom desks of Mrs. Lipscomb's AP Spanish class making small talk with my guy friends, I saw it as an opportunity that life was throwing my way; kind of like life was passing me the pigskin. When they dared me to come out for tryouts, this time my answer was, "Watch me."

Assuming there weren't any pads or helmets in the women's locker room, I hesitantly wandered over to the men's side, following my three guy friends while keeping my head down so not draw too much attention to myself. It took no longer than a couple minutes before one of the assistant coaches caught word of my presence and stormed in.

"Angela! You can't be in here!" he sternly reprimanded me, in disbelief that I had voluntarily entered.

"But Coach, how am I going to get fitted for my pads? I didn't see any gear on the women's side," I said like a smart ass.

He sensed the sass in my dispute. "Don't worry about pads today. Grab a helmet and cleats and git outta here."

Telling my story to the crowd, I added, "Most people can't really tell the difference between my polite sincerity and when I'm being a complete smart ass. It's one of life's most rewarding and satisfying gifts," I said with a wink and a smirk. A few of the casting and audio crew chuckled.

I remember walking onto the practice field that afternoon and feeling every eye fixed on me. Despite the judgmental stares and the primitive assessments of my athleticism, I remained my typical unbothered self.

"Hey, Ang!" I heard a voice coming from behind me. I turned around to see Coach Holden's smiling face. "So football tryouts, huh? This will be fun today, just have a good time out there."

Coach Holden's smile was like a universal welcome. He wore many hats. Not only was he one of the assistant coaches for the football team, he also a coached for the women's track team, and on top of all that, he taught world history at our high school. I'd never had him as a teacher, but he had always greeted me by name every time I passed by his classroom.

I thanked Coach Holden, appreciative of his sincerity. I saw that the rest of the students trying out had already taken a knee in front of our head coach, Coach Stapleton. I followed suit; monkey see, monkey do.

Coach S. stood before us, preparing to address the group, with his arms folded beneath his bulging chest. He was a tall, muscular man with broad, squared shoulders, standing stiff as a soldier.

Coach S.'s welcome speech began promptly at 4:00. His greeting, however, didn't begin with a smile. Every person on the practice field knew who he was, but he proceeded to introduce himself, name and title. My attention-deficit mind wandered away as he began to explain the warm-up.

I thought about all my friends suffering today at gymnastics practice, also commencing at precisely 4:00 p.m. They for sure had started their warm-ups by now. I visualized each one of my teammates so clearly that I might as well have been standing on the floor before them the same way Coach S. stood before us.

Each one of my teammates standing at attention. Shoulders back, chins up, perfectly spaced out between three identical rows of four. Every row full, except for one. There was a hole in the middle row where I had once stood.

I could hear our gymnastics coach's voice counting down. "Three, two, one, and tuck." Our daily warm-up began with ten standing backflips, which counted only if each one of us stuck the landing perfectly. If any one of us moved our foot even an inch, it didn't count. I looked down at the ground. For a split second, I expected to see the royal blue carpet of the floor beneath my bare feet. Instead, I saw a used cleat that was two sizes too big.

Shit, what did he just say? I refocused on Coach S., barely catching the end of the explanation of today's warm-up. *OK, fake it till I make it.* I followed the group of potential wide receivers and jumped in the back of their line.

From the end of my line, I judged my competition's athleticism by the way they moved. It's not unusual to hear people describe the way an athlete moves or performs a skill as seemingly effortless or "easy." From what I saw, it was quite possibly the complete opposite.

I was taken aback by how difficult they managed to make a grapevine with an arm circle look. It was what I imagined a bunch of not-so-sober giraffes on ice skates would look like.

"Angela Rummans is at football tryouts."

Word spread like a California wildfire that afternoon. It didn't take more than a half an hour before the spectators began to trickle in. A wall of curiosity formed as student athletes and coaches from other teams on the nearby practice fields arrived, filling in the sidelines, trying to discern which one of us had a ponytail hidden under their helmet.

They all wanted to know one thing: could a girl run a route and catch a football?

"You're damn right I did," I told the casting crowd with confidence. "I could have caught that football wearing these four-inch Weitzman stilettos."

I shifted my weight to the left as I kicked my heel up into the air and held it there for a split second. The room broke into laughter.

"I'd like to think my performance was impressive, but most importantly I was just proud of myself for getting out of my comfort zone and participating in a sport for no other reason than for the fun of it."

I remember walking off the field that day with my head held high, helmet in hand.

"Ang. Hey. Wait up a sec." I heard a voice coming from behind. It was Coach Holden again.

His radiant smile turned into words. "Great job today! Really fun having you out here. I think everyone really stepped it up today."

"Thanks, Coach," I said.

He continued. "Have you ever considered running track? You'd be great on our team. I was thinking the triple jump or the long jump, even sprints. You're quick and you got those long legs on you. Maybe even high jump too! What do you think, would you consider coming out for track this spring?"

Track? I thought. To be honest, this notion had never even crossed my mind. My preconception of track was a monotonous and somewhat boring sport. I couldn't see myself running around in circles, hopping over hurdles, or tossing around little heavy balls and metal frisbees.

"Uh, sure," I said hesitantly. "I'll consider it."

At the time, I hadn't the first indication of what this sport was all about. Had I been quizzed, I couldn't have told you how many meters were in a lap or even how many laps were in a mile, but I was open to anything life threw my way.

Once again, I wasn't sure what I had just gotten myself into and had absolutely no clue that what I had just agreed to was going to transpire into the beginning of my athletic career as a pole vaulter.

A new chapter had begun.

11

CHANGING SEASONS

When it's not tourist season on Hilton Head, the island becomes a beautiful little ghost town. The beach cruisers that once lined the bike paths disappear from our twelve-mile-long island. The shoreline sits pristinely empty, not a single sunburnt visitor or bronzed lifeguard under a red umbrella in sight. The flocks of shrieking seagulls and the colors of the ocean both become muted. The vibrant blue breakers are gradually replaced with grayish-brown rollers.

During these lifeless months, even the most insignificant bit of news could sweep through town like an offshore storm with little to no notice.

That was the downside of growing up on this tiny island. While it *was* absolutely beautiful there, it did seem that everyone somehow found out about your personal problems, sometimes even before you did.

While on my drive home from football tryouts that afternoon, my eyes were on the road but my mind was elsewhere, fixated on how in the hell I was going to approach my mom with this unusual, rather unexpected plea that maybe I wanted to play football my senior year. Partially because I'd had fun at tryouts and partially because, at that age, I lived to ruffle my mom's feathers a bit.

Like I said before, I was a difficult teenager.

In my mind, I ran through a multitude of possible scenarios of what her response might be. She had forbidden my older brother from participating in football, so all bets were off and I assumed the worst.

My mother was waiting for me in the kitchen when I got home that evening with both of her hands planted firmly on her hips. She had just turned on the burner beneath the black-and-white checkered MacKenzie-Childs kettle that lived permanently on our iron stove grate. The expression on her face said it all. I debated for a split second whether or not I needed to speak at all.

They say hindsight is 20/20, and in hindsight, I should've known the grapevine of gossipy Hilton Head housewives would have reached my mom long before I did. I should've just U-turned and headed straight to my room, where I was destined to spend the rest of my afternoon.

Well, it wasn't exactly the *fact* I had gone out for the football team that got me banished to my room. It was my sharp tongue and my attitude.

"My daughter will not play football," she said point blank. This came as no surprise. I had fully anticipated these to be the first words out of her mouth. "Your brother wasn't allowed to play football. What on God's earth makes you think that *you* would be allowed?"

I rolled my eyes as I pursed my lips with a look of disapproval and disgust. A look I learned from one of my gymnastics coaches.

"Vacuum cleaner," I mumbled under my breath.

"What did you say, young lady?"

My anger had reached a rolling boil. I went off. "*Vacuum cleaner!* You're like a vacuum cleaner! You suck the fun out of everything, *everything* in my life!"

I stormed out of the kitchen, attempting to make it to my room before she had the opportunity to send me there.

"You're grounded, young lady. Go to your room." Her voice echoed, following me down the hallway to my room.

I heard the kettle on the stove begin to squeal to like a stuck pig.

"I was already going there, but thanks!" I yelled back, slamming the door behind me. The loose brass hinges quivered as a clump of dust shook loose from the ceiling fan. It floated down, landing beside me on the maroon comforter of my unmade bed.

Laying on my back, I closed my eyes and swallowed my anger. Reducing my rage to a slow simmer, I brushed the dust off the side of my bed and grabbed my thick, once-white MacBook that was now wrapped in a curated collection of stickers.

I rolled over onto my stomach, flipped my laptop open, then propped myself up onto my elbows. I pecked "track and field" into Google and hit search.

The very first link that popped up on Google's search feed was Wikipedia's generic article outlining the basics of the sport. I clicked again.

Skimming over the first couple lines, I saw the obvious: running, jumping, and throwing competitions. "The name of the sport is derived from its typical venue." No shit. I jumped ahead, scrolling as my eyes tried to keep up.

I came across a word that caught my eyes, causing them to come to an abrupt stop. It was a word that had once been a part of my daily vocabulary: *vault*. The word before it was *pole*.

"Pole vault." I spoke the words aloud as I hovered my mouse over the word, highlighting the link in royal blue. I clicked and was redirected to another Wikipedia page.

Instantly, I was captivated by an image on the right-hand side of my screen. The picture was an action shot of a man

mid-pole vault. I could not stop staring; my eyes were captivated by this image.

I could totally do that, I thought. *This is it!*

Not only did pole vaulting look ridiculously fun, this sport
was essentially the combination of my two best events in
gymnastics: the vault and the bars.

Below this image, the women's records, both Olympic and
world, were listed beside a name I could hardly pronounce.
"Yelena Isinbayeva." I hovered my mouse over the name,
double-tapping my mouse pad.

A full bio of this pole vault prodigy appeared. Alongside it
was another image; a rectangular reflection of my future. I
focused my eyes on this photo. As my face drew closer to the
screen, I was stunned by the remarkable physical resemblance
of the woman looking back at me.

It was as if I was looking into a one-way mirror revealing
to me a glimpse of my future. Had the word "Russia" not
been plastered across the chest of her uniform, I might have
believed these thoughts to have been the truth.

I needed to know more. Scrolling down the page, the first
line of the next paragraph read, "Isinbayeva trained as a
gymnast from the age of five to fifteen." My jaw just about hit
the floor—well, the bed, in my current situation.

With this omen, my fate was sealed. My excitement was
boiling over as I continued to read. "She ultimately left the
sport because, as she grew, she was considered too tall to be
competitive in gymnastics, ultimately attaining a height of
1.74 meters (5'9")."

That's my *height too! This could not be any more perfect. Where has
this sport been all my life?*

I was starting to catch onto something here. There was a
lesson I was beginning to wrap my head around and firmly
grasp. This lesson was clearly demonstrating to me the divine
timing of all things.

Not only do we attract the things and the people into our

lives that we need, but they happen in what I like to call the "divine timing." By that I mean all will unfold when and exactly as it should—if and only if you can surrender and allow yourself to be guided. Aka, let go of the death grip you have on your life.

It was here I realized and fully trusted that this much needed inspiration was sent to me at exactly the right time I needed it to appear. Because I had escaped my comfort zone and surrendered control, I was able to trust in the unseen divine timing of all things. I allowed pole vaulting to enter my life and welcomed it with open arms.

That's all there is to it. By staying open and trusting in the divine timing and the magic of life, you can leave the details of how and when to be figured out and delivered to you.

And just like that, it was delivered to me on my computer screen via none other than Wikipedia.

You won't always see it, but it is still there. Most of the time—for me at least—it comes out of the dark, but trust that even when it seems like there is no light, the divine timing still exists to guide you through the darkness.

I exited my room before I was called and marched my little butt straight back into the kitchen where my parents sat in barstools at our kitchen high-top.

Both stools squealed as they swiveled, turning around to confirm my presence in the room.

There was a pause while no one spoke. I broke the silence with my announcement. "Fine, have it *your* way. I won't play football, but I'm going to pole vault."

12

DEFROST

My heart pounded audibly in my chest, so violently that the shell of ice surrounding it began to crack and shake loose with each powerful thud. It was a good feeling. It gave me the reassurance I needed to know that I did in fact *still* have a functioning heart somewhere in there.

Duhh-duhnn. Duhh-duhnn. Duhh-duhnn.

The rhythm was so loud that if the microphone I wore clipped to my baby-pink tube top had been just one inch closer, it would have picked up the sound of this drum in my chest, broadcasting the proof of its existence into the living rooms of millions of viewers who may've doubted it.

I could feel the freshly thawed blood pumping through every major artery in my body. I felt alive. Every breath I took was interrupted by the pounding of the drum that sat firmly pressed against the sides of my lungs.

"We're going to a tiebreaker round. Grab your boards. The answer will be a number." Julie's voice suddenly became muffled, like someone had cupped both hands over my ears. This loss of clarity in my hearing was common for me. It was my most consistent, telltale sign that my focus and nerves had consumed me.

"The person that comes closest to the correct number without going over will become the new HOH. In seconds, what was the total time of the 'Out on a Limb' endurance competition, from the official start to when Tyler hit the ground?" Her voice trailed off.

The second I heard his name in our "Ty"-breaker question, I knew I had this answer.

Ever since our first introductions on day one, Tyler was the one person in the house that I was somehow always aware of. If he wasn't there physically, he was there mentally. Every room he entered and exited I would constantly, yet unintentionally, follow his whereabouts. At any given time, if Julie had asked, "Where's Tyler?" I would have had this answer as well.

The fat black marker in my hand began to scribble as my mind went to my place of peace and happiness. I could so vividly recall the mental screenshot I had in my head of Tyler shivering and folded at the waist during this competition that took place in that "enchanted forest."

He was drenched in a combination of yellow honey-goo slime and rainwater. Gravity had begun to take its toll. It pulled on every part of his body except for his blonde ringlet curls, which stayed perfectly intact, covering his perfect face. His tanned arms, the one thing connecting him to the tree, were pulsating as he tried to concentrate.

My heart slowed as each beat softened. Thirty-six hundred seconds, about one hour, was how long I could handle being separated from him. I rounded down, making sure I didn't bust. My final answer: three thousand seconds. I held up my final answer as I held my breath.

"Three thousand seven hundred and twenty-two seconds. Which means congratulations, Angela. You are the next Head of Household!"

From where I stood, I couldn't see the other three house-guests left in my alliance, but I could feel each sigh of relief as I stepped out behind the stage. I was greeted with a few genuine hugs but, for the most part, a lot of forced smiles and fake applause.

Being the head of our house meant it was my duty this week to nominate two houseguests for eviction but not without an uncomfortable ten-to-fifteen-minute, one-on-one meeting with each and every houseguest.

I had my mind pretty much made up on who I wanted evicted from our house, but I decided to give everyone the opportunity to entertain me by spilling any extra info they wished to share.

Every mini interview was either a quick celebration with one of my allies or an uncomfortable five to ten minutes of being fed a stream of bullshit that practically burned my eardrums to hear.

The first couple of interviews were tolerable; however, there was only one person I couldn't wait to wrap my arms around. Finally, the door swung open and that curly head of sun-bleached ringlets emerged. My face lit up; I couldn't hold in my smile any longer. I could feel my cheeks getting warm as he checked to see if the door was completely closed, pulling it behind him until it clicked shut.

Neither one of us could contain our excitement any longer. He ran to me, tackling me with the biggest hug. Being wrapped in his arms had become my safe haven and every bit of my happiness. All of my worries temporarily melted away for those few moments. There had never been a hug that was long enough, and like all good things, it too came to an end.

The rest of the meetings dragged on a little past midnight. Both mentally and physically exhausted, I made my way upstairs to the luxury suite I'd won for the week and crawled into my circular princess-sized bed.

I reached out over the side of the bed to grab my headphones connected to a light blue iPod Shuffle loaded with nothing but Hootie and the Blowfish's greatest hits. The sound of Darius Rucker's voice never failed to bring me back. It was both the soundtrack of my senior year and my hometown, bringing me right back to a very specific time in my life.

I pressed shuffle and one of my all-time favorite songs, "Time," began to play.

Why did time make absolutely no sense in this house? On the days the backyard was closed off, we never saw the light of day. The oven's analog clock, our only clock, could have said anything and I would have believed it.

The forty-something days we had spent there felt like nothing at all, but at the same time, it felt like an eternity. There wasn't much that made sense anymore. It was late and my mind was exhausted, but I still made an attempt to rationalize these thoughts.

Time had always been the grand orchestrator of all things, and every action and every move we made was based around some specific time or timing of something, right? And if time is a measure of change and nothing appears to be changing day in and day out, how does time even still exist without an ebb or flow? How could an entire day pass by so quickly at times but a minute could feel like an eternity at others?

Why did the twelve years I spent in gymnastics feel shorter than the two years it took to go from a complete beginner to competing in the track and field Olympic Trials? Those two years felt longer than twelve. How does that make any sense? Was it because my life as a gymnast was an unchanging perpetual routine constituted from monotony, while pole vaulting was a fast-paced thrill ride? I have enough content to write an entire book about those two years, but I only have a couple chapters in me about those twelve years as a gymnast at best.

There's a very good chance that all these deep, outlandish thoughts were really just me beginning to lose my mind in this crazy house amid the bigger social experiment we were all a part of.

Even so, this song that I had listened to a thousand times

struck me differently, answering my question as to why those two years seemed far longer than the twelve I spent in gymnastics. It was because I began living with passion, courage, and intention. I was actually present, and I was *living* these moments. I wasn't just going through the motions blindly without a purpose as I had done for so long.

When I discovered pole vaulting, I rekindled a passion for my sport like never before. During those two years, there was a burning desire and a fire within me. Each individual that doubted me, telling me I was throwing away everything I had worked for to pursue pole vaulting, fueled my fire until it burned bright enough to illuminate every step of my journey.

My favorite quote by Maya Angelou goes a little something like this: "If you want me to do something, tell me I can't," and I'll do it better than it has ever been done before. This became the motto of my pole vault career: defy the odds and prove them all wrong.

In my mind, I saw those twelve years as training in preparation for the preceding two years—mentally, physically, and emotionally. The same way gymnastics had prepared me as a pole vaulter, pole vaulting in its own unique ways had prepared me for this game.

The more thought I put behind it, it seemed like every single event in my life had led me to my next stepping-stone. It was like there was one common thread, one finite string that weaved together each experience and thus forming the fabric of my existence.

The very next day, the nomination ceremony would take place, bright and early. I would have to nominate two members of our house for eviction. The thought alone of having to make an intimate speech the next morning caused my heart rate to accelerate once again.

The anxiety that began to set in weighed heavy in the pit of my stomach.

In this moment, I found comfort in letting my mind slip

off into my most vivid memory, when that anxious feeling of stepping out of my comfy bubble not only turned out to be all right but was also quite possibly the best thing I'd ever done for myself.

I was seventeen years old again, alone in my black Chevy Avalanche. Just a girl and her truck, foot on the gas, en route to her very first pole vault camp in Columbia, SC.

It was a peaceful memory, just me, myself, and I-95. A large Mickey D's sweet tea sat in my cup holder, and the only book I had ever voluntarily purchased in the front seat next to me: *From Beginner to Bubka, and Isinbayeva Too!*

13

FISH OUT OF WATER

S omewhere around Hardeeville, if you hang a right off 278 you'll end up on the infamous interstate I-95. The flattest, most lifeless, and boring road I'd encountered in all my years of commuting.

I had just the remedy for this kind of monotony: a cruise control button and a playlist that could give any millennial or child of the nineties *all* the feels. I plugged my excessively long aux cord into my iPod Nano and clicked on the playlist I had created the night before.

"Time" by Hootie and the Blowfish filled the cab of my truck.

The smell of rancid old grease and freshly fried hush puppies that had permeated my skin still lingered in my car. Only a few days ago, I had been greeting and seating our island's beloved tourists at my hostess job at one of Hilton Head's most renowned seafood restaurants, the Old Oyster Factory.

For a fleeting minute during those few weeks, it was fun getting to be just a normal teenager. I liked working. It felt good to have a purpose and a place where I was needed. I spent my mornings and early afternoons baking in my beach chair with my new favorite book at the time, the pole vault bible written by Alan Launder, *From Beginner to Bubka, and Isinbayeva Too!*

My evenings were spent slaving away at the beck and call of every entitled tourist and disgruntled retiree. And I liked it. Any downtime in between these two activities, and I was obsessing over my newfound passion, the pole vault. At this point, I'd never each touched a pole, but still I was obsessed.

The food and beverage industry is a real bitch, so naturally in my adolescent years I fit right in. I worked hard and was good at what I did. Working the seating arrangement at a restaurant was kind of like playing Tetris with people, tables, and chairs.

One piece of advice I have from this experience is if you prefer to not sit in the darkest corner of the restaurant next to the kitchen, I would strongly suggest you be kind to the hostess. Occasionally we'd get pleasant customers, but during those summer months, as the restaurant went on an actual three-hour wait, they were few and far between.

Those days were long gone now. I put in my two weeks and the world became *my* oyster. The feeling of freedom breathed new life into me. Just a few short weeks ago, I had found my shiny white pearl one day while scavenging the web. I discovered a pole vault camp for all levels, beginners to advanced, at the University of South Carolina in Columbia, an easy two-and-a-half-hour drive from my home in Sea Pines.

It goes without saying that pole vaulting is a rather small, niche sport with a tight-knit community of vaulters, coaches, and egos. In comparison, if gymnastics was the size of a grapefruit, pole vault was the size of a sesame seed. Actually, let's go with a poppy seed. I would soon learn that the smaller the sport, the bigger the egos.

Summertime in Columbia was like an inferno, a hell of a lot different than Hilton Head. There was no relief from the ocean breeze to cool off the heat of the summer. The stagnant dead heat, already thick and heavy with a humidity in the hundredth percentile, grew even thicker with my anticipation. A solid two weeks of anticipation.

I waited anxiously in the parking lot of the field house at the university. The thermostat read a sweltering ninety-eight degrees as I sat barefoot, Indian style in the front seat of my truck, contemplating when exactly I should grab my gym bag, put my shoes on, and enter my very first day of training.

I watched and waited until I saw several groups of camp attendees leisurely stroll into the building. Through my eyes, it looked like no one had come to this camp alone. Those first-day freshman jitters began to creep up as I thought about being the only one there without a buddy. I reminded myself of a time not too long ago when I was the only girl on the football field, and my anxiety melted away. I gathered my things and headed in.

The gymnast in me was accustomed to an overly structured, obsessively ordered practice. Upon entering, I wasn't even sure I was in the right place. I could clearly see the poles laid out across the turf, but no one seemed to know what we were supposed to be doing or who was in charge.

I shot a confused look at one of the adults standing around, hoping to receive some sort of direction or reassurance that we were all here for the same reason. The look on his face was a mirror of my puzzled expression.

I was somewhat relieved that we were all in the same lost and confused boat. I walked over to where the majority of vaulters sat, dropped my bag, and sat next to it, patiently waiting for the head coach to appear and address the group.

I couldn't stop staring at the array of pastel poles spread out across the turf like rainbow sprinkles scattered on a cake. Skinny ones, fat ones, short poles, long poles. Every color and every condition.

I'll never forget the first time I touched one. The University of South Carolina's field house smelled like hard work: a combination of sweat, mildew, rust, and something rotting. The only thing louder than the smell was the constant buzzing of the overhead LED arena lights.

That's going to drive me absolutely nuts. Jeez, what is wrong with these things? That is f-ing obnoxious, I thought as my mind wandered off, wondering when Coach G., former Olympian and supposedly the one in charge here, was going to show up.

I spotted an elderly man with a tuft of white hair walking toward us with a sway in his step.

That's definitely not Coach G.

"Hello all! Good morning. And welcome!" he shouted enthusiastically with a thick, unexpected Australian accent. No one said a word.

"I am Alan Launder."

My jaw dropped. *Alan Launder? Did he just say Alan Launder?* I stared in starstruck amazement. Was this *the* Alan Launder? The one that wrote the book that was currently sitting in the front seat of my car, the pole vault bible?

What looked like a few volunteer coaches and some USC student athletes gathered behind him as he continued to address us campers. I was stunned that Alan Launder was actually standing in front of me. Totally starstruck, I missed most everything else he had to say during his introduction.

Next thing I knew, I was standing shoulder to shoulder in a row of eager campers. I didn't know what the hell I was doing, but it seemed to me like everyone else did.

I was under the impression that this camp was for beginners too, but clearly I was mistaken. I'd never felt so much like fish out of water, too embarrassed to say that I had no clue what we were doing. I looked to my right and left and pulled the ole monkey see, monkey do.

The first activity was practicing the "pole drop." Trying my best to imitate the vaulters standing on either side of me, I raised my pole up to vertical, placing my left hand over top of the pole and the bottom hand rotated outward, tucked up against the side of my hip.

"About an arm's distance apart from the other hand," they said.

The hell does that mean? This can't be right. It feels extremely awkward. I began to shrink in fear of embarrassment.

As simple as it may look, dropping a fiberglass pole from vertical to horizontal takes the kind of timing and precision a tightrope walker needs on a windy day. Anything short of perfection in this sport could possibly be fatal.

One of the student athletes from USC, walking around with her nose up in the air, approached me. She snickered to herself as she condescendingly addressed the way I was holding the pole.

"Uh, your right hand needs to be flipped around underneath the pole, and *never* hold the pole totally vertical. It should be like at seventy degrees. Definitely not ninety degrees."

"Yeah, so should this field house, I'm fucking melting in here," I mumbled under my breath as she walked away.

This new handgrip felt even more uncomfortable and unnatural, and I was pretty sure I was doing everything wrong at this point. I was now more than sure that not a single other person at this camp was beginner like I was.

This realization immediately brought out a self-conscious, self-aware side of me. Negative thoughts began to fuel my frustration. Maybe I wasn't cut out for this all pole-vaulting business. I was used to picking up things quick: snowboarding, wakesurfing, skimboarding. It always came to me so effortlessly. This was a whole new beast. I simply could not get a feel for it, no matter how many times I tried to drop this stupid pole.

Finally, we had a water break. My head hung low as I stood in line for the Gatorade cooler to fill up my water bottle. As the lump in my throat continued to grow, every ounce of excitement drained out of me. Dehydrated and exasperated, I was genuinely disappointed in myself.

All I received was constant criticism: the timing of my pole drop, the way I pointed my toes when I ran. No matter how hard I tried, nothing I did was right or even remotely close. It was no different than being back in gymnastics. Nothing I did was right, and it was never good enough.

During the break, Alan Launder noticed me sitting off to the side by myself, cross-legged and picking at the plastic Astroturf with my fingers. I don't know whether he spotted the look of defeat on my face or he had actually seen something in me during our afternoon drill session.

His first words to me were, "Sheila! How many years you been jumping for?"

"Uh, about three hours," I sarcastically responded, still looking down at the fake strands of grass I continued to irritably pull out of the ground one by one.

I looked up at Alan just in time to catch a bewildered look wash over his face. He spoke again. "You've never pole vaulted before. You're a newbie—a beginner, you say?"

Like rubbing salt in my wound. I said, "Mm-hmm, yep, sure am."

"Wow! I don't believe it! I would have never guessed it."

I wasn't buying it, but nonetheless this kind gesture by the God of Pole Vault himself made me start to feel a little bit better.

"What brings you here? What made you want to try pole vaulting?" he asked.

I hesitated, thinking this was some sort of trick question. Instead of trying to formulate the perfect Miss America-style answer, I said honestly, "I was once a Level 10 gymnast, and, well, I thought pole vaulting looked fun. I wanted to feel what it's like to really fly."

Alan told me to stand up. So I stood up.

"How tall are you? About five—"

"5'9"." I said, interrupting him.

"Jesus, not so little. Seems a bit tall to be a gymnast, aye?"

I laughed, adding, "Only about a foot taller than the average Olympic gymnast."

He picked up a nearby pole and the long tape measure that was lying on the ground beside it. He said, "Keeping your feet flat on the ground, reach up as high as you can and grab the pole."

I did as I was told. He measured this distance from the bottom of the pole to where my hand met it.

Alan smiled. "You're going to be a hell of a vaulter one day."

14

POLE VAULT INNUENDOS

"Speed, strength, and fearlessness. You're fast, you're tall, *and* you can flip!" My look of defeat had been replaced with a diffident smile. Alan went on. "You're a perfect specimen, a coach's dream."

A genuine happiness flooded in. It filled my body and washed away every frustration and feeling of defeat.

Had Alan not pulled me aside on the very first day, I don't know if I would have been able to force myself to come back to camp that next day. I had spent plenty of time in an un-air-conditioned steel building, and the past three frustrating hours had not at all been what I had anticipated.

I've always believed that we as humans are in full control of what happens to us and where we end up in life. We control our destiny; but on the contrary, I'm also a firm believer in fate.

Through my eyes, fate and destiny are very different but are dependent on one another. These two words seem interchangeable to most. Fate, or *fatum* in Latin, means "that which has been spoken," and destiny, or *destinare*, means "that which has been firmly established."

While both may seem to mean the same and lend themselves to the idea of a predetermined future that we are unable to control, it's actually fate that's the one you cannot change, and it comes in many disguises. Sometimes it's a subtle omen, an opportunity, a chance, or even a short conversation. One time for me, it was bright yellow book titled *You Are a Bada$$* by Jen Sincero. An amazing read if you have the time—I highly recommend it. I stumbled across this book one evening while perusing a bookstore, killing time before a dinner reservation. It fell into my hands in the divine timing, at a point in my life I *needed* to read it.

Fate is what brings these opportunities and omens into existence, but we have the choice whether to act on what fate has presented us with, and *that* is our destiny. Destiny lies in our own hands, guided by the decisions we make in life. Only when you are clear about your dreams, goals, and other aspirations can you rely on your destiny to guide you in the right direction.

Fate guided me to the Wikipedia page titled "Pole Vaulting." Fate pulled me aside that very first day of pole-vaulting camp. My destiny was up to me in both scenarios, whether I was going to act on the inspiration I had in these moments of choice.

It was my destiny to pursue pole vaulting no matter what my parents or anyone else thought. It was destiny that I return to camp that next day. Since I was clear about my dreams of becoming a pole vaulter, my destiny was effortlessly guided in the direction I needed to go in order to stay on the right path to achieve my goals.

Fate brought my college scholarship to the University of South Carolina into existence. It provided me with the opportunity to drop out of college to train for the Olympics. Fate accepted me into the Olympic Training Center all the way out in Chula Vista, California, and it handed me the chance to be on one of biggest reality television show of all times. Without the generosity of fate and my clear vision of what I wanted in life shaping my destiny, I wouldn't be sitting here right now behind my computer screen sharing my anything-but-ordinary story with you.

That first day in the field house, fate was disguised as an ounce of hope from Alan Launder himself, and my destiny was my journey to the Olympics Trials in 2012, two short years later. This little piece of hope, a three-minute conversation, set my sights on an Olympic dream.

The only thing that really limits us is the extent of our imaginations. Set your sights on even the loftiest of goals and let fate provide you with the omens that guide you in the direction of your dreams. Believe that nothing is out of reach, and you will be unstoppable at achieving even your wildest dreams. "Time decides who you meet in life, your heart decides who you want in your life, and your behavior determines who stays in your life." Let go of everything that ties you down, shift your destiny to what you truly want, cut yourself loose, and feel what it's like to really fly.

* * *

That very next day, I arrived at camp more eager than ever before. On this day, however, there was an unmistakable shift in energy and a noticeable tension among the student athletes, campers, and coaches. Everyone was moving about, but no one said a word. The only noise was the obnoxious buzzing of the massive lights that hung overhead, illuminating the artificial green turf.

I sensed something was off; the energy was different. But to be perfectly honest, it didn't take a clairvoyant to see this one coming. Yesterday, the field house felt so huge, but not today. It was all the egos in the room that had this place bursting at its seams.

Without hesitation, as soon as Alan spotted me, he immediately began making his way over to me.

"Angela! How are you, how are you feeling?" Alan asked with the most pleasant of smiles.

Before I had the chance to answer, he went on. "You're going to be with me today. We're going to head outside to the track to work on a few things."

"Uh, OK!" I said eagerly. I couldn't have been more excited to be getting a private lesson with one of the pole vault gods.

"After you warm up with the group, we'll grab a few poles and go outside. Does that sound OK?"

Of course that sounded OK. "Sure!" I replied.

All throughout the warm-up, my mind was off in another place. I knew something was up. Channeling my inner Sherlock Holmes, I paid close attention, analyzing the way the coaches interacted with each other. They didn't at all.

As the rest of the campers and I stretched and began to go through each set of running drills, A-skips, B-skips, high-knees, grapevines, there was no communication between the coaches. Alan Launder and the head camp coach totally ignored each other.

I had it narrowed down to two very obvious possible causes: someone had stepped on someone else's toes yesterday, or someone's ego had been badly bruised. Probably both.

Alan stood waiting with an armful of poles. When the warm-up was over and the rest of the campers split off into their groups, he handed me three poles. With my water bottle in one hand, I strategically balanced the weight of the poles on my opposite shoulder and followed Alan. He made his way to the field house's barely illuminated red exit sign that hung above the steel double doors leading down to USC's outdoor track facility.

As soon as we passed through this set of dented metal doors, he broke his silence to explain to me that his time was very valuable and was much better spent working with an athlete with raw talent who was eager to learn rather than trying to orchestrate a poorly organized and dysfunctional camp.

Mm-hmm, knew it! I thought. All my speculations were confirmed; toes had in fact been stepped on, and egos had most definitely been bruised.

I didn't answer. I walked alongside him and quietly listened with an occasional nod of agreement. Alan continued with his mild yet very entertaining venting session until we reached the track.

The wealth of information I was about to be hit with over the course of the next four hours was the most exhilarating, mind-bending physics lesson that not even my AP Physics class could have prepared me for. The angles, the exactness of each movement, even the laser-like focus required to execute each task to the level of perfection required was mentally and physically demanding, to say the very least.

We started with the *very* basics, a real test of my patience: how to properly hold a pole. How to place your hands, which fingers go where, how far apart and where on the pole to put them. I was chomping at the bit for a little action, but I knew these fundamentals were imperative.

In every exercise to follow, precision was of the utmost importance. The next exercise was dropping the pole from vertical to horizontal. Then from this horizontal position, placing the tip into the menacing steel box that resided at the end of the runway.

From the outside, an exercise such as a pole drop while standing still looked simple, but it was anything but easy.

It felt counterintuitive to allow only gravity to move the pole from vertical to horizontal and to wait patiently for that perfect millisecond when the pole had reached exactly horizontal to raise my hands overhead to place the tip into the box. Keep in mind that this was to eventually be done while running at full speed.

The timing was crucial. If I was a split second off, if my

hands didn't end up in the proper position to be ready for takeoff, the results could be tragic.

Everything in pole vaulting causes a chain reaction, like dominoes. A single wrong position or sloppy technique at the start of your vault could end in a torn rotator cuff or concussion, but I loved that challenge. When it came to form, I was more than a perfectionist; I was a technician.

Surprisingly, I wasn't discouraged at the 2 percent accuracy rate of my pole drop. Alan even seemed overly delighted in my progress so far that day. It was all I needed to stay motivated.

After our lunch break that afternoon, I sat on the outdoor track watching as Alan began digging two small holes in one of the sand pits used for long jump. He proceeded to stick two poles in the ground on either side of the runway. Between these two poles, he strung a neon-orange bungee cord, forming what looked like a mini football goalpost.

Upon completion, he motioned for me to come over. Once again handing me a pole, he articulated that my task was to jog down the runway with the pole in my hands and stick the tip of the pole into the sand. Then, while still hanging on to the pole, hoist my 5'9" frame over that bungee crossbar, let go of the pole, and land back in the sandpit.

I visualized this task in my head. *So, I'm basically kicking a field goal but with my body, right?*

A long, drawn-out "OK" left my mouth as I took the pole from him. I couldn't tell if I felt more like I was auditioning for a role in Tarzan or I was in training for the next season of *Ninja Warrior*.

Without any demonstration, I went for it, clearing the orange bungee on my first attempt.

"You see? You're a natural!" Alan shouted joyfully as I reached down and emptied the sand out of my Nike compression shorts.

It became a game for me. With each attempt, Alan would

inch the bungee up, and with each attempt, I managed to shimmy my way over the bungee for a clearance. The look of delight on Alan's face after every clearance was all the reassurance I needed.

At the end of practice, while I packed up my gym bag, Alan asked, "I would like to have a word with your mum, if that's OK? Would you give me the number I can reach her on?"

"Sure! It's 843 . . ."

I thought about all the times I'd gotten a phone call home from a coach or a teacher. Nine times out of ten, it meant I was up shit's creek. Actually, make that ten out of ten times. I can't recall a single time I'd ever gotten a good phone call home.

I tried my best not to jump to any conclusions, but still, I *needed* to know what this phone call was all about.

As soon as I reached my aunt Cissy's house in the outskirts of Columbia, where I was staying during the camp, I parked in her driveway and dialed my mom. A dull panic twisted the insides of my chest as the sound of the busy signal filtered through my phone.

After the sixth try, she finally answered the phone. "Hi, sweetie! How is camp going?"

Not bothering to acknowledge her question, I blurted out, "Finally! Did you talk to Alan? Did he call you yet?"

"Yes, he called me. I actually just got off the phone with him."

I was already aware of this.

"So what did he say?" I hastily questioned, starting to lose my patience.

"Whatever you did today at practice—the sandpit drills, I think he said? Is that right?"

"Yep, mm-hmm. And?" I added anxiously.

"Well he was very, *very* impressed with how quickly you've been picking everything up. Actually, I think his exact words were that he was 'floored by your natural talent.' He said something about the last athlete he'd seen that compared to your stature and natural ability was some Russian girl? Yalenia Bayevia? I think that was her name."

Despite my mother having just butchered the name, I immediately knew who she was talking about. Yelena Isin-bayeva, the same Russian pole vaulter whom I'd seen an uncanny resemblance to that very first day I googled the words "track and field."

It was fate that she had appeared at the top of my search, and destiny had come creeping back into my current reality by conjuring this Olympic athlete yet again.

15

SHILLY-SHALLYING

Alan Launder had just compared *me* to the world record holder, the world's greatest pole vaulter in women's history. Closing my eyes, I exhaled, letting out the biggest sigh of relief and fully deflating my lungs as I sank into the driver's seat of my truck.

I needed to know everything. "What else did he say?" I asked hastily, trying to stay calm.

"Well, some of the pole vault terminology I didn't quite follow, but he wants me to come up to Columbia at the end of camp so we can sit down and discuss some possible opportunities for you for the rest of this summer."

Pausing, probably to take another sip of her red wine, she finally went on.

"He said he'd be coaching at a few more camps at Duke and App State and a couple clinics in Tennessee, and he wanted to extend the invite for you to come with him to do some demonstrating. He really wants to continue training you and wants you to stay on track with the step-by-step progression of this method he teaches, or something like that."

"Can I go? Please, Mom, can I?"

This time I could hear the smile in her voice. "You never cease to amaze us, Ang. Of course you can. I can bring up whatever you need to take with you. What clothes should I pack you?"

The last thing I was concerned about was packing a proper wardrobe. I could hardly think straight. I had just been offered the unthinkable. An opportunity I wouldn't have imagined in my wildest dreams.

"Uh, I don't know. I'll text you a list later. I just got to Cissy's, call you tomorrow."

"OK, sweetie, have a good—"

Interrupting her again at a thousand words per minute, I asked, "Oh wait, wait, wait. What time are you going to be here tomorrow?"

"I think Alan said for me to come around 3:00, 3:30," she said.

"OK, cool. See you tomorrow. Love you, bye!"

And there I stood, with my ten toes hanging over the edge of the cliff. Without even a moment of hesitation, I was ready to jump. I had faith that even though I couldn't see a net or the ground below me, one of two things would happen: the net would appear to catch me, or my parachute would open and guide me to my destination safely.

Shilly-shallying: the act of being indecisive, also known as hesitating.

Say that ten times fast. Hesitation or "shilly-shallying" is like holding the key that unlocks the ball and chain that's strapped to your ankle and not doing anything with it.

As long as you let the shackle stay locked on your ankle, you're obviously not going anywhere fast or at all. That ball and chain is going to continue doing what it does best, holding you in one stagnant, fruitless place.

Setting yourself free and making the choice to take that very first step is just as easy as deciding to turn the key. It's as simple as deciding what it is you really want.

When you take a step back and look at it in that light, shilly-shallying seems pretty silly.

Hesitancy had never been a character trait of mine. I was clear about my goals and I always knew just what I wanted. When this opportunity that was in perfect alignment transpired before me, I didn't need a minute or even a few seconds to make my decision to take the leap and trust that the net would appear.

Had I stood there hesitating, I could have come up with a million reasons why I shouldn't go, why I should leave that ball and chain strapped to my ankle. If we take a closer look at the root of each and every "why I shouldn't," there is one common denominator: the underlying fear of failure.

It's so important that we realize that even when we fail, we are still moving forward, growing, and making progress toward our goals.

Nowadays, the meaning of failure is something I have learned to reprogram in my brain. It no longer takes on a negative and disappointing connotation, invoking a feeling of defeat. I see failure as one of the most important parts of my personal growth. I choose to learn from my failures, thus making them stepping-stones to success.

I can't encourage this enough. Set exceptionally lofty goals for yourself, because it forces you to grow into the person who is able to achieve them. Growth happens when we learn from our mistakes and our failures, and we never give up. One of my favorite quotes illustrates this concept quite perfectly: "The most difficult roads often lead to the most beautiful destinations."

Sitting in the driveway of my aunt's house, my memory went in and out. I was there, but I wasn't really. I was still processing, taking note of what was going on around me, but my mind was elsewhere in the process of transitioning into the next chapter of my life.

I don't remember physically going inside my aunt's home

that night, having dinner, showering, or even going to bed. I was already in my happy place, living the life of my dreams when I drifted off to sleep that night, processing all the possibilities and envisioning myself clearing the winning bar at the Olympics.

* * *

Still lying in my HOH bed and dreading the nomination ceremony the next morning, I pulled the covers over my head, closed my eyes, and drifted off into my favorite recurring dream, my temporary escape in this game we played twenty-four hours a day, seven days a week.

It was an exact location with a particular person.

N 32°06"35", W 80°48"58" was a place both Tyler and I once called home.

There are few places in the world more beautiful. Where the land meets the Atlantic and the people speak slow with a slight southern twang, hanging onto every word: our little shoe-shaped island called Hilton Head.

Across the Calibogue Sound, the sun had just dipped behind Daufuskie Island way off in the distance. The beach to our right curved off into a point from the strong current of the Sound, forming the tip and giving Hilton Head its shoe-like appearance.

The gulls welcomed us home with their cries. Our only company as we lay on the beach in front of the water tower was an occasional fiddler crab minding his own business and a twist-off bottle of one of my favorite Cabernet Sauvignons.

In front of the round mandala tapestry we laid on were two trails of footprints leading from our blanket down to the ocean and back. I sat staring out at the sea, counting the orange crab pot floats marking the traps beneath them. The pink watercolor sky turned red.

Half on the blanket and half in the sand, Tyler reclined

back, propped up on his elbows beneath his suntanned shoulders.

The ocean was forever unchanging, and the beach seemed pretty much the same, but this trip home was different. Something about it felt complete . . .

"Wakey wakey, houseguests! Rise and shine! There are fresh batteries in the storage room. Please change . . ." Bob had interrupted my dream at the best part.

"Damn it, Bob. I don't wanna." Still dreading the nomination ceremony that was now only a couple hours away, I rolled back over and covered my face with a down pillow in preparation for the wake-up music that was about come blaring through the loudspeakers.

*"Meant to Be" by Bebe Rexha filled my HOH room and the rest of the house. The wake-up song of the day was always changing. The only constants in this house were my first thought every morning and my last thought before drifting off to sleep. These were always the same. At any given moment, even if he wasn't physically present, he was there mentally.

In a month and a half, we'd gone from complete strangers to allies to friends, and now I was so completely infatuated with him that I could only imagine my life with him in it.

16

UNLOCKING THE FUTURE

With privilege and power comes responsibility. As Head of Household, I was faced with an important decision to make. This week, the fate of one of my fellow houseguests rested in my "ice-cold" hands. It was my job to select two houseguests for possible eviction.

Once I had made my strategic decision about which individuals I chose to nominate, it was up to the rest of the members of the house to vote between these two houseguests to determine who they wanted to get rid of.

Before the nomination ceremony began, I sat alone in my luxury HOH suite, staring at a white plexiglass case full of orange keys. When I say "alone," what I mean is in a room by myself with about ten cameras recording my every move from every angle.

In front of me, there were ten keys labeled with the names of each member of our cast in uppercase bold letters. Each key represented a member of our house and a possible nominee.

Choosing a houseguest to nominate was as easy as removing their personalized key from the case and inserting it into a little box. Making my mind up on who I wanted to nominate had been even easier, and I was confident I had made the right decision.

As I reached toward the first key to make my first nomination, I recalled thinking that all along, making those hard life decisions really was just as easy as selecting a key and placing it into a slotted box. From career choices to college majors, even choosing where to call home—it was really as uncomplicated and painless as choosing what I wanted and then deciding that it was time for me to have it.

I envisioned each key representing a career choice instead of a name. Actor. Physician. Entrepreneur. Model. Teacher. Lawyer. Chef. Athlete. Superintendent. Stewardess.

"This is what I want." I would pick up a key.

"And now I'm ready to have it." I would turn the key in the box.

Or even if each key was inscribed with the name of a university. I thought back to a particular time during my adolescence when I was preparing myself to make what seemed like the biggest, most stressful, life-framing, daunting decision: choosing a college.

In my untamed imagination, the pressure of choosing a school felt like an offshore storm brewing in the back of my mind, slowly closing in on the shoreline. As the clock ticked down, this dark cloud moved steadily toward the forefront of my mind.

There were so many factors and criteria to consider: geography, size, the athletics' division, public vs. private, the majors offered, and most importantly, how the *hell* was I going to afford this shit?

Contrary to popular belief, I have never been handed or expected to be handed anything in my life.

I knew one thing for sure: that, despite having quit gymnastics, I had a dream that was still very much alive, and this dream involved particular criteria that outweighed all the others. I wanted to attend a Division 1 school in the South-eastern Conference, and I wanted to be on a team.

Calling it a fixation would have been an understatement. I spent years working myself up into a tizzy about achieving this dream on a daily basis to such an extent that this dream lived on long after my gymnastics career had ended. I had drilled this plan into my head with so much positive energy surrounding it, vibrating at the highest possible frequency, that this dream couldn't possibly die.

Without knowing it, through these vivid daydreams I had tapped into what some refer to as the law of attraction. I've never been fond of labels, so call it what you want.

At any given moment, I could close my eyes and see myself sitting in front of my letter of intent, staring at the large, awe-inspiring SEC logo embossed in royal blue and gold heading the page and, with a pen in my hand, giving it my best John Hancock. There wasn't a single night I went to bed without replaying this vision at least once in my head. Each vivid visualization brought this dream into existence.

I had big dreams, and I knew they were big because at times they absolutely scared the shit out of me. There were plenty of times that the fear of failure due to my Type A personality would set in and attempt to take over. The type A in me manually tried to override every step and institute a plan A, a plan B, a plan C, and even an "if shit hits the fan, abort mission" plan D.

The only thing that could overshadow the control freak in me was my wholehearted belief that I would arrive at the right place at the perfect time, allowing my dream to unfold in the divine timing.

From the very first time I touched a pole to my time spent traveling from college to college training with Alan Launder, I trusted in the process and had an unwavering faith in the power of the divine timing of all things.

From where I stood, I couldn't clearly see the destination,

but that's exactly it! I didn't have to because I was clear about what I wanted, and I allowed the events in my life to align themselves and unfold, thus bringing my dream into reality. I never planned out my next step or how I would take it. But when I was ready to take it, it appeared. All I had to do was take that ever-so-frightening first step. As soon as I found the right footing, the next step would appear, and then the next.

The memories flooded in of a time when each step came at me so fast, it felt like I was playing a game of hopscotch.

I was loving life, living in the fast lane. The summer I learned how to pole vault was a whirlwind of crazy. The opportunities transpired out of nowhere and the reward came so fast. Before I knew it, I had just won my very first outdoor track meet, jumping a height of 12'2" and clearing the Division 1 college scholarship standard.

This journey ended in a sea of possibilities. The floodgates of college options had opened. I had every key to every division of every conference I wished to choose from, bringing this dream into a very real existence. I had a scholarship opportunity to almost any SEC Division 1 school my heart desired.

This was the first time I realized it really was as simple as becoming clear about what I wanted (picking up the key), putting it out in the universe, and deciding I was ready for it to return to me (turning the key) in the perfect divine timing.

My key read the University of South Carolina.

My advice is if the key doesn't fit, don't ever force it. What flows will flow. Trust the process, stay the course, and stay positive throughout your journey. Continue vibrating at your highest frequency, and in return the things that are meant for you and that share your common frequency will materialize, guiding you to your desired destination.

The experiences I took away from this summer are to this day some of my most cherished memories. I owe it all to the one who believed in me even before I did, Alan Launder.

I am both grateful and blessed beyond measure to have been touched by his greatness. The joy, positivity, and the belief he instilled in me through his coaching were as invaluable to me as an athlete as they were to me as a person.

Alan Launder passed away in London on August 31, 2014. Rest in peace, Alan. Thank you for your guidance, these experiences, some of my most unforgettable memories, the laughs and the challenges, and, most importantly, thank you for the impact that you continue to have on my life.

17

THE UGLY TRUTH

Right when I thought things couldn't get any more stressful in the *Big Brother* house, I was put on slop. To be totally transparent, because it was my turn, I actually volunteered in order to keep our house the peaceful little "democracy" that it wasn't.

Raising my hand to volunteer, I thought, *This is it*. This would be the true test to determine whether I was fully healed from an illness I had suffered from so long ago. This highly restrictive diet I was about to sign myself up for—combined with the high-stress environment we were living in—just might be enough to reopen the wound.

All I could do was believe that the strength of my internal voice was loud enough to keep this illness silent. My mind raced with thoughts of uncertainty. Would my disorder come out of hibernation this week? Would the week ahead hold the moment I relapsed? This game had tested me in so many ways, but *damn*, I didn't see this one coming.

The term we so often used in the house, "being on slop," meant that for an entire week, seven days and six moons, the only thing we were able to consume was a concoction of fortified oatmeal mush. The smell was putrid, and the taste and texture were hardly tolerable.

I know you're probably wondering just how appetizing this off-white mush meal we called slop was. I can assure you it tasted just as good as it sounds. Imagine eating papier-mâché during its still-malleable, half-dried state.

My biggest fear—taking precedence over being evicted from the house—sadly became the possibility of a relapse of an eating disorder that came close to destroying me and shattering everything I had worked so hard for in my athletic career.

These were the memories I had suppressed and feared the most. For all my fellow Harry Potter fans, if had I been at Hogwarts instead of the *Big Brother* house and encountered a boggart, it would have transformed into a withered clone of me eight years ago, thirty pounds lighter with brittle bones and thinning hair.

Without ever having any formal therapy for my eating disorder or the knowledge of how to properly perform a boggart-banishing spell, all I could do was swallow these feelings, stuffing them down into the depths of my being in hopes that these harmful behaviors would never be regurgitated.

Each day I spent on slop was a reminder of what those restricting thoughts and patterns felt like. My only relief was to constantly remind myself that this was only temporary and I was doing it to prove to myself that I was stronger than this illness now. With this mindset, I fought through each and every passing day.

I confronted each memory with this reassuring affirmation, but despite my mindset, the memory vomit came up. I was covered in the memories and the pain.

* * *

It was fall 2010, and I had hit a new, emaciated rock bottom.

An eating disorder that led me to one of my lowest points.

It wasn't long after I joined the University of South Carolina's track and field team that I also unknowingly joined another group. Comprised of over thirty million people, both men and women, we were all suffering from a common illness: an eating disorder. An illness that left a tender scar I wasn't sure I would ever be able to fully get rid of.

The seeds of this possessive sickness were planted early on while I was still a young gymnast. The obsession to achieve perfection in both my performance and in myself physically was projected onto me by a particular gymnastics coach. That one coach ripped off the blindfold, exposing to me a *false* reality: that perfection was something attainable.

Almost ten years ago, she opened my eyes to the self-abusive side that comes with chasing perfection. A side that's eternally fueled by every self-scrutinizing assessment of myself. As my critical, dissatisfied eyes saw every one of my "imperfections," this fire burned brighter and brighter until that flame sucked the life straight out of me.

Years ago, I had been convinced that losing weight would make me a better gymnast. I thought my skills would be easier to execute had I been just a couple pounds lighter. My highly competitive nature and this insatiable need for perfection cultivated this illness. It followed me throughout my adolescence up until my freshman year in college, where it almost destroyed me.

I turned the dial to hot. One foot at time, I cautiously stepped into the stream of steaming water. Standing on the tiled floor of my freshmen apartment shower, steam filled the shower as I drew the curtain shut behind me.

I closed my eyes and let the almost-boiling water run down my face and wash over my hair. It cascaded down my shoulders and back, instantly turning my skin red. I reminded myself that this was the weed-out phase of our track team's fall training. They want to see who was weak. Who was going to drop and just give up.

"I'm not going to be one of them. I'm going to make it through this," I told myself.

This day felt like I had been dragged through hell and back again. Barely holding myself upright in the shower I shared with my teammate and fellow pole vaulter, I had reached a new level of fatigue. My mind, body, and spirit were running on empty.

Earlier at track practice, I'd just barely made it through another one of our grueling preseason running workouts, followed by an evening lift at Williams Brice Stadium's football facility.

Standing there in the shower, I felt like I was still holding that 185-pound barbell across my shoulders. It took everything I had left in me to hold myself upright. My legs began to tremble as the fatigue mixed with steam went straight to my head. For a minute, I thought I was about to pass out.

I sat down, practically collapsing to the floor of the shower, holding my head between my hands in preparation for everything to soon fade into blackness.

I lifted my head from my hands. Sitting upright and straightening my legs, I ran my fingers through my hair. A clump of my hair came out, clinging to my wet skin. I sat staring, too tired to even panic at what I saw. A wad of my long, brown hair interlaced in my fingers and ran down my forearms.

"What the hell? Oh my God. What is happening to me?"

My gut told me exactly what was wrong. I knew the answer, but I continued not to listen to that little voice in my head. The voice of my illness was so much louder.

As a freshman on the track team, I felt like I had something to prove. I wanted to be the fastest, strongest, and fittest.

In my pursuit of what I deemed perfect, I began to restrict my diet, thinking that was how I would become the fittest and thus achieve greater speed and strength.

It started with a thirteen-hundred-calorie limit. I dropped a couple pounds immediately. A couple turned into five, five turned into ten. Before the end of my fall semester, I had lost almost twenty-five pounds.

My clothes hung from my bony frame. I remember not leaving for class without carrying an extra hair tie to secure the side of my Lululemon yoga pants just to keep them from falling down. It wasn't long until my daily attire soon became our baggy track and field warm-ups. A men's small hid my skeleton perfectly.

Thirteen hundred calories plummeted to eleven hundred. My meal planning and preparation had become a meticulous science. Breakfast was exactly half a cup of instant oatmeal. I would weigh out exactly forty grams of instant oats, not a gram over or under. If I knew we had a rigorous workout that day, I might just add a handful of blueberries, but not without weighing each berry. Eventually I began adding a dash of cinnamon to my morning oats—not for flavor, but because I found out cinnamon was a metabolism booster.

Lunch was an iced coffee, black, and a bowl of leaves drenched in the lowest-calorie salad dressing I could find at the nearby Publix. Before practice, an apple. After lifting, a half a protein bar I'd grab from our weight room.

Depending on how many calories I had left for the day, dinner was either a can of broth-based soup or a frozen prepackaged meal so I could easily track the calories.

After study hall, if I needed to quiet my growling stomach, I had a small thirty-gram bowl of Fiber One bran cereal because I knew fiber swelled in your stomach, creating a false sense of fullness. I knew all the tricks.

I began weighing myself more often than my food. Eight to ten times a day was normal. I was consumed with constantly tracking both my body weight and every single calorie I ate. I had an app on my iPhone I used to log everything. If I ate a stick of chewing gum, I added five calories and weighed myself after. It became a sick obsession.

During my freshman year in college, the roots of this disease had grown so deep that they became intertwined, wrapping themselves around my most dominant personality traits at the time—the perfectionist, the control freak, the fierce competitor, and the stubborn Aries I was—thus making this disease nearly impossible for me to beat.

The combined pressures of classes and track season fast approaching was more than I could handle, and it continued to build until I was overwhelmed with an intense feeling of loss of control in all aspects of this new college life I was trying to navigate through.

In my attempts to regain control over my life, my diet became the thing I had complete control over. It was the one thing I, and only I, could fully orchestrate.

To make matters worse, we had a coach that was adamant and overly concerned with our diets, keeping close tabs on our physiques at all times.

I have memories that are still burned into my mind.

We were at an away meet at Texas A&M. My teammates and I stood around in the lobby of the hotel ready to head to dinner. A coach turned to us with a stern look on his face.

"Salads!" he said, pointing to each one of us.

There was another time I still haven't forgotten. It was late afternoon in the training room, before my teammates and I plunged into an ice bath.

Tara looked at me with a perplexed expression on her face and asked, "What are all those little bruises all over your thighs, your arms, and your stomach?"

Looking down, I hadn't any idea where they had come from. I shrugged, lowering my torso into the ice-cold water.

"I have no idea," I said, puzzled.

It was normal for my teammates and I to stand around at practice and suddenly feel a pinch on the back of our arms. It was our coach performing the classic skin fold test, gauging the amount of fat that surrounded the area we referred to as our "bat-wings."

This test was preceded by a mild interrogation about what we had been eating lately. One day during this questioning, a light bulb went off. I realized then that *I* had caused all these faint little bruises. Unconsciously in class, study hall, on bus trips—wherever—I pinched my way through every area of my body, analyzing my amount of body fat. These bruises were caused by performing countless skin fold tests on myself over and over again.

My body was deteriorating fast. By the time spring semester and our outdoor track season had rolled around, I had fallen victim to the female athlete triad: disordered eating, amenorrhea, and early onset osteoporosis. My period became so irregular it eventually stopped all together.

My low estrogen levels due to my poor nutrition had caused the third tier of the triad, early onset osteoporosis. My bones became so brittle that my feet were riddled with stress fractures, making training and competing so agonizing that it was almost impossible.

Everything I put myself through, all this punishment I inflicted on myself, was all intended to aid my performance and make me a better athlete so I could run faster and jump higher. Instead, it came close to destroying me.

The pressure and stress caused what I thought were good intentions to spiral out of control into this horrible disease. I had no energy, low self-esteem, and was in constant pain. I suffered, as did my ability to compete at even close to my full potential. I trained through the injuries, but my performance during my freshman year was far from what I was capable of.

The thing about an eating disorder is that the road to recovery is an ongoing journey. Anorexia and all other eating disorders are like a double-edged sword. It's a counterintuitive, ass-backwards mindfuck unlike anything I've ever experienced in my life. Food is both the medicine and the poison, making the road to recovery a living nightmare. It isn't a substance that can just be cut out cold turkey and avoided. For a person suffering from an eating disorder, food is our poison, and if we quit using our poison, we wither away until there is nothing left.

For me in this world today, I have constant reminders. Each and every hateful Instagram post, body-shaming comment, or cyberbullying tweet is a reminder of the scar that I'd been left with years ago. I call it a scar because it's a wound that's healed, and even though I can still see it, it can't hurt me anymore.

* * *

As the clock ticked down to midnight on my last day of being on slop, the eating disorder I once considered to be incurable was powerless. Food was no longer able to control me or hold me hostage in a living hell like it used to.

I proved to myself that I was stronger than this disease. My inner voice had become so loud that it was no longer a part of me. Reliving these painful memories again allowed me to connect all the dots I needed to understand this disease. Everything made perfect sense.

I understood who and what was behind my false sense of perfection and what really caused these harmful patterns. This did more than empower me; it set me free. The simple things that could have once triggered a full-on relapse left me completely and totally unbothered.

If you or someone you love struggle with disordered eating, contact the National Eating Disorders Association (US) at 800-931-2237 or the National Eating Disorder Information Centre (Canada) at 866-633-4220.

18

ASTERISKS AND OMENS

"August 17th," I said. "That's my dad's birthday. It's coming up really soon," I added as I spun myself around in a swivel chair, entertaining myself as an eight-year-old child would.

Around and around I spun, sitting at the *Big Brother* house's kitchen island and beginning to feel a little dizzy. It felt good to feel something, anything at all.

We relied on our most primitive sensations as our main sources of entertainment: touch, smell, taste, sight, hearing, pain, and balance. Any sort of stimulation was more than enough entertainment. It was all we had.

I looked to my right. Tyler sat motionless in the chair next to me, staring straight ahead. The expression on his face hinted that he was just about to say something. His lips even parted a bit, but instead he paused for a split second, refocusing his eyes up toward the ceiling of the *Big Brother* house.

I watched as he continued staring up toward the heavens above. His face softened as his expression subtly changed. I could tell his mind was churning, and as crazy as this may sound, in that moment I knew exactly what he was thinking. I knew why he had paused, and I knew what he was about to say. *The astronomical odds of it.*

He looked back to me and began to speak. I wanted to interrupt him, wrap my arms around him, and tell him, "I know." But instead, I let him speak.

"That's the same day my father passed away," he said. I smiled back at him, keeping my words to myself. I wanted to say something, anything at all to comfort him, but there were other houseguests around and I couldn't risk having anyone catch on to the fact there were so many undeniable connections between the two of us on so many levels. Since the very first day we met, the universe had been dropping hints that had not gone unnoticed.

As far back as I can remember, I've incessantly tried to figure out this crazy world we all share, like it holds secrets from us. I believe that if I think long and hard enough, all its little idiosyncrasies will eventually line up and make perfect sense.

Ever since I was a little girl, I've always had this innate feeling that whenever these minor coincidences occurred, it was a sign confirming that I was on the right path. Instead of dismissing these as insignificant coincidences, I learned to pay close attention to when inexplicable similarities grabbed my attention.

Another thing I started paying closer attention to was the random, vivid memories I had stored in my head. They seemed to be totally random, with absolutely no significance behind them. But for some odd reason, they remained painted in my mind so vividly that it was like they had giant asterisks all around them.

I can still distinctly see this one particular memory of my brother and me. He was about eight and I was about six. It's so clear that it's almost like a moving picture in my mind that I can go back to at any time.

It was fall, around mid-October, but not yet Halloween.

My costume was going to be a pink Power Ranger that year, and I was overly excited about it. Earlier that day, my dad had raked all the fallen pine straw and dead leaves—oranges, yellows, and browns—into several piles spread out across our backyard. I remember him sternly warning us about the poison ivy growing on the fence that bordered the creek around the perimeter of our lot.

"It looks like three leaves," he said. "Stay away!"

My brother and I, we were the curious type. That afternoon, we stayed far away from the poison ivy but meanwhile stumbled across a couple of long, white PVC pipes in the garage. They were about two inches in diameter, just small enough for me to wrap my little hand around. We spent the rest of that fall afternoon running around the backyard with our makeshift poles, pretending to be pole vaulters and using the piles of freshly raked leaves as our landing pits. How either one of us knew what pole vaulting was at that age is still an enigma.

It is no coincidence I carried this vivid memory around with me for over twenty years.

Think back to a time you had a strange coincidence like this happen or a vivid memory that oddly stuck with you. One that was just a little too bizarre, a bit too random, so much so that it left you thinking, *Damn, what are the odds of that?*

That thought lingers on in order for us to find the greater meaning, whether it be the confirmation that we are on the right path or a sign that we need to take a step back and reevaluate the direction our life is headed.

So many of us, including myself, are guilty at times of just going through the motions in our lives and falling victim to the monotony of our daily, weekly, and monthly routines. With our heads down, days fly by.

While in this state of unawareness, that clever ole universe has no other choice but to hurl a foul ball at us in the form of an alarming coincidence, odd parallel, or memory. It's kind of the world's way of saying, "Aye, buddy, heads up!" Once it's caught our attention, it leaves us with this feeling that there has to be *some* greater meaning.

In the *Big Brother* house, I had taken note of each and every random, obscure little connection there was between Tyler and me. I knew that there had to be some greater meaning. This final instance, this bizarre parallel, was the undeniable confirmation I needed.

Even without any hard evidence from Tyler to confirm it, something told me we shared the same thoughts and the same feelings about each other, but we both denied it relentlessly.

As Tyler held his gaze at the ceiling, it was like I was listening in on an intimate conversation he was having with his father.

I could hear Tyler saying in his head, "OK, Dad. I get it already; enough hints. It's her!"

Was it a message from the universe or the heavens above? I'd say a little of both. I'd had enough. I was over trying to deny all the signs and hints. There was something about this one that seemed meant to be.

It's not every time that these signs are so straightforward that they make sense almost immediately. I was lucky these clues pointed in a clear, obvious direction. Most of the time, these hints aren't so crystal clear.

More often, it's like the universe presents us with a riddle to solve, which can take years before we're able to gather all the evidence needed to decode the message.

I never really put much thought into why I chose the University of South Carolina out of all the potential schools I had been blessed with the opportunity to attend. I just *did*.

I took the max five official visits to colleges during my search: LSU, Virginia Tech, Clemson, the University of Arkansas, and lastly, the University of South Carolina.

Beyond these five schools, I was lucky enough to have many others knocking at my door. While I was in the process of making this decision, at first I was beyond flattered by the amount of interest from college coaches.

That soon changed.

I anticipated the process of getting to visit schools, meet various teams, and talk to coaches would be fun and exciting. Instead, it was downright overwhelming and slightly miserable. The endless emails, Facebook messages (long before the DM was a thing), and constant phone calls made it an extremely stressful time in my life.

Every coach had their list of reasons why their school was better than the next. I hated the negativity and bad-mouthing that I was subjected to from a number of coaches about the next college. I felt like a lone french fry that a bunch of seagulls were fighting over.

I was still new to the sport, utterly overwhelmed, and I'd had enough, so I just pulled the trigger and picked one. Since the University of South Carolina hadn't been the college with the best offer, I sort of always assumed that I chose South Carolina because my dad was an alumnus and it wasn't too far from home.

It just so happened that my grandmother and aunt, whom I'd been very close with all my life, also lived in USC's college town, Columbia, SC.

It was never a coincidence or a random choice. I had a riddle to solve here, and soon everything would make perfect sense.

In 2011, after I had almost destroyed myself both physically and emotionally, I dropped out of college, forfeiting both my athletic and academic scholarships.

I was *so* bitter and resentful. I was angry with myself for having fallen short of everything I expected out of myself during my freshman year at USC.

I felt foolish for choosing this college, and I blamed everything and everyone for my regression, especially myself. All the toxic what if's soon set in, poisoning my spirits.

What if I had chosen LSU? Would I have developed this horrible eating disorder? What if I chose Arkansas instead? Would I have made it to NCAA nationals this year? I drove myself crazy running through all the other possible scenarios in my head, assuming the grass would have been greener anywhere else.

There were two imperative reasons behind the decision I ultimately made to drop out of college, forfeit my athletic and academic scholarship, and start over.

The first and foremost was I needed to get healthy more than anything else. I knew it would take major changes in order for me to fully heal from what I had been through that past year, and if I remained in my current circumstances at USC, I didn't think a full recovery was possible.

Secondarily, 2012 was fast approaching and I was on a mission. I had a dream that I wasn't about to just give up on because of a minor setback. If I wanted to give my dream of making it to the 2012 Olympics in London a shot at becoming a reality, I knew it would take everything I had in me and my full undivided dedication to this sport over the next twelve months.

Of all the people that told me I was throwing everything away and that I was about to make the worst decision of my life, there were three people that believed in me. They supported me unconditionally in my decision to put it all on the line and blaze forward, full speed ahead, to chase this dream. That was my mother, my father, and Alan Launder.

(I'm sure my brother did too, but he was doing his thing getting his engineering degree at Clemson.)

It wasn't until years after that something clicked. When I realized the true reason why I had attended the University of South Carolina from 2010 to 2011, the riddle was solved. My first and only year at the university was also the last year of my grandmother's life.

My grandmother passed away January 2012, a little over

six months after I left school. The following year, May 2013, my aunt lost her battle to cancer.

The year I spent at USC wasn't about pole vaulting, making it to nationals, or the future of my track and field career. It was about the invaluable time I got to spend with both my aunt and my grandmother. I was meant to be there in Columbia with them during their last years of life with us.

This realization was not only vindicating, but it also put into perspective what's really important in this world: our family. I have no regrets. I no longer see my college experience as a setback, and I am beyond grateful for every extra minute I was able to spend with my two guardian angels. It was truly meant to be.

19

URINE STAINS

"What. A. Week." I sighed with relief as I emptied my clothes from the dresser, drawer by drawer, stuffing each nicely folded pair of yoga pants into my black BB duffel bag. I raked the rest of my toiletries into a big plastic Tupperware and set it beside my bag just outside the doorway of the HOH room.

I took one final look around my Head of Household suite to make sure that I hadn't forgotten anything as I began to reminisce on the past week of my reign. Even with all the luxuries—my princess suite, my circular bed, private bath, shower, even my own toilet—it was the farthest thing from a vacation.

The week was a drama-filled emotional rollercoaster. We laughed, we cried, and we "backdoored" our alliance's target. We even met Granny, gained a peanut, and had a private chef whip up delicious vegan recipes at all hours of the day.

"Oh shit! My pillow!" I gasped, crawling over the side of the bed and reaching toward my favorite pillow I'd almost left behind.

Grabbing hold of my heart eyes emoji pillow, I tucked it under my arm as I closed the HOH door, locking it behind me. Back down the spiral staircase I went, carrying all my luggage in one trip. I've always been a one-trip kind of person: groceries, shopping bags, luggage, it didn't matter. I liked to make the most out of every effort, and naturally I never wanted any help.

"One, step, at a time. Do not trip. You can do it. One. More. Step . . . Yes!" I sang my spiral staircase song aloud, talking myself through each step. I had perfectly executed the treacherous trip down this staircase in heels during a nomination ceremony but a tumble with this amount of shit would have been fatal.

If the fall itself didn't kill me, the embarrassment would have most definitely destroyed me. I couldn't help from envisioning what that GIF would look like: a spiral avalanche of clothes, toiletries, hair-styling tools, arms, and legs flailing every which direction, all to come crashing down at the bottom of the staircase in a mangled mess. That GIF would surely follow me for the rest of eternity.

I passed through the kitchen as I made my way back to the blue room, where the communal beds were. The sink was overflowing with dirty coffee mugs. A half-cut red onion sat in the middle of the kitchen island next to a single slice of unwrapped Kraft yellow cheese. No plate, just cheese to table.

My face twisted into a look of disgust. "Gross," I mumbled under my breath, trying my best to ignore the filth.

I passed through the living room next. Scottie lay face-up on the circular orange-and-green couch, tossing an artificial orange into the air over his head and catching it again and again. I wondered how much longer before it hit him in the face.

By the time I reached the blue room, where I had previously slept, my arms were on fire from the weight of my belongings. The back bedrooms were empty aside from Tyler and Kaycee sitting in silence and staring at each other.

Barely making it to the bed, I happily let go of all my shit at the foot of the middle bed, where Tyler sat against the blue, upholstered headboard. A part of me felt like I was moving back home.

"Welcome back! Join the peasants!" Kaycee shouted, breaking the silence. Her smile and energy were always infectious.

Laughing, a smile flashed across my face as I collapsed on Tyler and my bed next to my pile of things.

"Thanks, peanut, it's good to be home," I replied to Kaycee.

Still grinning, I stretched my arms out over my head, taking it all in.

I looked up at Tyler, then back down to my pile of possessions, comprised of every single one of my belongings in the house. It wasn't a lot, but it was everything. All that was mine was sitting right here at the foot of this bed.

"Ugh!" I whined. "I do not wanna unpack all this. I'm just really not feeling it right now," I contemplated aloud, debating how long I could continue to procrastinate.

Examining my pile of things brought me back, filling me with a sense of familiarity. Every item of importance gathered together, packed up, like I was ready to go somewhere. I could still feel the anxious anticipation and subtle apprehension that came with seeing everything I owned all piled up together. This was the familiar sight that denoted a new beginning.

I don't have enough fingers to count the number of times I saw all my possessions packed into the back of my truck ready to embark on a new adventure, a new town I would soon call home. One particular town came to mind. One that I called home for about three years, good ole Rocky Top, home of the Vols: Knoxville, TN.

* * *

It was 2011. I was officially a college dropout and, to my

parents' dismay, I had no plans of ever dropping back in. I'm still a firm believer that college isn't for everyone. It wasn't for me. I wasn't going to be another cow in the herd, grazing my way through a four-year program just to be able to check the degree box off the list. I didn't need a degree to grant me permission to embark on my journey in pursuit of my goals.

It didn't take a bachelor's degree to figure out that I could skip this step and save a couple years of life and the debt of student loans.

I was seeking a different type of knowledge. I reached out to an old friend, Alan Launder, whom I had stayed in contact with during my time at the University of South Carolina. I'll never forget his first words to me.

"I told you not to go to that college."

"Hindsight's always 20/20," I replied sheepishly. "I'm sorry, Alan. You were right," I added, swallowing my last few ounces of pride.

It went without saying that things hadn't quite worked out for me at USC. It was no one's fault but my own. He knew it. I knew it. We all knew it.

I was sure he had been following all my performances at my collegiate track meets, and I was also sure he wasn't the least bit surprised when he received my call from out of the blue.

Like I said before, I usually had a plan A, a plan B, a plan C, and an "if all else fails and shit hits the fan" plan D escape route for most situations in life. This time was different. I had no backup plans to fall on. But luckily, plan A worked. A stood for Alan.

I pleaded for help, asking him, "Where can I continue training? What coaches do you recommend? Where should I go from here?"

I leapt, and luckily for me, the net appeared right on time. It was about damn time something went my way, and just like the saying goes, when one door closed, another opened. I was unaware, but Alan had already opened the next door and left it slightly cracked for me.

There was a long pause before he replied. "Angela, I've been in talks with a coach in Tennessee—Knoxville, Tennessee, that is. He's an old friend of mine, Dmitri. Been coaching for years. All levels. "

The angst began to lift. He continued. "He is coaching one other girl right now, post-collegiate. If you recall, we met this gal ever so briefly in North Carolina at the Duke camp."

I interjected. "Susan?"

"Yes!" he exclaimed. "Susan is living there and training with Dmitri full time at the moment. And Dmitri knows all about you. Even before this possibility came about, I spoke to him about you. I proposed the idea of you training with him over the summer even before catching wind that you had left the university. He was open to the idea of training you and Susan together if you are able to move to up to Tennessee."

Even through his thick Australian accent, I could hear the tone of his voice turn. "If you're serious about your training and making it to the London Olympics next year, you will take my advice this time and *not* pass up this opportunity."

A bit thrown off by the sudden severity in his voice, I stammered, "Yeah, uh, of course!"

"Very well then, I will follow up with Dmitri. Why don't you talk things over with your mum to see how soon you can get yourself up to Knoxville."

June 29, 2011. Not even one week later, I gathered all that was important from home, packed my belongings into the back of my truck, and took yet another leap of faith. I was confident that this time the net would once again appear to catch me the same way it always had.

* * *

Four hundred and twenty-three miles later, I pulled into the complex of my soon-to-be apartment home with my new roommate and training partner, Susan.

I pulled the address up again on my iPhone to confirm: 100 Western Village Way, Unit 303.

"Yep, this is definitely it!"

I leaned my head out the window and tried to see if 303 meant that it was the third floor. I so desperately hoped that it would be on the first, if not second, floor.

Through the darkness I could somewhat see the dimly lit sign above the apartment doorbell labeling the unit number on the first floor. 103.

"Shit," I mumbled as I focused my eyes on the floor above. 203.

Unit 303 was, in fact, the third floor.

"That's OK," I said, reassuring myself. "I'm sure it's a lot safer than being on the bottom floors."

I was completely drained from the seven-hour drive from Hilton Head to Knoxville, TN. Both my car and my own internal gas light were on E. There was absolutely no way in hell I was going to get my queen-sized mattress out of the bed of my truck and up three flights of stairs at ten o'clock at night in this state of exhaustion.

"I'll sleep on the floor," I decided. "Just for one night."

I grabbed my pillow, comforter, and overnight necessities and headed up to the elevator-less top floor. My legs were stiff from the drive, and with each step, my legs felt like they were made of solid lead.

I pressed the doorbell button under the sign for 303. Through the thin aluminum door, I heard the doorbell ringing inside.

"Grab Bailey!" I heard a girl's voice shout.

Grab who? I thought. *Am I at the wrong door?* It was too late to walk away now.

Moments later, the door swung open.

"Hey! How was the drive? Welcome!" Susan beamed.

Over her shoulder, I saw some dude standing in the living room holding one pissed-off cat.

"This is Jarred, my boyfriend," she added, turning around. "And my kitty, Bailey."

Susan reached out to pet the calico wad of fur Jarred was struggling to maintain. The cat broke its eye contact with me for the first time since our introduction and let out a long hiss, exposing its four sharp teeth to all of us.

"Stop it!" Susan snapped. "That's enough, Bailey!"

My eyes widened. I didn't even attempt to hide the look of sheer shock on my face. The only thoughts running through my head were: *Cat? Bailey? Boyfriend?* Three roommates—was I moving in with a family? *And that's no "kitty." That's one fat, angry cat.*

"Uh," I replied hesitantly, trying to ignore the many elephants in the room. "The drive was pretty exhausting. Those winding roads through the Smokies are no joke!"

I walked inside the carpeted all-in-one living room, dining, and kitchen area. Still holding onto my luggage, several yellowish-brown stains on the carpet immediately grabbed my attention. I opted not to set my bags down on any surface.

The stench confirmed the culprit. *Those are from you, little kitty. Mmm, cat urine.*

The forced smile on to my face began to fade. I looked up from the floor as Jarred took a step toward me. Resituating the cat on his left side, he stuck out his hand.

"Hey, Jarred, nice to meet—"

"Let me show you your room!" Susan interrupted.

I followed Susan to my room, keeping one cautious eye on Bailey.

"This is your room!" she said, opening the first door we came to. "Across the hall is our bathroom."

I walked inside what seemed to be a large, empty closet with one small window. The yellowish carpet stains continued into what was going to be my room.

The walls of this oversized closet had a gaudy sheen with a strange, sponge-painted texture. One small, curtainless window looked out to the limbs of a pine tree. There was no curtain rod or hardware, just a rectangular glass hole.

I felt a sneeze coming on. Trying to hold it in, I looked up toward the dusty ceiling fan. Two out of three bulbs were burnt out.

"I'll let you get situ—"

"Auuhhhhchuuueee!" It finally came out.

"I'll let you get situated," Susan repeated. "Let me know if you need anything." Her voice trailed off as she walked away.

I stood there, trying to rub my itching eyes with an armful of luggage. I looked down at the floor as my eyes welled up with tears and the lump in my throat continued to swell.

This was it. This was my new home, and these were my new roommates. Susan, Jarred, and Bailey.

I laid my white Anthropologie comforter down over the stained carpet. It stretched from corner to corner, covering the entire floor space of the room. I was hopeful but doubted that even a queen mattress would be able to fit in here.

I set my pillow and duffel bag on top of my blanket. I reached down into the bottom of my duffel and grabbed the cord to my phone charger.

I set my alarm for 7:00 a.m. and plugged my phone into the charger. Tomorrow was my first day of practice, bright and early.

I could hardly wait to meet my new coach and start training again.

"Auuhhhhchuuueee!" With one last sneeze, I drifted off to sleep.

20

THE UNICORN

"Zyrtec or Claritin?" I asked myself, standing alone in the allergy aisle of the twenty-four-hour CVS Pharmacy on Kingston Pike.

This would usually have been a question for none other than my mother, but it was 6:30 in the morning and I would have felt bad waking her up for such a simple, unnecessary question.

Non-drowsy Claritin it is. Extra strength. I grabbed a small bottle of eyedrops and the largest bottle of Fiji water on my way out. On my way home from the drugstore, I downed the recommended daily dose for adults and children over the age of six.

I arrived back at the apartment just in time to help my roomie, Susan, carry her blue tube-shaped bag of poles, measuring approximately fourteen feet long and about eight inches in diameter, down from our third-floor apartment. It wasn't all that heavy; I would guesstimate fifteen, maybe twenty pounds. But the awkward dimensions made the trip down three flights of stairs nearly impossible. The 180-degree turns on a narrow staircase with a fourteen-foot-long object were a real bitch.

Sweating and out of breath, I set my side of the poles down beside her Toyota Prius, marked with several Team USA Olympic rings stickers plastered to both the bumper and rear window.

"How the hell did you do this by yourself?" I asked, still panting like a dog after a long session of fetch.

"It wasn't easy," Susan said, handing me one of two Tennessee-orange ratchet straps.

"What do I do with this?" I said, staring at this contraption of engineered metal, ribbon, and rubber-coated metal hooks and wondering how it was going to attach this to that. Perplexed, I looked down at the strap, then to the pole bag, and finally back to her gold Prius.

Awaiting her response, I proceeded to watch in silence as she power cleaned the pole bag to chest height and rolled it on top of the roof racks on her car. She meticulously wrapped the orange strap around the blue tube, underneath the roof rack, back around the tube, and finally securing one black hook to the other one. She pulled on the gold metal thingy again and again. It made a noise like a rusty pepper grinder as it tightened with each tug.

"Nice!" I exclaimed, thinking she deserved a gold star for that performance. I smiled, handing her the other ratchet strap. "That's all you, girl. I'm not sure I caught all that."

I stood back and took in one of the most ridiculous sights I think I've ever witnessed: her gold Prius with a blue fourteen-foot-long tube of poles fastened to the top. It was Toyota's newest model. The Toyota Unicorn hatchback, Team USA edition.

I bit my upper lip, trying to hold in my laughter, but it wasn't long before I cracked.

"You mean you—" The laughter escaped. I covered my mouth trying to compose myself again. "You mean you actually are going to drive with it like that? It looks like you're about to engage in a medieval joust!"

Tears streamed down my cheeks. My own jokes never failed to crack me up.

"What's funny?" Susan asked, not amused.

"Nothing. It's almost 8:00. We should head out."

* * *

As we pulled up to Tom Black Track, I flipped the passenger seat visor down one last time to check if my puffy red eyes I had woken up with had gotten any better.

They weren't totally back to normal yet, but they were much less swollen than they had been earlier. My red eyes read more "I'm just really tired" than "I have severe cat allergies and I slept in feline urine last night."

From a distance, I could see my new coach, Dmitri, pacing back and forth on the track. He waved to us from a distance.

Typically before I meet someone, I tend to have some sort of visual in my head of what they will look like, sound like, even act like. I've always been a visual person, and most of the time I was pretty good at imagining what I was about to walk into beforehand. But boy, was I off on this one.

He beamed. "Hello ladeez! How are you?" His words had a heavy accent. We crossed over the twelve lanes of red rubber track into the grassy infield to greet him.

"My name is Dmitri!" He stuck out his hand with the biggest, most animated grin on his face. He was well dressed in a silver silk, button-down shirt, black dress pants and calfskin Ferragamo loafers. The Gancini bit had me baffled.

The image of what I expected our coach to look like and act like was shattered into little bitty, finale-sized confetti pieces. My anticipations were so far off.

His energy and eternal happiness radiated almost blindingly. His accent wasn't the standard Russian accent I was used to, but at the same time it was strangely familiar. It was Russian mixed with a hint of Australian. There was a distinct exuberance I recognized as well. Where had I heard this before?

It finally came to me. Hit me like a ton of bricks. I bit down on my upper lip and looked down at the shaggy grass beneath my feet. I knew if I held eye contact a moment longer, I would surely erupt into convulsing laughter.

It was undoubtedly the voice of Borat.

Borat.

Is this real? Am I dreaming? I have got to be sleeping on the floor of Susan's guest closet still.

Both eyes began to water—this time not because of my cat allergies. My mouth twitched. I held my outburst in, squeezing all my muscles with my eyes tightly shut. Pulling myself together, I replied, "So nice to finally meet you!"

Susan and I proceeded to unpack the poles from her blue tube for our jump practice that morning. I needed something, anything to distract me and divert my attention away from the voice of Borat.

As we unpacked our poles, Dmitri continued. "Okeey. Today, ladeez, we are going to start weeth some short approach dreels. And then, we'll make our way back to the longer full approach jumps. I jeest want to geet a better idea of where you ladeez are at. How does all that sound, eh?"

I nodded, still avoiding all eye contact.

"Sounds good, Coach!" Susan added.

That morning, Susan and I had an amazing jump session. I mean a *phenomenal* jump session. My legs felt good, and I was firing on all cylinders. I got into my groove quickly and was finishing jumps I didn't even know I had in me.

Summertime in Knoxville, TN was truly something special. The air smelled sweet and the Smokies were very much alive and green. The white dogwood trees that lined the outdoor track were in full bloom and beginning to shed their petals like summer snow. Dmitri was an added breath of fresh air. He was positive, fun to work with, had so much great feedback, and his insight seemed to really click for me. Sometimes you just need to hear things a different way for things to sink in.

At the end of practice, Dmitri asked if we could meet later that afternoon, possibly at Barnes and Noble, so we could sit down and go over a tentative schedule for the remainder of the summer and into fall.

"I have a job. *I* have to work." Susan turned to look at me as she went on. "I'm working tonight, till seven, so I—"

"OK then!" Dmitri interrupted. "7:15 tonight, we meet! The Barnes and Noble next door to the Health Shoppe you work at, Susan. Sound good?"

"Yep!" I said.

"That's fine," Susan concluded.

The fifteen-minute ride home from the track back to our little apartment complex was a quiet one.

I sat in silence, trying to figure out why the sudden attitude after we both had a great practice. Why the need to turn to me and emphasize that *she* had to work? Was she upset that I didn't have a job? That my family was helping to support me at the moment? I couldn't put my finger on the reason, but I could feel a subtle tension and an acute animosity that I couldn't quite get to the bottom of.

As we pulled into the complex, Susan broke the ambient silence to ask me if it was OK if I took the poles in by myself today since she was running late to *her* job.

I didn't mind. "Sure!" I replied.

As I dehorned her Toyota Unicorn, Susan ran upstairs to grab a change of clothes and fill up her water bottle. I struggled up every stair. Flight after flight, eventually I made it to the third floor, out of breath again, with a couple of new nicks and bruises on my limbs.

A couple hours and a hot shower later, I not only managed to get the poles up three flights of stairs but my mattress as well. For the first time, I was grateful for our third roommate

Jarred, because that queen mattress was not going up those stairs willingly.

Having my bed in my room made it feel one step closer to home. I just lay there, exhausted and motionless, listening to my favorite Hootie album and staring at the empty wall where no flat-screen TV could ever fit.

A text popped up on my phone, interrupting the usual nostalgia from Darius Rucker's soft southern rasp. It was from Susan.

"Hey, Ang! Thanks for taking care of the poles for me. Eddie, my boss, said if you wanted to come in today before we meet with Dmitri, he'll do a BodPod test with you to get your body comp stats and sit down with you to go over a general nutrition plan. It's a pretty cool little test. I like to do it before summer training so I can track my progress over the fall."

I replied, "Thanks, Susan! Can I come by around 6:00? Does that work?"

"Yep! I'll let Eddie know. Bring a pen and a notebook to take notes. He is a wealth of knowledge when it comes to nutrition."

I thanked her but couldn't help wondering if she was really being nice or if she got commission on booking BodPod appointments. I wasn't sure, but either way I desperately needed help when it came to my nutritional needs. That was the one thing that I was sure about.

21

THIS MEANS WAR

Two slices of low-sodium Ezekiel bread, two egg whites, one whole egg, and precisely one cup of fresh organic spinach. Eddie from the Health Shoppe had my nutrition plan down to a science. Every meal consisted of just the right ratio of carbs to protein to fats and included some sort of dark leafy green.

I was eating six small meals a day, one every three hours, supplementing with protein powders, downing spoonfuls of flaxseed and fish oils, and beginning each morning and ending every evening with a palmful of vitamins. And wait for it . . . I was consuming over twenty-five hundred calories a day! Over *double* my previous intake.

At first it was mortifying. Just seeing "2-5-0-0 cals" written out was enough to make me want to puke. I was dubious that this amount of food, supplements, and vitamins could possibly fit in my stomach all in one day. However, after a couple of days realizing that I actually had enough energy to get through these grueling two-a-day workouts and then some, I was all in.

Due to my severe allergies, I suffered through those first couple of months from what felt like a chronic upper respiratory infection. In my desperate attempt to stay out of the house and away from that damn cat as much as possible, I found a job at a nearby sushi restaurant as a lunch-shift hostess. The shift fit perfectly between our 8:00 a.m. first workout and our 4 p.m. afternoon practice.

It wasn't much. Actually, it was almost nothing—eight bucks an hour, three to four hours a day. But it was enough to put an end to Susan's "woe is me, I have to work" dialogue that played in my ear like a broken record.

Ironically, the sushi bar was right across the street from Dmitri's office. Explaining to my coworkers how I knew this exuberant man that often came by during my shifts was always a fun little challenge. I so desperately wanted to say he was just my hairdresser that worked at the salon next door or the barista from Gourmet Market across the street. But all of those options would have been a big fat lie. He was my pole vault coach.

"You? Pole vaulting?" they would say, the usual intro to an avalanche of questions.

"You're training for the Olympics? Wait, what? I didn't even know that pole vaulting had an Olympics? That's the one in track where you run with that long, bendy pole and try and catapult yourself the highest?"

"Exactly! You're so smart. That's exactly what I do!" I said, gathering an armful of menus to pretend to place elsewhere.

I thought maybe if I made myself look busy, I could end the potentially hour-long conversation about how I got into pole vaulting, why I wasn't in school, how often I had to train, how many hours, where I practiced, what did I do in practice . . . The interrogation would go on and on if I allowed it.

My coworkers, even the obnoxiously nosy ones, became my first friends in Tennessee. They were my ears to vent to about everything: practices, roommates, cats, my coach.

Sam, one of the many servers at the restaurant, was my

closest friend. We immediately bonded over our love for avocados.

"I just eat avocados these days like it's going out of style," she would say, adjusting her boobs to accentuate her cleavage. The first day we met, she showed me the tattoo she was most pleased with.

El Petron was tattooed in an Old English font underneath her left tit. *"El Patron!"* Sam exclaimed proudly. "It means 'the boss!'"

I could never bring myself to tell her that whoever was the boss of that tattoo spelled *patron* incorrectly. It was supposed to have an *a*, not an *e*.

I was so grateful to have her as a close friend. Some days I could hardly wait to come into work to tell her the latest Susan story.

It became a thing. Sam was often more excited to hear the latest episode of "The Struggles with Susan" than I was to vent about the level of bullshit I had to put up with. I couldn't make this stuff up if I wanted to. Between her, the cat, and the boyfriend, I was living in a real-life sitcom.

Before long, a few other employees began tuning in for story time. The last episode had left off with a petty "I have to pay all my own bills, wahh wahh wahh" comment during a casual conversation between Susan and me about who our cell service provider was.

Sam came marching up to the hostess stand. "So, what do you got for me? I need a story. It's *so* slow in here today, I'm bored as hell!"

Drew walked up behind Sam and chimed in. "Yeah, whatcha got for us?"

"Boy oh boy! Do I got a story for you guys today!" I could see the anticipation sparkling in their eyes.

"So last night, I get home from a long practice, and I am beat! I mean the kind of tired that I could just collapse at any moment. I'm a little bit hangry too at this point, and the only thing I can think about is scarfing down some leftover chicken for dinner, taking the quickest hot shower, and getting in my warm cozy bed.

"I get home, inhale my dinner in legit less than three minutes, go to get in the shower, and our shared bathroom is occupied. Jarred's in the bathroom. Turns out he's got food poisoning and not doing so hot.

"Susan tells me this as she passes by with a load of laundry in her arms. I'm like whatever, I won't shower. Gross, I know, but I wasn't going to wait around for whatever's happening in there to be over.

"I get in my bed, stretch my legs out underneath the covers, and suddenly I hit a wet spot. I'm like, 'What in the actual fuck? Why is my bed wet?'"

"Hold on!" I interrupted my own story, turning to the group of guests that just walked through the glass double doors. "Hi! How are you guys? How many are we, four?"

"Yes, can we have one of those tables outside?" the woman replied.

"Of course, right this way," I said, motioning for the guests to follow behind me.

As soon as I sat the guests, I hurried back to my hostess stand. Sam and Drew stood anxiously waiting, both ignoring the table I had just seated.

"OK, where was I?" I asked, returning to my post.

"Uh, I think you just got in bed and something was . . . wet?" Drew reminded us all.

"That's right!" I went on. "I get in my bed, my little slice of heaven that I cannot wait to come home to, and there is this massive wet spot that I just rubbed my legs into. I'm talking not just a little damp; it was a small, soaking-wet puddle. I'm like *hell* no. Instantly, I had a pretty good idea what it might be, so I rip the sheets off, and lo and behold—"

"Wait, stop right there!" Sam interrupted. "I really gotta go greet this table. They're starting to stare at us!"

"All right, all right. Go!" I said.

"You gotta tell me," Drew inquired with a slight smile. "It was cat piss, wasn't it?"

Smiling back, I nodded. "But it gets better," I added. "Just wait."

Sam hustled back. Halfway back to the hostess stand, she grinned and pointed. "Drew, you got a piece of pickled ginger on your shoe."

"Peeling it off." He thanked Sam, and I went on again.

"After I rip the sheets of my bed, I find a yellow—yellow-brown, actually—puddle that's about a foot and a half in diameter. Not only has it soaked through my sheets *and* my down mattress topper, but it's well into the mattress too."

They both stared at me, mouths wide open, like I had just pulled a rabbit out from under the stacked menus.

"Gross, huh? But it gets better. So, I call out, 'Susan, uh, I think your cat peed all over my bed.' Soon, she enters my room to investigate the scene and leans down over the yellow urine stain. She takes a whiff and affirms in her mousy little voice, pushing her glasses further up on her nose, 'Yep! That's definitely pee.'

"I'm standing there, mind you, with cat pee still all over my legs like, 'No fucking shit, Sherlock.' And she has the nerve to say, as she leaves, 'Sorry about that. My clothes should be out of the dryer in an hour, then it's all yours. Don't forget to clean the lint out of the tray. You forget a lot of times.'

"I'm telling you, icing on the cake. I'm like seeing red at this point. I don't just want to strangle her disgusting, inconsiderate little cat but her too! For her lack of empathy and for just being a selfish bitch! OK, not really. I took that a little far, but I was really mad, OK?

"She had the nerve to remind me to clean out the lint tray! Bitch, your fucking cat just ruined my mattress and I can't even shower because your boyfriend is either shitting his brains out or vomiting up his lungs. What am I supposed to do? Sit here with cat pee on me and patiently wait for your clothes to dry? You are out of your *mind*, woman!"

I'm heated again, but at this point, Sam and Drew are rolling. Slowly, I begin to see the humor in the level of ridiculousness, and my anger soon fades to laughter.

"So, I'm livid. And through all this anger I get a second wind. It's late now, like 8:00. I head down to the local PetSmart. It's in the shopping center right across the street, and I am out for blood at this point.

"What I really wanted to do was ask for the largest rat trap they sell that can be used for stray cats, but instead I inquired about a spray repellent for cats. They had just the product I was searching for. It's called Keep Off. You basically spray it everywhere you don't want the cat to go. Something about how they don't like the smell of it and won't even dare to go near it. It even comes in a convenient aerosol spray too!

"So . . . guess what I did?" I announced.

Tears stream down Sam and Drew's faces. Neither one of them could pull it together long enough to form an answer, so I went on with my story.

"I covered my entire room, dining room, and kitchen with it! Yep, everywhere that cat didn't needed to be! Used all ten ounces. I haven't seen that cat since," I noted proudly.

Just getting it out in the open through Susan Story Time was a cathartic release. I didn't realize it then, but releasing these bottled emotions was so beneficial to my unconscious mind. By bringing these emotions into my conscious awareness, I was letting go of my ill will by means of laughter.

These venting sessions kept me sane, allowing me to bear through the hard times and put up with the bullshit I had no choice but to deal with. By seeing the humor in my stories, I was able to cope with my situation, and it allowed me to spin a potentially unbearable situation into something that was laughable.

I learned quite a few life lessons living with this motley

crew. I learned patience; I learned to laugh at the things you can't change; and I learned to never be quick to judge, because you never know what people are going through.

A couple weeks down the road, I learned while eavesdropping on a conversation Susan was having with her father that her family had cut her off financially right before I moved in. Immediately, it all made perfect sense: those petty comments about having to work and why she let an additional roommate move into the mix with her boyfriend and cat. It was so she could afford her new financially independent life.

By no means is that a reason to treat someone with disrespect, but it made me really think about how easy it is to pass judgment without knowing what someone else might be going through.

I vowed that next time I saw a driver whipping through traffic, I would take into consideration that maybe their wife was laboring in the front seat. Or the next time a car came flying around the corner of a parking garage, maybe they were trying to get away from a dentist that had just sexually assaulted them. The next time a woman walked into the sushi restaurant and demanded to be seated in a booth immediately, maybe she had a day from hell. You just never know.

22

THE RAPIDS

L ife is a _____. Which word came to mind first? A highway, a rollercoaster, a bumpy road, a wild ride, or a real bitch?

For me, I fill in this blank with the word "river." I see life, at least my own life, to be an ever-flowing river. Sections of this river of life are a smooth, steady ride. And like most rivers, sometimes out of nowhere, the river starts winding and makes an unexpected turn, taking us in an entirely new direction we hadn't anticipated.

Once in a while, the gradient of our geography steepens and the water starts gaining a lot of momentum. It doesn't take long for us to begin feeling out of control. The once calm, steady stream turns into whitewater rapids, and out of nowhere, we free fall down what seems to be Niagara Falls.

For a few moments there, we lose sight of all of our surroundings and plunge deep down into a pool of dark water, not knowing which way is up or which way is down, thinking we may never come up for air.

Lucky for us, the human body is relatively buoyant, and we will eventually float to the surface, dead or alive. When we do come up for air, suddenly we are in a whole new place.

Just like that, with the blink of an eye, everything has changed. Without even a warning, yesterday's normal doesn't exist in our world today. No matter how hard we try to swim upstream back to an earlier place we passed by, the river continues flowing. Our only option is to continue to flow with it and move on. Life happens just like that.

I'd be lying if I said that when my river's pace was smooth and steady, I stopped to take a moment to appreciate the beauty of everything around me. To really take it *all* in, realize just how far I had come, how grateful I was for where my journey had led me, and witness all my blessings before me in the flesh. With so much positive momentum, it's easy to get caught up in the thrill of the ride.

It took me a lot of time contemplating how or if I could properly write this chapter. The memories are still painful to relive, but on the flip side, the writing process is like medicine to me. Its healing power is truly amazing. Putting my thoughts to paper and articulating my emotions and feelings into words where I can see them feels like I'm weaving the canvas for my life to be painted on, and once it's complete, I'll take a few steps back and see the bigger picture.

I couldn't allow myself to take the easy route and leave this series of unfortunate events and gut-wrenching memories out. After all, they were responsible for the cultivation of this indestructible, fearless, "no fucks given" attitude that allowed me to temporarily withdraw myself from my current reality.

The events that take place in this chapter not only changed my attitude but also shaped a new perspective and allowed me to tap into a higher, almost masochistic mentality that allowed me to push myself to a place where the impossible was tangible. My twelve-month journey from being a victim of anorexia to the US Track and Field Olympic Trials wasn't a miracle; it was a mindset.

Life has a way of sending me over the edge when I least expect it, taking me from sixty back down to zero. Every time it's happened, the circumstances are always similar. Things would be going far too well! And I'll have forgotten to count my blessings. As the saying goes, "When you take things for granted, the things you are granted get taken."

There were two phone calls. Both from my mom. Both beginning in the exact same way. I picked up the phone like any other phone call from home.

"Ang?" she said. "Are you done with practice for the day?"

I remember thinking this was an unusual way for her to ask how practice went. I was used to an exuberant, "How high did you jump today, sweetie?"

I could tell by the tone of her voice something was off.

"Yeah, I'm home now," I replied.

It was January 2012, the start of my first indoor season training with Dmitri and Susan in Tennessee. And boy, was my river flowing! Fast!

I'd been dragged through hell by the ponytail that fall. I had made it through the hardest training regimen that, at the time, I didn't think was humanly possible to endure. I'd even recovered from an eating disorder and hadn't murdered my roommates' cat yet. I'd gotten faster, stronger, more technically sound than ever before.

My biggest accomplishment had gone unnoticed. I had gained a confidence in myself as an athlete in both my abilities and my performance. It was something I hadn't had before, and I took it for granted. To be honest, I didn't even notice this huge accomplishment until *poof*, it vanished. I repeat: "When you take things for granted, the things you are granted get taken."

In the blink of an eye, everything changed. I didn't say two words after I heard the news.

"Um." She paused. "Granny passed away this morning."

I didn't speak, I couldn't make words. Instead, I hung up the phone and I turned it off.

I thought I was strong. I was clearly physically strong, I knew that. I could bench press more than multiple times my body weight. I was mentally strong, obviously. I could fight through a tough workout and hang on mentally longer than my body was willing to last.

My coach always told me, "Like a chain, we are only as strong as our weakest link." What I didn't have, unbeknownst to me, was emotional strength. That was my weak link. That was my Achilles heel.

Losing my grandmother was my first real loss. I didn't have the support and wasn't in a place where I could handle the emotions that came flooding in from this unexpected loss. The five stages of grief kicked in fast: the denial, the anger, all the toxic what if's that soon followed.

I pretended it wasn't real, that my river was still on the same steady course as yesterday. That things were just fine and dandy and I hadn't just plunged into the darkest waters fathomable.

My refusal soon turned into pure rage. "How can this happen? It wasn't meant to be like this!" I said over and over, sobbing alone in my closet-sized bedroom, sealed off from any light.

"She was supposed to see me compete at the Olympics! This wasn't a part of my plans!" I screamed into my pillow.

The grief was debilitating, and it sucked every ounce of life out of me. It stole all my motivation from me and took my invaluable confidence with it. My once enthusiastic "can't even sleep I'm so excited for my 6:00 a.m. workout" attitude turned into a twenty-five-pound dumbbell pressing my face into my pillow wet with tears.

I was far from fully recovered from this loss when the second call came. Exactly one month and one week later.

My mom called. "Ang? Are you done with practice for the day?"

I remembered the last time she began with that line. The tone of her voice alluded to the worst.

"Yeah, what's wrong?" I asked.

"Sarah Creech passed away. It was an accident. She had an asthma attack. It was too late when they found her."

I'd never seen or heard my mother cry before this minute, but through the phone I heard the tears in her voice. The sound was unbearable. How could I possibly be strong when the strongest woman I know was so broken, and the other two were *gone?*

I felt robbed, like something had been stolen from me. Two of the strongest women in my life—my grandmother and close friend, both who I looked up to—were taken from us all too soon. Every aspect of my life turned to doubt; in particular, whether I'd be able to feel real happiness or be motivated again.

I wish I could say that the events that followed brought light into my life, but that was not the case. The depression spiraled out of control, and my coach was anything but empathetic.

"She won't know you're not there," he said, forbidding me from attending Sarah's funeral.

At the indoor track meets that season, where I'd been so excited to compete in front of all my old coaches and against my old teammates, I no heighted not once but three times in a row—in front of *everyone.*

The excitement and anticipation I had to prove to myself and everyone that doubted me—all those who told me I was making the biggest mistake of my life dropping out of college —were crushed. Most importantly, I so desperately needed to prove my competency to my parents and show them that it wasn't all for nothing, and I wasn't able to.

I lost every bit of confidence and faith in myself and began to second guess every decision I had made to follow through with chasing my dreams.

The grief came in waves. Once these waves washed over me, drained me of all my tears, and left me feeling totally empty, something changed. Amid this nothingness, a new part of me was born. This part of me wasn't exactly a sweet, bubbly ball of positivity.

I wish I could say that a switch flipped and just like that I turned into a mini Tony Robbins, but that wasn't at all the case. It was a dark, masochistic, and unmerciful person that was born. I jumped like there were no repercussions for mistakes, like paralysis wasn't a possible outcome. I walked into every practice wondering how much pain I could put myself through during this workout. With this mentality, I was able to push myself to a place where the impossible was tangible.

I must have been heartless, right? My beating heart had just been ripped straight out of my chest. I didn't worry about trying to heal it. Worrying would have just been another fat assumption. An assumption that tomorrow would be there for me to experience some type of agony, and I was well aware that tomorrow was never guaranteed.

A thorough psychological analysis might suggest that maybe I had reached the final stage of grieving, the acceptance phase. It might make sense to say it was all apathy at this point, that I simply didn't care what happened, but that would have been a lie too.

Perhaps I hadn't been able to pour my heart into something until it had been ripped out of my chest first, and I learned what emotional strength really was. The kind of strength I lacked before. Despite this heartbreak, I chose not to give up on my dreams. Through the hurt, I developed a mindset that was unstoppable and fearless in the pursuit of my dreams. This indomitable will was my emotional strength.

I showed up to that last track meet, the one I *had* to go to in lieu of Sarah's funeral, and joined the "no fucks given" club. I didn't care if I snapped my pole into three different pieces mid-jump. I didn't care if I landed on my neck in the steel box or if my ankle snapped at takeoff and the bone protruded through my skin. I'd witnessed all of these things happen in competition before my eyes. Those used to be the thoughts that invaded my mind in competition.

Why had I ever worried about a potential unsightly outcome, letting my parents down by my performance, or not qualifying to the indoor national track meet? All along, these worries were also insinuating that tomorrow had always been promised.

Today is a God-given gift, and tomorrow is in no way a guarantee. At any given second, our soul can vanish from this earth in the blink of an eye. Life is fucking fragile.

The more time I spent thinking about life—how fragile it was, how we have just one chance to really live—the more it sucked the worry and fear right out of me.

I was grateful that I was here, that I was able, and that I had every opportunity laid out in front of me to live my life to its fullest and drain it for all it was worth. I was going to wring that bitch out until it was high and dry.

I didn't clear a single bar until this final meet, my last opportunity to qualify for indoor nationals, the meet Dmitri forbade me to miss.

I missed Sarah's funeral that Saturday afternoon, but she got to watch my track meet. Her and my grandma both, front row seats and a bird's eye view. God had other plans for them as angels, for reasons we'll never fully understand.

There is no such thing as a full recovery from this loss. They were both the type of women that can never be forgotten, but I realized that whether or not they were physically here with us, life would continue to move on, the river would keep flowing, and we had to live our lives to the fullest in honor of them.

What had I been waiting for? I gave it everything I had in me that Saturday afternoon at the meet: no mercy, no fear, no hesitation, no fucks given whether the outcome was good, bad, or downright ugly. I turned my brain off and I just competed.

I didn't qualify to indoor nationals, *but* I cleared two bars that meet. Two more than I had cleared all season long. I walked away from that meet with two things: a sense of peace and a vengeance to turn my dreams into a reality.

23

NO HEIGHTS

W hat takes three tries, ends before it ever started, is high off the ground, sometimes hurts physically, always hurts emotionally, and looks like three small x's when you see it on paper? Here's a hint: it's a pole vault term, and it's one of the few that is not a PG-13 innuendo.

It's called a "no height."

No heighting is an important term, and it is imperative I define it in elaborate detail in order for you to fully understand what the hell went on that warm June day at the 2012 Olympic Trials in Eugene, Oregon.

When an athlete no heights, he or she fails three times in a row to clear their opening height, and for them, the competition ends immediately. They are out. Donezo.

The competition continues as the bar is raised to the next height. All athletes that have cleared the previous height continue in the competition and have another three attempts at clearing this higher bar.

When everything is on the line, generally most people will have some sort of physiological reaction to this type of stress. Examples include but are not limited to: an elevated heart rate, adrenaline production, increased breathing, or decreased digestive activity. Stress is both a biological and a psycholog-ical response to a given situation. It wasn't until just recently that I had started feeling these signs and symptoms again.

The casting interviews didn't do it, *Big Brother* move-in day didn't even do it, but the first sign of one of these symptoms happened during an extremely important tiebreaker round of a Head of Household competition.

Right after my HOH week, I landed myself a spot on the block next to my best friend, Kaycee. This meant that I had a pretty good chance, given the circumstances, of being evicted from the house that week. The veto competition would decide my fate.

It was a Saturday, if I remember correctly. I woke up that morning to my heart pounding uncontrollably. There was nothing I could do; no amount of controlled breathing would lower its tempo. The more I tried to calm myself down, the more I got worked up.

My anxiety was like a boomerang with a homing device set to one particular individual. Trying anything to calm my mind and quiet my nerves, each scenario I ran through my head was like throwing a boomerang out. And in each scenario, it returned right back to one person. Yup, you guessed it: Tyler.

If I or someone I was aligned with didn't win the veto today, I was going home. *What if I get evicted before I have the chance to tell him how I really feel?* My mind spiraled. I imagined myself having to pack my bags and leave him all alone in the middle bed we shared in the blue room. These thoughts were enough to send me over the edge. If you want to know where your heart lies, pay attention to where your mind wanders. Or in this case, *who* your boomerang returns to.

I say this with conviction: sometimes the stars *do* align. That Saturday afternoon, they did. If you watched season 20, you already understand what I'm getting at here.

I wasn't meant to go home that week, and what happened

during the OTEV veto competition was visible proof of that. It was the kind of shit that doesn't just happen by coincidence. CBS All Access has the hard evidence. (#NotAnAd. But go subscribe and watch it.)

The morning leading up to this epic competition was pure hell. The same apprehensive kind of hell I felt the night before the Trials when I realized something about myself was off. I don't remember what exactly happened, if there was a certain event that caused this sudden awareness or if it was just something innate that I sensed was off.

* * *

Seven whole years, an extensive sport psych assessment, and a lot of expensive therapy sessions later, there is still not one clear answer as to what caused the numbness and the out-of-body experience I felt on the day of competition at the Olympic Trials.

The last memory I have was the night before the meet, lying in bed and trying to sleep in the three-bedroom Airbnb in Eugene, OR that my mom, my coach, and I all shared.

I had rolled over and grabbed my phone from the nightstand and opened my favorite sports inspiration video on YouTube, "How Great I Am." I could practically recite the entire clip verbatim. Out of the thirty-something million views and counting, I accounted for at least one thousand of them.

This video never failed to send chills down my spine, raise goosebumps on my arms and neck, and make me feel like I could run straight through a brick wall—but this time it conjured *nothing*. I went to sleep that night praying that this too shall pass, preferably before tomorrow morning.

I would have given anything to feel a fraction of the emotional bomb that exploded in my chest at the Olympic Trials on the day of my veto competition several years later.

The morning of the BB competition, I closed my eyes and immersed myself in this memory I have from the Trials, hoping I could call forth the numbness and soothe my rattled core.

There I was, lined up shoulder to shoulder with the 2012 Olympic Trials pole vault finalists in the infield of historic Hayward Field. My blue, white, and lime-green Nike spikes were planted firmly in the red rubber surface. The same surface that lay over top of the basement where the first pair of Nike shoes were constructed and the multi-billion-dollar athletic company began. I was standing at the birthplace of *legends*.

The national anthem began to play. I looked up to where my mom and coach sat and forced a smile on my face to the eighty-five hundred spectators that filled the stands to watch us compete. I can hardly describe the emotions I had in this moment, because to this day I struggle to understand them myself.

It was like I couldn't connect to what was going on around me. Almost like I was witnessing myself living the moment without physically being there. As if my mind was just recording the memories for me to experience at a later date.

It was the closest thing I've encountered to an out-of-body experience. My brain was playing cruel tricks on me. Like this life I was living wasn't mine. Like I had lost control of it, and the part of me that made me human had left. Numbness, blankness, and a body not capable of feeling emotion were all that remained.

"Motivationless or amotivation," my sports psychologist called it; the reason why I no heighted. He said, "It's just science. The chronic stress that this competition put on you taxed your limbic system, which is what's responsible for your emotions. And *that* left you physically and emotionally depleted."

As I stood on the runway moments from taking my first attempt at the opening height of 4.25 meters, 13'11", I white-knuckled my fifteen-foot fiberglass pole in my right hand. I felt the rough, chalky athletic tape in my palm and a subtle head-wind at my face. That was all.

My once intrinsic motivation to compete for personal reward and the pure satisfaction I got from all the little victories at some point was turned to an extrinsic motivation during my summer training for the Olympic Trials.

This extrinsic motivation was fueled by the need to prove myself, to make up for the guilt that gymnastics had left me with, to justify myself dropping out of college, and to still my need for validation. The perfectionist in me still based my self-esteem and self-worth around my performance. I still needed to feel like I was enough. I needed the title Olympian to feel that I was enough. How f-ing crazy is that?

I was headed down a spiral staircase that led to a path I had been down before as a gymnast. Each step down, as my intrinsic motivation turned to extrinsic motivation, I was one step closer to the road to burnout. The last step before the eroded path, the path gymnastics had once led me down, was where I landed. I was in a place of amotivation or, as Webster's defines it, "a state of lacking any motivation to engage in an activity, characterized by a lack of perceived competence and/or a failure to value the activity or its outcomes."

Before my first two attempts at 4.25 meters, the opening height, I didn't even have the motivation to try and convince myself that everything was OK and would turn out all right. I just went through the motions, doing everything I had repetitively trained myself to do. I had my cues in my head. All I had to do was relax, drive out of the back, stand up, and jump. But for some reason, my legs felt heavy and my body felt uncoordinated.

It was now my third and final attempt. If I didn't clear this bar, it was a no height at the Olympic Trials. Still I felt nothing. No last attempt nerves, no adrenaline. Nothing but a cold, hollow numbness. I pushed hard out of the back and began my countdown. As each left foot struck the track, I counted.

"Nine, eight, seven, six, five, four, three, two, one, and jump!" Me and my Olympic dream were up in the air.

My arm brushed the bar on the way down and the crossbar fell with me into the pit. When I stood up, the crowd clapped out of pity, and I was out of the meet.

As I stepped off the pit, the first place I looked was up to my coach and mom sitting in the stands. I mouthed the words "I'm sorry" to them as I walked with my head hung low back to the end of the runway to pack up my things.

What happened that day is what I consider the perfect storm.

It was the perfect combination of physical, emotional, and psychological problems, including the loss of my own personal autonomy. This created a recipe for disaster at the pinnacle of my athletic career.

At times I have wondered if I had understood what was going on, would I have been able to prevent it, to salvage my performance? If I hadn't shut out everyone and everything that didn't directly aid my performance, if I had allowed myself a life outside of pole vaulting, would I have reached this point of no return?

What if I had realized that the root of my motivation had suddenly changed and noticed that I had begun to resent my coach? Resent him for trying to control me, for not letting me go to Sarah's funeral, for telling me what I should eat, when I should sleep, how I should think, feel, act, be, and want. Resent him for treating me like an animal he was training to race in the derby. If I hadn't let this sport consume me, would I have ended up in this position?

The answer is yes. I would have somehow ended up right here, in this exact same place. Because the events that followed this painful experience led me to finding my path in the business world and discovering the entrepreneurial spirit within me.

24

LET'S MAKE A DEAL

"I would go crazy in this house without you guys," Tyler said, breaking the silence.

It wasn't the typical, tense first-date type of quiet self-awareness. It was the kind of quiet calmness that made you feel like you could just be yourself without any sort of judgement. It was one of those few moments that the cameras all suddenly disappeared. He was all that existed to me and I was all that existed to him.

You know that feeling of total completeness? Like if this moment lasted an eternity, you'd be totally OK with it? I felt it between us for the first time, but I didn't know what to do with it. At the time, I didn't know where to find the words to articulate how it felt to me, let alone to him.

Had I been able to find the proper verbiage suitable for that level of vulnerability, even without the cameras, it scared the hell out of me.

After a long pause, I added, "Same. I would die."

I thought about how effortless it had been falling for him yet how seemingly impossible it was to find the words or the courage to admit to it.

"Goin' crazy, just being in the have-not room," Tyler said.

The past several days we had been separated due to a punishment imposed on Tyler by the current HOH. He had been confined to a special room to sleep in and therefore wasn't able to sleep in our shared bed in the blue room. The separation anxiety I felt was real, but the burning question was if he felt it too.

"I miss you—and, uh, JC," I blurted out at the very last second.

The little voice in the back of my head came over my internal loudspeaker. *Damn it, Angela! How are you just going to throw JC in there like that? Why was it so hard for you to admit that you just miss him? Is it necessary for you to be so damn stubborn all the time?*

I stuck my toe in the pool of vulnerability and pulled it right back out before I even had a chance to test the waters. Admitting to myself had already been an arduous task. Now I just had to figure out another way to slide in some kind of nonchalant hint and see just how he took it.

Missed opportunity number one, the voice in my head went on. *You scared little—*

Tyler interrupted me amid my self-loathing. "I know JC—I'm sure he's loving that I'm a have not. He is *loving* that I'm a have not," Tyler repeated himself.

"Oh yes! Absolutely," I said, laughing to mask the disappointment in myself.

There was another long pause. As my smile started to fade, Tyler lifted himself off his chest, repositioning his weight onto his elbows. No longer making eye contact, he went on.

"He's definitely caught us cuddling before."

Ugh, finally! Someone lifted up the covers to reveal the elephant that had been in the room—or in our case, the bed —all along.

OK, I thought, *it's time to direct this conversation where I need it to go.*

Laughing again, I replied, "Oh, I know he has. Pretty sure

Kaycee has too." I could feel my cheeks flushing warm. Laughing was my only way to buffer this feeling of raw vulnerability.

"Have you talked to her?" Tyler asked.

"No," I said with red cheeks.

"Stupid! This game! Dude!" he shouted, shaking his head. "I hate everything. My God!"

This surge of emotion that had been triggered was the frustration of having to deal with the aftermath of what had happened between us. I knew just where he was going with this now.

We both laughed, and it was then—I can pinpoint it here —I knew these feelings were mutual.

"So annoying! Gosh, you're so annoying, Angela!" This was probably the first time, last time, and only time I loved hearing that I was annoying, because I knew precisely the feeling he felt. Having to hide our feelings constantly and always pretend to act uninterested in each other was beyond annoying and slowly driving the both of us crazy.

He went on with his rant. "You're the worst!" Tyler exclaimed.

"You're the worst." I followed suit.

"You're the worst," he retorted.

"You're the worst, *worst!*" I enunciated each "worst," emphasizing the next just a hair louder than the last.

The playful banter was like a ping pong ball between us. Back and forth and back and forth, the innocence and the infantility of it all. How an ally could turn into a friend, then into a crush, and now into this.

"You're. Way. Worse." Tyler finally ended it. It wasn't like me to let someone have the last word, but obviously he was different.

We both laughed out loud together as I buried my face in the pillow in front of me.

"Can you just go back in time and not tell me the part of your story when you went to Hawaii by yourself?"

Looking up from my pillow, I quietly mouthed back to him, "Nope. Sorry."

"Take that back. You didn't actually do that, did you?"

"I did. I'll show you pictures when we get out of here," I said, inching just the slightest bit closer. I spoke as if we were in some kind of jail—an emotional prison, if you will.

He chose his words strategically. They came out slow. "We'll take new pictures."

Deny, I could no longer. These were the words that I lived to hear.

"Deal," I concurred, deep in thought as the memories of Hawaii came flooding back in.

Every storm runs out of rain and every story has its turning point. Although I had taken one last attempt to save my pole vault career, my adventure to Hawaii was mine.

* * *

I wasn't going to give up. I was not a quitter.

I told myself I was going to make one last valiant attempt to salvage what was left of my track and field career after the unfortunate tragedy of the 2012 Olympic Trials. A short while after that painful no height, I reached out for acceptance into the Chula Vista Olympic Training Center.

I told myself, *Maybe a change in scenery, a new training regimen, different coaching, and better facilities are what I need to resuscitate my passion for this sport that I have invested all of myself in.*

Well, that was the surface-deep, embellished story I had convinced myself to be my truth at the time. But below the surface of my subconscious, the root of the problem went way deeper.

It wasn't until years later that my therapist helped me dig

down to the root of my problem, which allowed me to gain the awareness I needed to understand what had really happened.

I was running away.

25

TUMBLEWEEDS TO GREENER GRASS

I f you were just about to search where Chula Vista, or "Chula-Juana" as my teammates and I used to call it, is located, I'll save you the trouble.

It's thirty minutes south of San Diego, CA, minutes from the border of Tijuana, Mexico.

Pull out your dusty compass protractor set from middle-school geometry class. On a map of the US, place the pointed end on either South Carolina or Tennessee. Your pick.

Now stretch the pencil end out to Chula Vista, CA. Slowly rotate the compass around so that it draws a circle on your United States map. You will notice within this circle you have just drawn that there are not many places within this geographical circumference I could have moved to that were farther away from home than southern California.

Coincidence? I think not.

During the summer outdoor season leading up the Olympic Trials, I jumped a PR (personal record) of 4.40 meters, which also happened to be *exactly* the Olympic B standard. This height was just enough for me get accepted into the Chula Vista Olympic Training Center.

Three weeks after receiving my acceptance into the track

and field program, during the most miserable thirty-one-hour road trip across the country, I saw my very first tumbleweed rolling across the highway somewhere near El Paso, TX while entering New Mexico. That was also the very first time I had ever seen the border of Mexico. It was a sight I'll never forget.

Interstate 375 runs parallel to the border of Mexico for a couple miles. So close that my cell phone picked up the Mexican service provider Telcel instead of Verizon.

The difference from the left side of the highway to the right was eye-opening. From where Mexico began on the left to where our country lay on the right, it was nothing short of heartbreaking.

I can still picture it. The houses with every window busted out and the rusty holes in the roofs. The trash scattered among the children playing barefoot in the half-paved streets.

Makes and models of cars I'd never seen before: broken, rusted, and disorderly cars strewn halfway in the roads and street corners. Not because they had been parked there, but because that's where they quit working and there were no means of fixing them.

Just over the fence on the US side, brand-new automobiles whizzed past at eighty miles per hour, almost taunting the citizens on the Mexican side of the highway. It felt insensitive.

This trip from Tennessee to California was a rollercoaster of emotions extending from the highest of highs to the lowest of lows. The expectation and excitement of a new beginning to the anxiety and angst of the uncharted waters ahead. All the way down to this feeling of sadness and guilt that I experienced passing through El Paso, TX.

I was able to just pack up and go when a better opportunity with greener grass presented itself to me. I was guilty of having taken that kind of freedom for granted. I imagined what it would feel like living in the conditions I witnessed and the cruelty of being able to clearly see what seemed like greener grass just beyond the fenced highway that separated us.

During this three-day journey across the country, I had an excess of free time to do nothing but think and be alone with my thoughts. A road trip alone or any sort of traveling solo is a therapeutic experience that I highly recommend. I know it might seem scary at first, but I'm telling you, traveling alone can be life changing.

When you can remove almost all distractions for a prolonged period of time and be alone with your thoughts, eventually the clutter clears and the unwanted thoughts filter out. We're left with a clear picture of what's really important to us. We realize what really brings us happiness and fulfillment in our lives. Be mindful of what that is. That is your truth.

Without ever realizing it, commuting had always been my form of mediation ever since I was a child. The ninety minutes I'd spent in the car each way to and from gymnastics practice five times a week was the only time I had to heal. This block of time was how I dealt with stress, controlled my anxiety, thought about what it was I wanted, and allowed my thoughts to illustrate the blueprints of my life. It was where my internal dialogue was born. The good and the bad.

I so wish I'd had enough time during that cross-country drive to dig down deep, come to my truth on my own, and figure out what was *really* driving me. It took a licensed therapist to lead my archeological hunt to dig down deep and investigate the site at which my most toxic belief was buried.

She asked me questions like: "When do you feel happiest? What are some things you are good at? What does it mean to be good or good enough? Who do we need to be good enough for?" And the kicker: "What do you feel you need to do or accomplish in order to be good enough?"

These questions revealed the buried truth, my deepest root: I felt *I* wasn't enough as is. I realized that I would never be able to satisfy that hunger because there isn't an end point to reach. There was no finish line or final destination. No matter how much I accomplished in my life, this end goal would never come into sight.

The belief that I wasn't enough had both hands on the wheel and was still driving me. It had been driving me as far back as my memories go. This common yet incredibly toxic belief is what drives so many of us.

The letdown I experienced at the Trials magnified all the issues I'd been dealing with throughout my life, such as feeling that I was not worthy, thinking that I had to prove my worth, and ultimately, thinking that I wasn't enough. On top of that painful no height came a sense of overall failure.

I recognize now that I felt being an athlete at the Olympic Training Center would in some way provide the worth I was searching for. I thought that if I put enough distance between myself, my coach, my family, and the people I felt I had let down back home, it would help numb this sense of failure I was left with.

In the back of my mind, I hoped that by running away and starting over in a new place, the grass would be greener. But in all actuality, Chula Vista had no grass at all.

26

THE OTC

When I think about all the things that could be more diverse than the cast of a reality TV show, while there aren't many, one does comes to mind: a track team. Just like our country, as a team we are a melting pot. We come from every walk of life, consist of every religion, gender, sexual preference, socioeconomic background, and ethnicity. And despite our different beliefs, values, and upbringings, we are a family. One big, happy, slightly dysfunctional family.

Ask any athlete about their fellow teammates, and they will likely use the word "family" in some way and in some language. *Familia, sem'ya, gia đình, familie*—they all mean family.

We laugh as a team, cry as a team, push each other through tough practices, compete against each other, and lift each other up—all as a team. Those unbreakable bonds that form among teammates are how we get through it. It's how we manage incredibly demanding schedules and physically brutal training regiments.

The camaraderie of my teammates and this family feeling were what I missed the most leaving the University of South Carolina. Walking into my first team meeting at the Olympic

Training Center, I desperately hoped that I could find that again.

I sat down in one of the empty chairs toward the back of the room. The designated team meeting room was already full of some of the world's most talented track and field athletes. Standing in the front of the room were all the event coaches. I immediately recognized a few familiar faces: Coach Al Joyner, Brittney Reese, and Will Claye. Some of the United States' best jumpers. *Ever.*

Looking around the room brought back all those new-school, first-day feels. It was undoubtedly a melting pot. To better illustrate the caliber of athletes I was surrounded by, imagine if the Avengers formed a track team. This would have been it.

I would be lying if I said I wasn't intimidated as hell walking into a room saturated by pure talent and athletic greatness. Every man and woman in that room looked like they could either pick me up and throw me at least thirty yards, jump clear over my head, or run circles around me.

And then there I was. The most basic-looking, skinny little Carolina girl in the back of the room, just waiting for someone to turn to me and ask if I was in the wrong room. Fortunately for me, that didn't happen. What did happen, however, was that one by one we went around the room and introduced ourselves: our name, alma mater, and athletic accolades.

The first person stood. I could tell by the room's reaction and casual tone of her voice that she was an OTC vet and this wasn't her first rodeo.

"What's up, I'm Brittney," she said. "Olympic gold medalist and seven-time world champion. Ole Miss!"

Oh, wow, I thought. *Is this a joke?*

I wanted to shrink down in my chair and hide. I wished I had an invisibility cloak that I could throw over my head and disappear.

Great. What was I going to stand up and say? *Hey guys! Me here. My name's Angela, and you're probably wondering if I'm at the wrong team meeting, but I'm not. I pole vault. I'm a US Trials participant, and I also participated at the University of South Carolina for a little bit too?*

OK, well that felt like I was like bragging about getting the "A for effort" award. Oh hell.

As each athlete stood up and gave their verbal bio, I grew more and more anxious as my time to present myself ticked down. I sat squirming in my seat, trying to figure out the best way to articulate my accolades and lack of education.

Before my turn, I gave myself a little much-needed pep talk. *OK, Ang,* I said. *You're here because you qualified to be here. Pull yourself together. You've been through much worse. You got this. Don't choke this time.*

I chose to keep my speech short and sweet. "Hi y'all! My name is Angela Rummans, I was an Olympic Trials finalist in 2012, and I went to the University of South Carolina." Generic, easy, and to the point. I sat down quickly, before my face had the chance to turn bright red.

I replayed what I had just said over in my head, over-analyzing every word I had just spoken. *Did that make sense? Did I say it right?* Honestly, I sort of blacked out and don't remember anything I'd said or the next few athlete names or accolades whatsoever.

The tallest guy in the room suddenly stood. As my attention shifted away from my self-analysis, I thought, *He's* got *to be a high jumper. I bet he can dunk standing still.*

His bio consisted of only five short words. Those five words confirmed to me that I was going to fit in just fine here and that Jeremy was about to be my very first friend.

Stoically, without cracking even the slightest smile, he said, "Jeremy Taiwo. Decathlon. Gryffindor House." The entire team meeting erupted into laughter as he sat back down, unfazed by the roar of the room.

* * *

After the team meeting, I took a self-guided tour around the grounds of this 155-acre, state-of-the-art facility that was home to both US Olympians and Paralympians.

The training center was everything I imagined and more. Driving through the gates alone felt like a religious experience. Just beyond the gates, leading into Olympic heaven, flags and flames danced to the rhythm of the dry desert wind.

Front and center, a futuristic sculpture held the infinite Olympic flame. In the background of this symbol of greatness, the American flag waved in the wind, accompanied on either side by the California state flag and the Olympic rings.

I'd browsed through countless photos on the internet beforehand, and no static image could capture the magnitude of this sight. Or the grandeur of the rest of this facility that extended out over a hundred acres.

Some of the teams had already begun their preseason training. From a distance, I could see the rowing team was out on the lake practicing. I walked down the hill to the track. I stood there for a while, captivated by the Paralympic track and field athletes getting in their mid-morning workouts. I had never actually seen them practice in person. It was fascinating.

There were athletes sprinting by with blades for legs, faster than I had ever seen a human move before. There were both guys and girls in wheelchairs racing around the track, guiding their wheelchairs perfectly centered within each lane, making it look effortless. There were even blind athletes running at full speed, side by side with their guides that gave them auditory directional feedback.

If you ever have a chance to tour an Olympic Training Center or watch a Paralympic athlete compete, it is a truly humbling and inspiring experience you should not pass up.

I was lucky enough to get to know many of these athletes and train alongside them. They were also a part of the diverse track and field family I made at the OTC. Each one in their own unique way, despite their disabilities, was a ray of sunshine that could outshine the California sun even on its hottest day.

Their eternal happiness had its way of healing. On days when I was physically exhausted and dreading the workout, Marc, one of the visually impaired athletes, would come over to me and say hello, asking how I was doing today. Rain or shine, he greeted each one of us every single day. Even when the real answer would had been "Sore and worn out," suddenly I was "Doing great, Marc!"

They were not only amazing people but also incredible athletes. Imagine sprinting at full speed and leaping into a sand pit with a blindfold on. Not only staying in a narrow track lane and taking off the ground at just the right time but trusting that the sand pit would be there upon landing. We had one member of our team who actually competed wearing a blindfold. He won three world championships and earned four Paralympic medals wearing that blindfold.

I can attest that these so called "disabled" athletes train just as hard, if not harder, than the rest of us. In actuality, they were so very able. They didn't let a "disability" disable any part of their lives or hold them back from achieving their dreams.

There was no physical or even visual impairment that was able to hinder their athletic careers. They were elite-level athletes despite their disabilities. These were the athletes that inspired us all to become stronger, better versions of ourselves. They showed us there really is no excuse.

Most importantly, they showed us all that we can be fearless of failure and that an excuse is really just an obstacle imposed by our fear of failure.

So, what's holding you back? What's your excuse?

27

SPOON-FED

"Somewhat-OK Sundays, Monotonous Mondays, Typical Tuesdays, Weird Wednesdays, and Terrible Thursdays," we called them. In the *Big Brother* house, the word *Thursday* and the phrase "uncontrollable debilitating anxiety" were interchangeable. I know that might sound a tad dramatic, but hey, we're dramatic here. That's why we were handpicked for reality television, duh.

There are only about two-hundred-something people in this country that can attest to this: the BB Alums. Our own little fraternity. Even though it's really all just a social experiment, living in the *Big Brother* house feels so much like real life. Being evicted was the equivalent of being exiled from Earth. I don't expect you understand that, but just go with it.

Thursdays to us meant a couple things: another eviction ceremony, another member of our cast exiting through those double doors, getting to see what Julie Chen was wearing, and most importantly, the crowning of a new HOH.

This particular week, the Monday monotony had extended all the way through Thursday. It was an unusually quiet week leading up to the eviction ceremony, and this Thursday felt like any other. The usual ten o'clock wake-up call, the mechanical morning routine, and of course let's not forget "Anybody want some eggs?"

Other than coffee, breakfast, and our morning poops, really nothing happened out of the ordinary until the evening. For the most part, the day was spent aimlessly moving about the house and slowly stirring in the communal bathroom.

We took our damn sweet time to get ready. Why? Because there wasn't anything else for us to do.

By this point in the season, we had mastered the art of spending an entire day showering, shaving, layering on makeup, applying deodorant, tweezing our eyebrows or any other unwanted hairs, curling our hair, gluing false eyelashes on, and ironing the outfit we'd picked out last Monday. You'd have thought we were getting ready for the Met Gala or something. This process that once took me less than an hour now took a solid six.

The hours dragged on slowly. With the backyard being closed off, our only clock was the one on the oven and whatever was left of our biological clocks.

Finally, the time came to gather in the living room. I took a seat on the circular couch, accompanied by the remaining castmates.

All right, let's get this over with, I thought.

Haleigh stood up first, giving her well-rehearsed eviction speech. As always, she was well spoken and gave a beautiful speech. Perfection. Just as we expected. Like her, the words she spoke were classy and innocent. Those two words were always the ones to come to mind when I thought about Hails.

She thanked all the important people and loved ones in her life: God, her family, and of course CBS and the producers of *Big Brother*. Within her speech, she discreetly touched on the reasons why we would be wise to keep her over her counterpart.

While she spoke, I thought about how much of myself I saw in her. She was so far beyond her years. Despite her being on the "other side" of the house when it came to the game, I always thought of her like a little sister and wished that she had ended up in our alliance.

The second nominee stood and began to present what he had prepared for us all. Partway through, his speech took a delightful little detour.

He turned to the current HOH and said, "As far as the HOH . . . the first time I realized how spoon-fed you've been your whole life was when you were braggin' about drivin' a Range Rover and how you wear a fake engagement ring at the grocery store." He paused for dramatic effect. "Just relax. I promise you're not all that."

Guess who the HOH was? Yep, yours truly. Another personal attack for the second week in a row. Silly me. I should have expected the unexpected.

His words bounced off me like rain on a tin roof.

My unbothered mind had already wandered off, taking a stroll down memory lane to remind myself how "spoon-fed" I'd been my whole life.

As my mind wandered, I stumbled upon a distant memory when I was bitten by one of the most infectious bugs: the entrepreneurship bug.

It happened during a soul-searching window of time after the tragedy of the Olympic Trials and before I moved to Chula Vista to train at the Olympic Training Center. I had left my coach, Dmitri, and joined a group of post-collegiate guys that had been training at the same facilities in Knoxville, TN.

Each one of these twenty-something-year-old dudes was a college graduate with a degree and a wild entrepreneurial spirit that was very much alive. They were just as passionate as I was about pole vaulting and shared the same Olympic dreams as I did; however, for a couple of them pole vaulting felt more like a transitional stepping-stone post-college, pre-Silicon Valley.

Being the only girl at practices was . . . let's go with interesting. It was fantastic in some ways, like forcing myself to push even harder in practices. If I could kind of keep up with them during a running workout, I was doing phenomenal for a girl.

I cherished the few times that I outperformed one of them in a random drill or an exercise and held onto those precious moments like gold. That kind of victory wouldn't just make my day; it made my entire week. You bet I called home bragging about it. There was just something about outperforming a guy that never failed to light me up. I celebrated all these little victories all along the way.

While this training situation was beneficial when it came to my performance, it also had its disadvantages. It didn't take long for my emotional state of mind to harmonize with theirs. I got even better at repressing and hiding any emotional expression, especially around them.

The saying goes, "We are a product of our peers," and the hole I punched through the drywall after a particularly frustrating practice was pretty solid evidence. It's normal to be influenced by our environment, so for that reason I will say it probably wasn't the best thing for me to be surrounded by only testosterone all the time.

There was some good that rubbed off on me that I am forever grateful for, and I owe this inspiration to each one of my training partners. I do believe that people are brought into our lives at specific times for a specific purpose. This was one of those times.

Each of my male pole vault peers had at least one small business they owned individually. Some of them ran multiple businesses and still figured out how to make time to train forty hours a week. Impressive, right? There were countless times when just being at practice felt like I was the host on an episode of *Shark Tank*.

It was the best education my twenty-one-year-old self could have received at the time—not to mention it was free, which is about all I could afford. I got more out of eavesdropping on my training partners' conversations than I did out of an entire year of college.

I figured out what a profit margin was and why it was of the utmost importance in running a small business. I learned what ROI stood for and what a decent percentage for that was. I was educated on all the best websites out there to host an e-commerce business and how the logistical side of the small business actually functioned. I took mental notes on which label printer was the best for printing shipping labels and which payment-processing providers had the lowest rates.

I was enthralled. It didn't take long before this fascination turned into inspiration. I wanted a business that I could call my own. I thought, *If these guys can do it, I can too. If I can keep up with them in the athletic space, then I can do it in the business space.*

I might be stating the obvious here, but starting a business when you're broke is hard—not impossible, just really hard. I had less than three hundred dollars to my name at any given time, and that wasn't quite going to cut it. My product needed to comply with two guidelines: it needed to be something I could make myself by hand, and it needed to not have materials and startup costs that would break the bank.

One afternoon between practices, I was perusing the aisles of our local Michaels craft store for ideas, and as I narrowed down my options, the jewelry supply aisle immediately grabbed my attention. Unfortunately, the supplies weren't exactly cheap.

Growing up, my mom had been in the jewelry industry. She taught me how *real* jewelry was made. I knew how to solder and the impressive process of turning a wax model into precious metal, also known as lost-wax casting. At about the age of three, I learned the twelve birthstones by month at the same time I learned my colors. (Thank you, Mom.)

"Yes! I can start a jewelry business!" I thought this was a no-brainer.

I ran a quick formula through my head, adding up the approximate cost of materials to make a pair of earrings and what I thought I could sell them for. In layman's terms, my math determined there wasn't enough meat left on the bone. The gross profit margin just wasn't worth the time. Nonetheless, I never fully gave up on the idea of starting my own jewelry company, but for now I put it on the back burner.

"OK," I said as I kept browsing, "what's something I can afford? Something that I could make from home without torches or a soldering kit? Something I won't need to buy renter's insurance for?"

I wound up in the scrapbook aisle. All the rows and rows of colorful papers with unique textures, patterns, and prints grabbed my attention. At only cents per sheet, this was much more my speed and it left a lot of room for error. It's practically free! Free was affordable. You know what else was free? Starting an Etsy shop.

A couple months, a two-hundred-dollar investment toward the necessary equipment that was most likely put on a credit card, and a lot of trial and error later, the business that would one day evolve into Paper'd Moments LLC joined Etsy.

I threw a lot of shit at the wall before something stuck. There were all kinds of art to begin with. Three-dimensional paper hearts cut out of maps, monogrammed signs and quotes cut out of fancy patterned papers. There were pop-out flowers with song lyrics printed on the petals arranged inside little shadowbox frames, branches adorned with paper cutouts of birds, and eventually the addition of vintage maps. While often difficult to find, those maps were the shit that stuck.

Customers had begun contacting me, wanting to request custom orders with specific maps and personalized wording. I knew then that I was onto something. If they were willing to go out of their way to special request this item, there was clearly a hole in the market here.

Every little hole I found, I filled with one of my products.

My customers were the ones that pointed out each hole to me. Real estate closing gifts, the paper anniversary—you name it, Paper'd Moments filled it.

I realized the infinite value I could add to an item if I was able to form an emotional connection between the consumer and the product. If I could visually recreate a moment when a couple first met, got engaged, or married with an inexpensive medium like paper, I could charge a substantial amount for this item.

As the maps finally started catching speed, Paper'd Moment's slogan became "art that tells a story."

By no means was it smooth sailing all the time. I ran into obstacles constantly, but I chose to see every obstacle as an opportunity to grow and perfect my company. I rolled with the punches, and my company evolved and grew as the outcome.

A couple of months in, I came within inches of just giving up. Almost every order I shipped out was arriving to the customer bent and badly damaged. I was beyond discouraged, spinning my wheels and constantly shipping out replacements to no avail.

I needed to figure out a new way to ship my art that would provide greater protection but also wouldn't significantly increase the cost of postage or cut into my margins. I researched different mailers and eventually found a wholesale company that manufactured mailers out of a particular inexpensive and sturdy material in bulk quantities. The packaging I found would protect my art through the transit process. This obstacle opened my eyes to the benefits of buying inventory in bulk. Greater quantities meant greater profit margins.

My business was growing by the month, and before I knew it I was able to pay my own rent, which was huge! In 2014, when my business moved with me out to California, it became my creative outlet when our schedule at the Olympic Training Center was just brutal. Meanwhile, on the side, I worked on creating a line of nautical-themed jewelry that I would one day co-own called Naut & Chain.

My business of making "art that tells a story" gave me my freedom. When I did eventually give up my pole vaulting career in 2015, after a year at the Olympic Training Center, it was all I had. When I was cut my off financially after letting go of my sport, it was the spoon that fed me. It gave me the financial independence to be able to move from the training center to LA on my own.

Six months after retiring from track and field and moving to Los Angeles, that two-hundred-dollar investment broke six figures in annual revenue. I bought the Range Rover that I'd always dreamed of having. The sport version in Fuji white.

It was a huge deal for me. I think we can all remember that first big purchase and what it meant to us. I loved that thing. She's got a lot of miles on her now, but I still love her the same way I did the first day I drove her home to my apartment in downtown Los Angeles.

I never had a business plan or any type of formal education on how to run a business, but I figured it out. Yes, a business degree would have probably been helpful, but it is *not* a necessity by any means.

When I needed to know something, I googled it, phoned a friend, asked for advice, called up customer support, or watched YouTube videos. Nowadays there isn't much you can't figure out on your own with a quick search. "I don't know how" is no longer a valid excuse.

We have everything we need at our fingertips, degree or no degree. I found the opportunity in every obstacle, and I was willing to make sacrifices to focus on growing my company. I never really knew what the next step was going to be, but when I was ready to take it, it appeared. What I had driving me was the vision of the life I wanted to create for myself. I let the universe work out the fine details I needed to bring this vision to reality.

I genuinely loved creating art that was so personal and meaningful to my customers. The messages I got from customers telling me the recipient cried upon opening their gift made it so worth it. Every trip to the post office felt like I was shipping out nostalgic happiness in tangible form.

My advice to you is to find something that you're passionate about and enjoy doing. The joy that comes from doing something that you love allows you to raise your vibration. This positive energy will fuel your motivation to turn your idea or product into a company and, furthermore, will drive your company to new heights.

You don't need a revolutionary product that's going to change the world, and you absolutely don't need to try reinventing the wheel. If you can that's great, congratulations, you'll end up with a seat next to Mark Cuban on *Shark Tank*.

To be perfectly honest, it can be the simplest idea. Take the business Potato Parcel, which ships potatoes in a box with Sharpie messages written on them. That business made it onto *Shark Tank*. Yeah . . .

Although it may be scary and uncomfortable, all you have to do is take that very first step. Hit the ground running and never look back. Surround yourself with positive, like-minded individuals who boost you up, are ambitious, and full of energy. Throw all that shit against the wall, and I promise you something will stick.

> Surround yourself with the dreamers and the doers, the believers and thinkers, but most of all, surround yourself with those who see greatness within you, even when you don't see it yourself.
>
> — STEVE JOBS

28

THE BREAKUP

Have you ever caught yourself saying something your parents used to say? You know, those one-liners that still evoke some kind of an emotional response. There's a few that come to mind so clearly, it's like I was just thirteen years old yesterday.

Something along the lines of "we'll see," "because I said so!", or "don't you make me pull this car off the road!" If you just read that last line with the same exact tone and emphasis your parent(s) once used, I'll take that as a yes.

In the next Head of Household competition, I caught myself shouting one, maybe three, of these familiar phrases like a broken record. "You got this! You can do it! Don't give up!" I had a good reason, though; I needed someone from our alliance to hang on just a little bit longer than the rest of them.

Hanging on and refusing to let go in this situation was an absolute must. It wasn't just the best option; it was the only option we had. However, ever so often there comes a time that hanging on for dear life isn't so ideal. In some cases, letting go doesn't always mean that we're weak. Sometimes it shows that we're strong enough to let go.

The year I spent training at the Olympic Training Center was one of those times. I heard these motivational words from my parents on repeat over and over again, like the same three songs on perpetual shuffle. After every hard practice and every upsetting no height, I was hit with a "you can do this, Ang, don't give up" from both my mom and my dad.

I have this vivid image still in my head, so clear I could paint it. I was taking a left turn out of the athlete entrance of the training center onto Wueste Road. I was on the phone with both parents as I followed the winding road along Lower Otay Lake. The sun had mostly set, and the sky had already changed from its ordinary blue to a pinkish-orange hue. Come to think of it, the only time I really got to see that bright blue California sky was on the facility grounds during practices and of course Sunday, our *one* day off.

Practice started early and ended late. By the time I reached home, the sun had already dipped behind the Pacific horizon. The demands of our packed schedule didn't leave a whole lot of time for anything other than training, eating, and sleeping. But this was everyone's full-time job here, their career, and it was up to me to figure out a way to balance my training with the demands of my company.

Our weekly schedule made my past workouts in Tennessee look like a damn walk in the park. Our four-part warm-up alone was a workout in itself. It took just under an hour and covered a couple miles in combined total distance. It included thirty different kinds of shuffles, directional skips, lunges, cariocas, dynamic stretches, and—as if that wasn't enough—let's not forget the twenty "short" 30-meter acceleration sprints.

I clearly recall the unpleasant surprise I got the first day we ran through this hell of a warm-up prior to our running workout. I actually thought this warm-up *was* the running workout and that after the weight room, we would be done for the day. Little did I know we had hardly scratched the surface of the day's training agenda. We still had hurdle mobility part one, tempo runs, rack strength, weight room day two, plank series, foam rolling, and our cooldown recovery routines.

A typical running workout was something along the lines of five sets of two 200-meter runs, with two minutes rest in between the first and second 200-meter legs, and six minutes between each set. We each had designated times that we had to hit the 200-meter runs under, and I assure you it was no ten-minute mile pace.

Go out to your local high school's football field. Run all the way down to one goalpost, touch it, turn around, and run —don't jog—all the way back. Rest two minutes, and then do it again. That was one set. Four more to go.

After our warm-up and running workout were complete, if we were lucky and not bent over a trash can vomiting, we got to eat lunch and would head up to the OTC cafeterias. That, however, was only the case if time permitted. Some days we had so much on the agenda that lunch became "how many Clif Bars can I shove down my throat while walking from the track up to the weight room?"

The weight room was a whole new beast entirely. It was another full workout, specialized for our particular event. These workouts were so specific that we needed folders and charts to keep track of it all: the weight, the reps, even the bar speed. And I could never find that damn pencil at the bottom of my gym bag.

There was this one slightly mortifying time where we had some kind of power clean set straight into one-legged box jumps. My body just wasn't feeling it that day. Granted, it had been a long hot day. When I went to jump, my legs didn't follow. I obviously ate shit and the team got a good laugh at the expense of my bloody shins. It was totally embarrassing, but I was at that level of fatigue where I didn't have two shits to give.

By the time we finished up in the weight room, it was already late in the afternoon and we still weren't finished for the day. After weights came plank series one or plank series two, depending on the day. Our afternoon concluded with a trip to the training room where we would cool down with preventive therapy exercises. Essentially this was physical therapy for the injuries we hadn't yet acquired. To me, I always felt like it was putting it out in the universe that we were expecting to get injured, but I did them anyway.

There was one thing that I did look forward to, which now looking back on it seems so outlandish because it's something most normal people would find torturous. (If this doesn't go to show how demanding these days were, I don't know what else to say here.)

It was contrast therapy. Also known as the wretched ice bath. We would start in the cold tub and then go straight into the hot tub, then back and forth and back and forth. I lived for that feeling. That relief breathed the life back into me.

The funny thing about the dreaded ice bath was how surprisingly easy it was to open up and get to know the person next to you. Ironic, isn't it? When things are shrinking up, it's easier to open up.

I think it's something about sharing the pure agony of the icy water that creates an unusual bond. I got to know a lot of the athletes from different teams pretty well while standing there in my biker shorts and sports bra, nips harder than an industrial-grade diamond. The rugby team, both men's and women's, were pretty darn cool. The men's side formed the Cold Tub Choir and often serenaded us through our suffering.

It was routine for me to catch up with my parents on the drive home. These conversations never failed to unfold into just another venting session as I dropped hint after hint of how demandingly miserable my days were.

Nine times out of ten, it was dark by the time I got home from practice, and the rest of the energy I had left I spent catching up on what had gone on with my business that day.

I persevered through the fall, just barely hanging on. I

remember waking up on almost any given Sunday, our recovery day off, and not even being able to muster up the energy to roll myself out of bed.

Allow me to contradict myself for a minute here. I was living, but I wasn't *living*.

As the days passed, I was just going through the motions, trying to push through to Sunday. In the meantime, while wallowing in my agony and unaware of the world happening around me, I lost whatever was left of my emotional expression.

I quit feeling much of anything at all. I was far too drained to have any kind of deep emotion. Things I had once cared about just didn't matter to me anymore. Regardless of whether or not I had been worn thin, I was never even present enough to be able to experience those feelings anyway.

Life happens in the present. When we are not present, we are not living. While training at the Olympic Training Center, the present equaled pain and fatigue more often than not. Thus, I trained my mind to dwell constantly in the future, looking ahead to my one day of relief, or the only thing I had to really look forward to: Sunday, my weekly destination. The problem was that when Sunday actually came, I was worn so thin I could barely function.

I realized that this wasn't life. I was alive but far from living. I can't say this enough: life is happening in this moment, the present, as your eyes scan the pages of this book. Not in the past or in the future. When we're not present, we're not able to see the bigger picture to realize or even experience what is really important: our happiness.

Things started to get better when our track season began in January. The training load lightened up a bit and being able to travel to meets all over the country on weekends was the breath of fresh air I needed.

I wish I could say all the hard work that I put in during my fall training paid off and I was setting personal bests every weekend, shattering records left and right, but that was not the case.

It's almost humorous for me to reminisce about how hard I trained versus how terribly I performed. It was a season of no heights, back to back to back. I only had one meet that entire season in New Mexico in which I didn't pull out a no height. Every other time, when I did nothing but no height, Jeremy was always there to help me pick up the pieces and talk me through it. Another testament that goes to show there are people brought into our lives when we need them the most.

His friendship meant so much more to me than just being the teammate to pick me up when times were hard. He opened my eyes to the concept of mindfulness, or the mental state we are able to reach when we focus on ourselves in the present moment. We shared a lot of common beliefs about creating with our thoughts, believing that all is possible, the power of gratitude, and the beauty of living in the moment.

These are the spiritual concepts that I have always believed in and that have made sense to me as far back as I can remember. Sometimes it takes someone close that you have a real respect for to be the influence that really solidifies these powerful concepts. I owe that to him for helping me instill these beliefs firmly in my being and giving me the strength to change my mindset for good.

* * *

It was a cold day in Geneva, OH that also just so happened to be Valentine's Day. This marked the day my athletic career and I broke up for good. It wasn't the messy, drawn-out-divorce-type breakup; it was quick and clean, leaving me with no strings attached and one last no height to my name. On February 14, 2015, I competed in my very last track meet.

Walking into that competition, by no means did I expect it to be my last.

There is nothing worse than the flight home after a big fat no height. It's a truly special type of torture.

I sat alone, staring out the window into the darkness on my Southwest flight home. Reflecting on the past year, how much work I had put in and all my poor performances, I thought about what the training center really meant to me and what it had done for me.

The more I thought about it, I eventually arrived at an answer. It did a lot of things for me: it gave me physical strength, it gave me emotional strength, it gave me a sense of family out in California. But most importantly, it gave me closure. It provided me with the kind of strength that I needed to be able to let go.

This time, though, I didn't see letting go as giving up. My perspective had since changed, and through this clearer lens, letting go wasn't a sign of weakness, it was a symbol of my strength.

I was able to see it for what it was worth, the growth this experience gave me. The Olympic Training Center was the closure I needed to walk away from my sport. So that's what I did. With my head held high and an awakened sense of optimism and mindfulness.

So what did I do next? I booked a plane ticket to Hawaii and said fuck it.

"I am ready to *live*."

29

FIND YOUR FUEL

For some of us that have grown up on the water and around boats, we develop a kind of innate sense for the rules of the waterways. For those unfamiliar with the boating world, it might be news to you that there is such thing as maritime "rules of the road."

Fact: The wide-open ocean is not an unsystematic free-for-all. Just because there aren't roads to follow and traditional triangular yield signs doesn't mean rules don't exist.

There are actually a lot of rules. There's even a boating hierarchy—a vessel pecking order, so to say—beginning with power-driven vessels, which have the easiest time and most controlled ability to maneuver. Then come sailing and fishing vessels, the kind with all that elaborate netting. Next come the vessels such as the buoy tenders and those massive aircraft carriers that are restricted in their ability to maneuver. Essentially, the more agile your vessel, the lower down on the totem pole you are.

But wait, there's more. There are all kind of rules about head-on and crossing situations, most of which are pretty obvious because they mirror the rules of operating a motor vehicle.

You're probably starting to wonder where I am going with all of this. Just stay with me here. I am no professional mariner, but I do know that if you don't follow the navigation buoys and markers, you'll probably end up high and dry, running aground—or, in layman's terms, end up with your boat up on a sandbar. I've spent hours on a sandbar. Stranded in the Atlantic, with no cell service, waiting for the tide to come back in to free our vessel. It's a lot like being in the *Big Brother* house, come to think of it.

If you've ever heard somebody use the term "high and dry," welcome to its origin. In the 1700s, when a ship was stuck on dry land after the tide had gone back out, these ships were referred to as being high and dry.

Enough boating and history lessons. Let's bring it back to the present. To a conversation that left *me* high and dry.

* * *

"Mom, I'm, uh, not going to pole vault anymore," I said, opening the conversation with a can of worms.

No answer came from the other end of the line.

"Mom, are you there? Did you hear me? I'm done pole vaulting," I repeated.

"What?" she said.

"I'm quitting pole vaulting, Mom," I announced for the third and final time.

"What do you mean you're quitting?" The cadence of her words quickened. "What do you think you're going to do? Why do you want to quit all of a sudden?"

I could already tell this wasn't going to go over well, just as I had expected.

"Well, first off, it's not all of a sudden. I've been miserable for months now. I know—" Pausing to take a deep breath in, I exhaled to compose myself. "I just can't keep giving up month after month of my life, constantly unhappy, hoping that one day I'm gonna have some kind of breakthrough that makes it all worth it. There's not—"

"But you've come all this way. You've put in so much work, Ang. You're going to give up now? You're so close to—"

Clenching my phone now, I shouted, "What don't you understand about I. Am. Miserable!"

There was a moment of silence. I could tell that she was at a loss for words. It was starting to sink in that I was serious this time and this was no boo-hoo cry for attention. She also knew very well that when I had my mind made up, there was nothing anyone could do to sway me. Not a thing.

As my words began to resonate, with jeering exaggeration she asked, "So you're just going to give it *all* away, everything you've ever worked for? It was all for nothing?"

'Yep. Sure am. I'm gonna give it *all* away, Mom."

"What do you think you're going to do then? You don't have a college degree, and we're *definitely* not going to continue to support you living out in California not doing a thing."

I pulled the phone away from my ear until her voice was hardly audible. I thought about one of my favorite, most personifying quotes. Maya Angelou said, "You want me to do something, tell me I can't." The words "you can't" poured lighter fluid on the already blazing fire within me.

I hadn't expected her to jump at the idea, but all my life, my parents had been behind me with every major life decision. This one, however, was going to be the one that I was on my own with.

"Are you going to go back to school then? You don't have anything to fall back on, you know that? You dropped out of college, remember?"

No, I forgot, I thought. *Yes, I fucking remember.*

"Remember I have this business? You remember it pays my rent?" I retorted. "Look, I don't have it all figured out yet, but I'm going to focus on growing my business. Also, some of the girls at the training center are signed with a sports modeling agency in San Diego and LA, so I'm going to try and see—"

"Well, you better figure it out because we will *not* continue to pay for you to live out there. We agreed to help support you when you dropped out of college only because you were—"

I'd had enough. I pressed the red "end call" button as I collapsed onto the couch. It felt good; oh so satisfying.

"Watch me," I said aloud, tossing my phone down on the sofa beside me.

For the next two weeks, we didn't speak. There was a hostility in the form of silence that separated us. It was the longest stretch of time (other than the ninety-nine days I spent in the *Big Brother* house) where we didn't communicate *at all*.

It was the first time I didn't have the support I had hoped for and desperately needed at the time. I'd had so much more I needed to say to explain this hard decision so that she could understand where I was coming from, but I didn't get to. She wasn't open to hearing it.

I was dead set on quitting, and she was dead set on not having it. That was the downside of being a clone of my mother; I was just as stubborn as she was, if not more.

Another thing I meant to mention to her was that in a week I was going to be departing the continental US alone on a trip to Hawaii.

Later that afternoon, I got on my laptop to google some of the local modeling agencies in San Diego and ones that specialized in sport and fitness modeling in LA. I submitted myself to the new faces department of several modeling agencies and held my breath, hoping for the net to appear.

Before I left for my unaccompanied trip to Hawaii, I was not only signed with my first agency in San Diego, but I'd even been sent out on my very first audition.

30

EUTIERRIA

As the remaining passengers boarded the plane, I sat in my window seat toward the back, picking at the split ends of my hair while I kept a close watch out of the corner of my right eye. As each person approached my aisle, I held my breath, hoping to get lucky enough to have an open seat next to me. My odds were looking promising.

I looked up just in time to see the stewardess closing the cabin door. Nobody was left standing in the aisles. *Yes! Not one, but two open seats next to me!* I thought. I had the whole aisle to myself to sprawl. *It's about damn time things start going my way.*

A couple of hours passed, and every time I checked through the oval double-paned window, all that was visible was the flat, unchanging, navy Pacific Ocean beneath us. The occasional cloud coverage resembled the aftermath of a bag of spilled cotton balls, casting dark shadows of similar shapes and sizes over the sea. We were far too high to catch even a glimmer of the sun reflecting off the ocean.

"Mai tai or mojito?" the stewardess asked. Smiling, she added, "Complimentary."

"Uh, mai tai?" I didn't know what either was, but I liked the name better.

"Oh, and are you twenty-one?" she added, handing me the cocktail.

"Yeah, I am, thanks," I remarked.

This complimentary cocktail is a little sugary for my taste, I thought as I stretched my barely twenty-one-year-old legs across the two seats next to me, acting like I was some kind of coach-class royalty.

I took full advantage of that extra personal space because I knew the Banana Bungalow hostel in Wailuku would be limited, at least from what I had seen from the Travelocity photos. My unisex "dorm room," as they called it, had four to six beds and no bathroom. I prayed none of my bunkmates were snorers.

A short cab ride later, I arrived at what I thought would be my home for the whole next week. It was cute—quaint, but cute. The girl behind me was also checking in alone.

Deciding to jump out of my usual comfort zone with a bit of liquid courage, I turned around and introduced myself. "Hey! My name's Angela. Are you here by yourself?"

She smiled stiffly, nodding.

"Cool, me too!" I added.

"We'll just need one signature from you right here," a woman with dreadlocks working behind the front desk said, pointing with a pen to the highlighted line. I scribbled down a quick signature and turned back around.

As the girl's face softened, she asked with a familiar heavy accent, "Where are you from?"

"California. Where are you from?" I asked back, wheeling my luggage out of her way so she could get to the check-in counter.

"San Fran. Well, originally I'm from Sweden, but I've been working in San Francisco. My visa is almost up so I wanted to see Hawaii before I go back."

"Oh, no way! I used to have a teammate from Sweden. I knew I recognized your accent."

"Your name?" the woman behind the counter asked. I suddenly realized I had forgotten to ask the girl's name.

"Valerie," she replied to the woman.

"After you're all checked in and settled, you want to go explore? Maybe head to the beach?" I asked.

"Sure! I have a rental car. It's parked out front. There's this beach I wanted to drive to. It's about a thirty-minute drive, about forty-five kilometers," Valerie said as she reached into her tote that hung from her shoulder and pulled out a guidebook from the bottom of her bag. Flashing the book for all to see, she exclaimed, "We should go!"

She signed off on her paperwork and off we went.

I like to call this traveling with *un*intentions. When you allow the world to lead you to the path that you're supposed to end up on, a short conversation in the lobby of a hostel can turn into an afternoon adventure.

My solo Hawaiian adventure for me didn't include guidebooks and definitely no maps. Instead of plans, I had goals. I was going to talk to every stranger I met, say yes to every opportunity that presented itself, enjoy the unexpected, and let the tropical winds take me to what I was meant to see. At the end of my trip, I hoped to have a clear mind and know exactly what my next big move in life would be.

My first day in Hawaii never actually ended. I found myself in a caravan at 3:00 in the morning with a group of friends I'd made from our hostel, heading up to the top of Haleakala, Maui's iconic volcano that sits 10,023 feet above sea level.

The drive up was not for those with a weak stomach or prone to motion sickness. Thirty-seven miles up winding serpentine roads with unbarricaded shoulders dropping straight off into the darkness isn't for the faint of heart. At each pothole we hit, I'd say a little prayer of gratitude in hopes that the rusted axle of the beat-up caravan wouldn't fall off and send us down the side of a cliff.

I'm pleased to announce we arrived just before sunrise, safe and sound. Standing atop the volcano, ten thousand feet above sea level and above the first layer of clouds, felt like heaven. All of a sudden, out of the darkness, the sun poked through a crack in the clouds, instantly illuminating the sky and turning everything around us a shade of golden orange.

There could not have been a more perfect, more mindful way to begin my first full day in Hawaii. When you observe a sunrise or sunset, you can't help but be fully present in that moment. A sunrise is like a gift from the present. Earth's favorite star melts away our worries and our stresses in its fleeting moments. Its captivation becomes all that exists, and it never fails to pull us back into our present mind.

So this is what it must be like watching the sunrise from heaven, I thought. This was God's view.

Later that morning, after a quick nap in my bottom bunk, I microwaved a packet of Quaker instant oats I had stowed in my suitcase and set out determined to learn how public transportation worked.

The front desk offered me a chart outlining the bus schedule, folded up like one of those glossy travel brochures. The woman with dreads told me that if I took a right out of the hostel and walked a quarter mile up the street to the stop sign, then the closest bus stop was on the left. I couldn't miss it.

It was my first time on a bus—well, the public transportation type. Previously on buses, I had always been surrounded by teammates and knew where the final destination was. This time, I had no clue where I was headed and little understanding of when or where to get off.

I chose the first stop to get off and boarded another bus labeled "Pa'ia" in fluorescent electronic letters. The name reminded me of that yummy Spanish rice dish with all the seafood in it. I'd never heard of any of these places, much less heard them pronounced. But this one sounded nice, so I hopped aboard.

The bus to Pa'ia unloaded at the base of the town. One of the first shops I wandered into was called Lila. It was a small boutique selling mostly handmade jewelry and a curated collection of vintage-style clothing. As I perused the store, the girl behind the register kindly greeted me. Her necklace read "August."

I continued to wander about the store but couldn't help wondering if this girl, close in age to me, lived on this island full time.

I eventually turned to her and asked, "Do you live here? In Maui?"

"Yeah," she said, looking up from the doodle she was working on beside the cash register.

"Oh really? What's it like living here?" I asked. "I know you probably get this all the time, but do you ever get island fever? Is that a real thing—like that feeling you need to just get out? Sorry, I'm probably projecting my own past experiences," I said, brushing off my inquiry. "I grew up on an island. One that wasn't quite as isolated as this one, but sometimes it's how I felt."

"Yes! Oh my God, I totally do!" she announced with a slight smile of relief.

One thing led to another, and about a half hour of chatting it up later, we had shared our life stories with each other. While our stories were very different, August and I were so much alike.

Neither of us were meant for the straight and narrow path, and neither of us fit into the standard, socially-acceptable cookie-cutter mold. She lived her life the way I dreamed of living my own. She chased happiness instead of validation as her sense of fulfillment.

After graduating high school, she moved to Hawaii for no other reason than because it was absolutely beautiful and seemed like a fun next step. College wasn't right for her, she knew it, and she didn't allow anyone to convince her otherwise.

Gosh, I thought, *every time I moved, I was chasing a dream that sometimes wasn't even my own.*

"So our hostel is having this party tonight," I said. "If you're not doing anything later, you wanna come hang?"

"Yeah! Oh my gosh, that sounds amazing. I seriously never have anyone to hang out with here. I'm so in!"

"Yay! OK, how 'bout——"

"I get off work at 5:00," she interjected, "If you want, you can hang out around here and I'll drive us back over to Wailuku?"

"Oh yeah, that's perfect! I won't have to figure out how to take the bus back," I said, laughing. "Uh, I'm going to go grab a bite to eat, maybe take a quick nap on the beach, then I'll come back here a quarter till five. How does that sound? I don't want to distract you from your customers any longer."

"OK!" Her face lit up. The excitement was mutual.

* * *

Not a minute after five o'clock, we locked up the shop and headed back to my hostel in her early 1980s Mercedes, windows down, cruising along Highway 36.

Over the course of the next couple of days, we were practically inseparable. I totally jumped ship on the hostel I had booked and paid for in advance, which was the only solid plan I had prior to departure, and abandoned my weeklong stay.

We just started driving, and one adventure lead us to the next. For the rest of my week, we were pretty much homeless. Roaming around like nomads, climbing up waterfalls, and jumping from the highest rocks we could find. Simply because it was fun.

We took a drive through the Hana highway and camped in the rain on a beach in a not-so-waterproof tent we had borrowed from God knows who. We were well equipped with no food, no water. Just a box of cinnamon Chex and probably a handle of vodka.

Turns out neither one of us had any idea how a tent worked *or* how to set it up. After a valiant effort from the two of us, a half-hour-long struggle, and a short rain shower later, a group of Jehovah's Witnesses in a nearby campsite noticed the tussle we were having with our tent.

Two of the kindest young gentlemen and one of their wives came over and not only offered us help but also ended up giving us food and water as well.

After they basically put together our entire tent for us, they invited us over to their campsite to warm up by the fire. I'm not sure if they saw us practically drooling over the food they were cooking or if we looked famished. With both of us soaking wet and shivering, they offered us their food and some water.

Let me tell you, that hot dog was the best thing I'd ever eaten. They say hunger is the best sauce, but that ketchup, y'all, was somethin' else. There was only so much sugary cereal we could stomach, and the vodka hadn't quite been able to quench our thirst.

The rest of the drive through the Hana highway was the most memorable. We took it slow, stopped all along the way at every lookout point and possible activity that had potential to turn into an exciting adventure.

We eventually stumbled across the Waianapanapa Caves and ventured down into the darkness. It felt like we were leaving Hawaii temporarily and entering the underworld. The deeper we went, the colder and crisper the stagnant air around us became. The smell of musty earth was pungent. The stalactites hung like icicles from the roof of the cave and eventually disappeared into the darkness. The only flashlight we had, on our iPhones, guided us back to safety.

I later learned this cave was also acclaimed as the murder site of King Ka'akea and Princess Popu'alaea. I also regret to inform you that these caves have since been closed and blocked off to the public due to loose rocks and the death of a California visitor in January 2017.

Our diet for the rest of that week consisted mostly of banana bread we purchased from a roadside stand. I found that one small loaf of macadamia nut banana bread could hold me over for an entire day and only set me back a couple dollars.

We saw eucalyptus trees with bark every color of the rainbow, like something out of a Dr. Seuss book. August showed me that at that time of the year, when the ocean is particularly calm and if you listened closely, you could hear the whales calling to one another underwater at night.

I've said it once and I'll say it again: people come into our lives for a purpose. August came into my life to teach me that I could let go. By the end of my trip, I had accomplished my goal. With a clear mind, I knew exactly what my next stepping-stone would be and which door would finally lead me to my happiness.

At the end of this remedial journey, I ended up right where I was intended to be. It happened so perfectly that I couldn't have possibly planned it better.

Traveling alone, if you have the right mindset, can be life changing. Find the courage to let go of the need to control all the fine details. Let the universe be the gentle wind that takes you on an adventure of a lifetime. Let it breathe life back into you. You have to let go of the death grip you have on your life before you can really start living.

Spending a week in nature and in some of the most beautiful scenery on our earth has a profound healing effect.

Experiencing a sunrise from the heavens, nighttime swimming close enough to hear the blue whales sing, and exploring nature in its purest form is, in my opinion, the meaning of the term *eutierria*.

Eu meaning "good," and *tierra* meaning "earth." The term

by definition means "a positive feeling of oneness with the earth and its life forces." *Eutierria* was my gateway to happiness.

Ola I kea he lau makani. There is life in the gentle breath of wind.

31

MARK MY WORDS

"You'll model when you get out of here." I smiled, looking up at his perfect face. "Whether you like it or not. I *guarantee* you, you will," I said, reassuring him.

"For what? A Proactiv commercial?" Tyler asked sarcastically.

It wasn't funny, but still it made me laugh. The irony of it all. I wanted to tell him to shut the hell up and hold an unbiased mirror up to his face so he could see himself through my eyes.

Good lord, anyone's eyes. Perfect bone structure, eyes the color of springtime with flecks of gold. *Gosh, you are delusional!*

I wondered if that was a ploy or if he actually thought that he wasn't a perfect reincarnation of the statue of David.

"Mark my words," I said. "Mark. My. Words."

I was so excited, but excited wasn't quite the word I was searching for. That would have been an understatement. My internal thesaurus was away on vacation. *Animated, exhilarated, electrified?* No, no, and no. None of these would cut it.

What I'm trying to say is, I was beyond excited for Tyler, because I knew he had no idea the prosperity his future held. I knew it for certain. Never had I been more sure about anything.

It brought it all back. The unadulterated excitement and anticipation that came with every email from my booking agent and the pure joy I felt when I found out I had booked my first national campaign. The memories came flooding in.

* * *

Two days after returning home from Hawaii, while still holding a silent grudge between my mother and myself, I got the email. The subject line read "Please Confirm."

The casting I had attended before leaving for Hawaii chose *me* for the job. I had booked not just a one-day shoot but an entire week! When I saw the day rate, I just about fell on the floor. I was going to make more in one day than I had ever made in an entire week. I could pay my entire rent in just one eight-hour day.

I was dead set on not being the one to break the silence between us, but this news outweighed my resilience by far. I phoned home to Mom within minutes, spilling the news.

"Mom?" I said, when I heard the dial tone stop, thus forcing me to speak first. "Hello?"

"Hi, sweetie. How are you?" I could tell by the tone of her voice that almost all animosity had since faded.

"Figured I'd, uh, give you a call." I was trying to play it real cool and not act overly excited. I went on with my purpose for the call. "I booked my first job."

"What do you mean? Booked a job? You got a job? Where at?"

The words practically came spilling out of my mouth. "It's a modeling shoot. I booked a national campaign for an athletic wear company."

"Oh."

"Yep, just thought I'd let you know," I said, trying to still seem indifferent, like this wasn't the biggest deal to me and I wasn't jumping out of my skin with excitement. "If you don't hear from me much next week, it's just because I'll be busy during the day—job's all week."

I was well aware how cringeworthy this humble brag came across, but the words tasted like sweet revenge on my lips. I figured I'd also probably call again and check in around mid-week, maybe bitch about my headache from all the flashing lights from the cameras constantly in my face.

"Wow! That's really great, Ang," she remarked.

"I'm pretty excited, should be fun," I said, still with an apathetic tone. "Oh, and I'm going to probably just try and buy out the rest of this lease here so I can go ahead and move up to LA. It'll just—"

She gasped. "LA . . . Los Angeles?"

Satisfied that I had gotten the rise out of her that I was looking for, I went on. "Yeah, that's where I need to be. It's where everything is going on. I'm gonna move up there so I can go out on more castings and auditions and stuff like that. This is what I want to do, and LA just has that energy I need, you know?"

That, however, was a rhetorical question because I knew very well that she did not know. She did not know that I had spent the past week in Hawaii formulating the blueprints of my future, clearing out the clutter, and silencing my constant subconscious chatter. She didn't know that this plan had already been put into motion the minute I told her that I intended to quit pole vaulting.

What she did know was I believed in myself so deeply that a plan B had never even existed. This time failure wasn't an option, and I intentionally had no plan B, no plan C, and definitely no "if all else fails and shit hits the fan" escape plan. I had realized that these plans insinuated that I believed that failure was possible to some degree.

I knew and understood the reason that she hadn't been

supportive when I broke the news to her about the detour my life was taking. The answer came to me during my travels, and I'd since forgiven her; the salty Pacific Ocean had washed away my bitterness.

Looking down at the cherry-red infected wound on my knee I had recently acquired slipping on an algae-covered rock at the base of one of the waterfalls I'd jumped off, I finally understood. If my mom thought she could pour peroxide on something while it was just a small, festering infection, then she could prevent it from spreading.

It was never about whether she believed in me, and I knew deep down that she did all along. From a rational mommies-just-want-the-best-for-us point of view, she thought that if she was able to shut it down early and kill the dream before it turned into a full-blown career change, she might be able to save me from the heartache if I failed.

She was my mom, and like any loving mother she couldn't bear the thought of seeing her child fail yet again. It made perfect sense. Through her eyes, this time the risk seemed much greater than the potential reward. The ROI from her perspective was a percentage that ranged from not probable to unlikely.

There will always be two ways to look at every situation, and had I not understood that she was coming from a place of good and opted to take her advice and not pursue this passion of mine, by no means would that have been her fault or the fault of any other caring parent who can't bear the thought of watching their child fail.

It would've been my own fault because I didn't try to see this situation for more than the surface value. No one other than us is liable for choosing whether or not we pursue our passions, and no one other than us can pick a side of the coin or which lens to look a situation through.

The choice will always be ours. Do we choose the lens that sees the good or the one that fixates on the bad?

Staying in the present mind brings with it many gifts. Its gift to me was a bottle of Windex and a pair of noise-canceling headphones. In my present mind, I could look as a situation with so much clarity, it had a streak-free shine. It quieted the chatter and all the background noise so I could hear my own obstructive subconscious beliefs. Like that I was too young to own a successful company, or that I was too small of a fish to move to LA and dive headfirst into the largest pool inhabited by the biggest fish in the industry.

Our subconscious will always exist, but only in the present mind can we hear it think and speak. My subconscious was as quiet as a whisper, but a lie is a lie no matter how audible the voice is. If we don't silence this voice while it is still a whisper, it will eventually take root and grow louder. The only thing that can silence these thoughts is the actual truth: that if you believe in yourself wholeheartedly, the world is your oyster. You can do and be anything you want to be. You can reinvent yourself as many times as you wish. This is the truth that will set you free.

32

"BACKTIRES BIG FIME"

"What a *crazy* day," I said as I readjusted my towel. I reached out the other hand to hold his. I was still dripping with water from my shower, half on the circular HOH bed, unconcerned with the six or seven cameras in the room and unfazed that I was covered by a mere few square feet of terry cloth.

It had to have been well after midnight. It felt like hours had passed since twelve o'clock. The hell if I knew what time it actually was. My sense of time was two or three sheets to the wind at this point.

Tyler and I had honed our tactics to spend more time with each other without it seeming obvious to the others that we were in the early stages of an actual relationship.

One of our cleverer ideas was making a public announcement that we were headed up to the HOH room to shower in front of the other houseguests so that they would assume I was up there just taking my sweet time unwinding in the luxurious private HOH suite bathroom.

The truth was, I really hadn't needed to shower at all. I hadn't done anything active all day other than host and watch a HOH competition that, as outgoing HOH, I wasn't allowed to participate in. It was nice to be able to sit back and relax, but at the same time, it was a helpless feeling, not getting to play.

Tyler looked up from the red comforter on his bed and announced, "That's crazy, there's like three weeks left." He paused for a split second, his eyes narrowing. "Or four?"

"After this one, yeah, three weeks left," I agreed. I didn't count this week since Tyler was the current reigning HOH, meaning this week was going to be smooth sailing and hopefully stress free.

All we had to do for the next six days was sit back, relax, keep our mouths shut, and play our innocent little points game we had fabricated out of boredom and indignation.

Instead of getting irritated by the countless attempts of the other houseguests trying to weasel their way into figuring out what was going on between the two of us, we turned it into a game where we earned points, for the sake of our sanity.

The rules were simple. The more blatantly obviously the attempt, the more the points we scored. Every time one of the houseguests went rummaging in our business, they scored one to three points depending on the level of discretion. Any time Tyler or I stayed anywhere by ourselves too long, our daily point count would skyrocket so high we could hardly keep track.

"That's crazy," he repeated.

"Right?" I said.

"Whatever, we'll be here for a while," Tyler reassured me.

"I hope so."

"You're sleeping up here one of these nights, I don't care what anyone says. Well—if that's OK with you."

"Fine," I said. That was obviously what I would have preferred, but we both knew if that actually happened, our daily point count would set a new PR.

Stretching out on the bed, Tyler confessed, "That's why I couldn't sleep the past, like, five nights."

"Same," I said, laughing. "I was like, 'I wonder what Tyler's doing?'"

Tyler looked down at my hand still holding his. "Same. I was like, 'How can I get up there?'"

His grin turned into a sigh. "I swear when people try and do things to put us against each other it—"

"Backfires?" I said, finishing his sentence.

"Yeah. It backtire—it backfires big time. Backtires big fime," he joked.

Looking down at him stretched out across the bed, I laughed. "Words are hard," I said.

"I'm turning into you."

There was a long pause as I debated whether I had exceeded my shower time limit up here in the HOH room.

"I think they're going to start getting suspicious. I've been up here a while." But the longer I stayed, the less I cared about trying to cover my tracks.

"We'll figure it out. We'll figure it out by winning back-to-back HOHs for four weeks straight," he said, putting it out there in the universe.

"That sounds good. That would be pretty amazing," I added.

"I know. I know."

That was all it took. It seemed too easy, right? All we had to do was put it out in the universe, trust the process, and allow it to return to us the way it was meant to play out. We didn't just win the next four HOHs. We, as an alliance, won five in—a—row!

Back-to-back-to-back-to-back-to-back. Pardon my redundancy, but that kind of alliance domination deserves to be spelled out.

It had gotten late. The sun had to have been only a few hours away from its morning arrival. The fatigue had set in, and I was beginning to zone in and out of my current state of reality. My mind went astray, remembering all the pivotal times it really had been just that simple.

It happened that exact same way when I packed every belonging to my name and moved to the city of dreams, Los Angeles, CA. I put it out there while putting myself in the position for all my plans to root themselves in my reality.

I had this image in my head that LA was this conglomeration of beach cities, beautiful people, and vegan cafes all offering their take on latest trend of avocado toast. I thought the locals spent their Sundays riding their light blue Linus bikes from yoga class to brunch and back with baskets full of green juices. I pictured all the extraordinary houses the celebrities owned hidden in the Hollywood Hills and of course that iconic sign. I imagined the many tourists in those red, double-decker Starline buses taking pictures of all those high-end stores lining Rodeo Drive, where the only affordable thing was a keychain.

Through my unworldly eyes, that's what I thought Los Angeles was all about. I signed my lease sight unseen, picking downtown as the part of LA I would call home. I loved the vibe of downtown San Diego, and since I've always wanted to live in a little area of town called Little Italy, I hoped downtown LA would feel the same.

Downtown Los Angeles is mostly divided up into districts. There's the Arts District, the Toy, Jewelry, and Financial Districts—even a little area called the Piñata District. And let's not forget Little Tokyo and Chinatown, all within walking distance.

Naturally, I picked an area of downtown LA between the Fashion and Jewelry Districts. The apartment building I found was somewhat affordable, had a Starbucks across the street, and from the pictures I saw online, the lofts looked bright and airy. Natural light has always been a must for me.

It took me about a week or two of trying to find my way

around these parts on foot before I realized I was a handful of streets away from Skid Row.

I had gotten my first taste of our country's homeless problem while living in San Diego, but this was much more than a problem. What I saw was a crisis. What's even more heartbreaking is that the problem is steadily getting worse.

There are entire communities of people living in tents made of shopping carts and napping on flattened cardboard boxes all along the sidewalks. These communities extended block after block. They had no place to go; affordable housing didn't exist for miles around.

If you're living in downtown Los Angeles, you're either paying two to three thousand a month in rent or you're living outside the entrances of these pricey apartment complexes. This drastic separation reminded me of what I witnessed driving through El Paso along the Mexican border. I later learned that, according the US Department of Housing, Los Angeles has one of the lowest percentages in sheltering their homeless population.

Downtown is very much a work in progress and will be for a long time. While some parts are great, others need a lot of help. At the time, the streets around my neighborhood were dangerous to be out in at night, especially alone and as a young woman. I'd overheard stories in the elevator from my fellow tenants of people being mugged literally blocks from our building.

My experience while living here was not exactly the warm welcome I expected from LA. For a while, I hadn't even realized how so "not LA" it really was. I was so wrapped up in growing my business and focusing on my modeling career that it didn't hit me until late one night when I stepped out of my building to make a quick trip to the CVS Pharmacy across the street.

I'd most likely either run out of tampons or desperately

needed a bottle of red wine. There wasn't a whole lot else I would have risked braving these streets alone at night for.

These were no Alo yoga pants I was wearing. I remember I was dressed in baggy gray sweats multiple sizes too big, a T-shirt, and a royal blue LA Dodgers ball cap pulled down over my eyes.

The second I stepped out of the entrance of my building, an elderly man, who I identified as most likely homeless, rolled past me in a wheelchair right as I shut the door behind me.

At the top of his eighty-year-old lungs, he screamed at me, "White trash!" Then he proceeded to turn and come at me like he was going to try and ram me with his wheelchair.

I was shocked, startled, and scared shitless. I ran! As fast as my Adidas slides could go, straight into CVS, where I knew for sure a security guard would be standing at the entrance.

I don't remember what I needed at the store, but if it hadn't originally been a bottle of wine, it was now.

This traumatic shopping experience left me asking myself, *Where the hell am I? What is this place? This is not the LA I dreamed about. Where were all the healthy, happy people riding bikes and taking wheat grass shots? It smells like shit everywhere here.*

The smell haunts me to this day. Not the smell of shit, although that was a very common scent around my apartment building. It wasn't even a putrid or rotten smell that bothered me. It was the smell of the cleaning solution they used to wash the streets.

I'd never lived in a place where they washed their streets for their people to live in. It felt like putting a Band-Aid on the problem. It bothered me that this was their solution to the problem. Why wasn't whatever it cost to clean and sanitize the streets being used to create shelters and to house our people?

I have since developed a legitimate aversion to the scent of this "solution." Even to this day, anytime that smell comes anywhere near me, it brings back the memories I have of walking down the sidewalk and feeling sorry for these homeless people when I was en route to the post office during daylight hours to ship my orders.

I can honestly say that for the entire year I spent living downtown, I only went "out out" one time in LA, and that was only because a friend was in town. The only times I left my apartment other than for urgent shopping missions and post office trips was to attend auditions and castings.

These took place in casting studios all around Los Angeles, from Beverly Hills to Santa Monica, all the way down to Long Beach and Orange County. Going out on castings was like mini vacation from the caustic environment I lived in.

If you are familiar with the industry at all, you're already well aware that at casting calls and auditions for modeling and acting gigs, the directors often don't have a sweet disposition. The exception is just one casting director, whose initials are RK. She is f-ing amazing.

At the majority of castings I went to, the important people were the ones sitting behind a desk with a camera at their sides, quietly glaring at you with their judgmental eyes.

They're almost always on a tight schedule and have a specific agenda. If you're not what they're looking for, you'll get a "Thank you. *Next!*" I had gotten to the point that I even felt lucky to get a thank you preceding the word *next*.

At first, those words cut like a knife. As my skin eventually hardened, those words triggered nothing more than my classic eye roll and the persistent urge to give them all the finger before exiting the room and wondering why everyone had to be so damn harsh in this town. Even the homeless people around here were ruthless.

My skin didn't exactly just grow thicker. I realized something that was of the utmost importance and so very necessary for handling this constant scrutiny. It came to me one day as I was reading over my affirmations I had listed in the notes section of my phone. The words struck me differently this time: "create rather than compete." Stop comparing yourself and competing with others.

The fact: it was never *me*.

It wasn't my problem that I didn't have the bone structure that they were looking for. It wasn't my fault my hair wasn't the right length or color, and it absolutely did *not* mean that I wasn't good enough for their job.

It wasn't that I wasn't right for the role, the role wasn't right for me. It is never that you're not right for something; it's that something isn't right for you.

Yes, it may just seem like this is some ass-backwards way of shining a positive light on a given scenario, but let's take it a step further.

Think back to that one hard breakup you went through; how the rejection felt and who you blamed. Was it yourself, because they said you were unreliable, too much for them, or they simply just weren't ready to be settled?

Almost every reason comes back to highlighting the fact that *they* needed something more or something else. Did you hear that? *They* needed. It is not your responsibility to fulfill their needs, unless of course it's your child. If not, then they are not your responsibility. The same way it wasn't my responsibility to meet the criteria of each role and audition.

So next time you hear "it's not you, it's me," you can reassure them, "You're damn right; it's you, not me."

Part of my definition of "being unbothered" is knowing your self-worth, being mindful and independent enough to stand on your own two feet, and being able to see a situation for its actual value.

The lesson: know your worth.

At the end of my twelve-month lease downtown, I made a beeline to the west side of LA. I knew there was something else I was searching for. Something was missing, but I didn't know what.

I did it! I thought. I had everything I wanted and dreamed of: I had a successful company, employees working for my business, I was signed with modeling agencies across the US.

So . . . What in the hell was missing?

At the time, I ended up attributing this void to my location and the caustic living conditions of downtown LA. I thought, *Maybe I need the ocean near me in order to ground myself here in Los Angeles. That salty Pacific always has its way of healing me. Maybe I'm feeling like I'm not able to put roots down because it doesn't felt like home yet.*

Sometimes home isn't a physical location. For me, it was a person.

33

PARENTAL ADVISORY WARNING

This is the chapter I've been dreading. The one that's been in the back of my mind since I began writing this book. It's where the walls went back up, and this time they turned into impenetrable boulders.

I thought about just copying and pasting the two-thousand-word document I wrote and submitted to the district attorney along with the police report I had filed. That would have been much easier, and I wouldn't have to relive these awful memories. If I just wrote a couple paragraphs at the end of the document explaining the extent of the emotional turmoil, maybe I could prevent myself from having those recurring nightmares again.

That would have been the easy route, but that's not why I am here and that is not my purpose.

I am a firm believer that everything happens for a reason. Awful things sometimes happen for a reason too. There were two reasons why the following event became a part of my story. It wasn't until the boulders that went up were broken down that I understood the first reason. I came to the second reason when I typed out the words "Chapter 33."

Before I begin, I must give credit where credit is due.

Each and every one of you who reached out since I shared my story on national television (you know who you are), I thank you. To those of you who suffered from debilitating anxiety, depression, an eating disorder, loss of a loved one, or impenetrable emotional walls and my story gave you the hope you needed to begin healing, I thank you. And for the select few who found strength through my vulnerability that enabled you to share your stories of sexual harassment and sexual assault, I thank you. *You* gave me the courage to write this chapter.

What I need to tell you is that you are not alone, and these wounds are not a life sentence. As a victim, you are not to blame. What I came here to tell you is *me too*.

If you are under the age of thirteen, please skip ahead to the next chapter.

Here it goes.

* * *

September 2016, while I was still living in downtown LA, I stopped by one of my LA-based agencies in Studio City for a commercial audition. After seeing the client and a short meeting with my booking agent, I went downstairs into the lobby to get a coffee in the café and my parking validated before heading back home.

While waiting for my Americano, a man approached me. "Hi, I'm Dr. U.," he said. "What is your name, miss?"

"Angela. Nice to meet you," I replied.

"I'm a dentist. My practice is upstairs on the twelfth floor."

"Oh really! My agency is on the sixth," I said, smiling.

Taking a sip of his coffee, he asked, "Model, right?"

"Right."

"I thought so. A few of my clients work with the agency here too."

"Angela! Americano with steamed soy!" the barista shouted, sliding my coffee to me in a to-go cup.

"If you ever need any dental work—a cleaning, some whitening—you let me know. Here's my card." He reached into his pocket and pulled out his brown leather wallet. "Ah, I'm all out of my business cards. Oh shoot—uh, do you have an Instagram? You can follow my business so you know where to find us."

I pulled out my phone and proceeded to follow his dentistry business. I recall thinking how cute it was that this kind old man was using Instagram to promote his company.

"Cool, I gotcha!" I said. "Thanks so much, I really appreciate that. I'll definitely take you up on that offer. I have yet to find a dentist since I've been out here," I confessed.

"It was very nice meeting you, Angela. You are a very beautiful lady, by the way. Have a good day, and please let me know if you need anything at all. It would be an honor to have you as a patient of mine."

I slipped my parking validation into my back pocket and picked up my coffee. "Thanks, it was nice meeting you too." I turned to the door.

Later that afternoon, Dr. U. followed me back on Instagram. Over a year went by. I totally forgot this encounter ever happened until February 14, 2018, when I received an Instagram message from Dr. U. saying, "Happy Valentine's Day, Angela. Come in and get a free whitening. It would be an honor to have you as a patient."

I responded, "I would love to! Thank you so much. That is so kind."

I remembered him using the exact phrase "it would be honor to have you as a patient" the first time we spoke at the coffee shop months ago. It seemed like an odd thing to say, but I brushed it off.

He's a dentist, he's old, it's normal, I thought.

The next day, he responded, "Hey, let me know if you want to come in Friday afternoon. Text me at . . ."

I replied, "Sounds great!"

Friday morning, I confirmed the appointment via Instagram DM. "Hi Dr. U. Happy Friday. Is it still OK for me to come in today? What time?"

He responded, "Yes, sure, but I have a very particular patient at 5:00, kind of loud. Is 5:30 OK?"

I confirmed. "5:30 is great."

Friday at approximately 5:15 p.m., I pressed the glowing "generate ticket" button on the machine guarding the entrance to the parking garage. I'd parked in this garage at least ten different times for castings, meetings, go see's, and whatever else my agency had me doing. I drove in clockwise circles until I reached the vacant visitor-designated top floor, where I was accustomed to parking.

I crossed the street from the parking garage to the building and entered one of the four elevators in the lobby. I pressed the button for the twelfth floor.

Exiting the elevator, I immediately spotted the sign next to the door that read "Dr. U. Cosmetic & Family Dentistry."

A nurse at the front desk greeted me, handing me the new patient paperwork. I chose a seat in the waiting room next to the door and checked the time before putting my phone away in my purse.

5:20. Wow, I'm even a little early.

With the clipboard in my lap, I began at the top.

Name: Angela Rummans.

DOB: March 23, 1992.

I scribbled as fast as my hand could write, annoyed by this packet of paperwork I had to fill out for a teeth whitening. I reached the blank asking for my address.

Skip it, don't fill it in, that tiny voice chimed in out of nowhere, totally unexpected.

Thankfully, I listened this time. I inscribed an inaccurate

home address, one I had lived in a few leases back, as a dark, unsettled feeling washed over me.

Only a few moments later, I was startled when Dr. U. stepped out from behind the doorway, peering into the waiting room. I sat, legs crossed, not moving a muscle or saying a word.

His eyes closely examined me from under the dental head-piece he wore. He began scanning me up and down, analyzing every inch of me. His eyes moved slowly from my face down to my chest, hips, legs, all the way to the floor where my Fendi purse sat at my feet, then slowly all the way back up to meet my eyes again.

The moment of silence extended beyond my level of comfort. I sat still, frozen; now on edge. I stared back at Dr. U. as my stomach turned over. Uneasily, I watched as the corners of his lips slowly rose.

"I'll call you back in just a minute," he finally spoke as he turned away, disappearing into one of the rooms.

Ten long minutes passed, and he reappeared from out of the empty doorway.

"You can come back now," he said.

I stood up slowly, picked up my purse, and followed him into one of the exam rooms.

"You can set your purse down over there by the window. Have a seat right here," he said, motioning toward the reclined dental chair.

I sat down as I was told and leaned back in the chair, lifting one leg off the floor at a time.

"Ugh," he sighed. "This patient I just had."

He went on, shaking his head. "From a family of Gypsies, I believe. Needs a *lot* of work. I mean a lot. So much damage from all the drug use. It's a mess in there."

I was taken aback by this unsolicited, very personal client information. Wasn't there some kind of patient confidentiality he was supposed to abide by? I wasn't sure what to say other than, "Oh, wow."

"I have to use a lot of gas when working on this particular patient. It's how I know her damage is from drugs. The tolerance of this small girl just isn't normal. She screams for me to turn up the laughing gas at times too."

I didn't say a single word. He continued to vent. "But when I do give her what she wants, she starts telling me 'I love you' and all these crazy things. When I turn it down, she starts yelling again. What do I do? I don't know. But anyway . . . Let's get started on you."

He went on to explain the procedure. "First we need to protect your gums from the whitening chemical. Open up," he said. "We're going to put this plastic piece in your mouth to keep your teeth exposed and dry."

He stepped away to grab something out of one of the overhead cabinets, asking, "Now, how does that feel?"

"Um, good." I tried to speak as clear as possible despite having a large plastic device prying my mouth open.

"Good. I'm going to put this gel on your teeth." As he finished, he switched on the blue light overhead and pulled it down, almost touching my teeth.

"This is going to turn off after fifteen minutes. Then we check."

"OK," I murmured.

He handed me the bell he had been holding in his hand. "If you need anything, ring this bell and one of the nurses will come. I'm going to go downstairs for a quick break. I've been working for hours and hours straight. I'll be back in a short bit."

He left the room, and shortly after I heard the nurses in the reception area checking out of work, saying bye to one another.

After several minutes of not hearing anything—no voices,

no commotion from the lobby or reception—I realized I was alone in this office.

The blue light turned off, and minutes later, the dentist reemerged.

"How are you doing?" he asked, examining the progress. "Everything looks pretty good. Any sensitivity?"

"Uh—a little every now and again," I babbled.

"OK, I'll get the gas out of the other exam room. It'll make you more comfortable through the rest of your treatment."

Moments later, he returned. I could hardly see, but out of the corner of my eye, I could tell that he was wheeling in some kind of machine.

As he rolled the machine near me, he removed the blue light long enough to place the gas piece over my nose. The cords ran down the sides of my face, immobilizing my head against the headrest.

As I breathed in the gas, I instantly felt myself beginning to lose sensation in my limbs.

"I need to run downstairs one more time," he said. This time he turned out all the lights in the room as he left.

The room was now completely dark other than the blinding blue glow of the headlight illuminating my face. My internal sirens began to sound. *Alert! Alert!*

In this moment, I knew I was in trouble.

I felt myself slipping under. I told myself over and over, *Stay with it. Stay here, Ang. Just hold on. Be brave.* It wasn't enough.

I had given it everything I had, but I couldn't fight the anesthesia any longer. I was alone in the dark office under anesthesia. Eventually everything went numb, including my fear and, partially, my memory.

The next thing I remember, Dr. U. was back in the room.

"I'm going to show you how to use this machine here. I want you to put it on me," he said. "I've never felt it."

The blue light turned off, and out of the corner of my eye,

I could see his shadow reaching toward the machine to turn a knob. I felt the gas flow increase. He removed the device from around my teeth and left the anesthesia on over my nose.

Moments later, his face was inches from mine. His hand moved from my shoulder down to my chest, slipping underneath my shirt and my bra.

He began trying to kiss me. I could taste the cigar on his breath as I helplessly tried to pull away. I could barely move, my body was numb, and my face was trapped underneath the device administering the gas.

He began groping my breasts with his hands.

As I pulled his hands away from me, I screamed, "Stop! Stop!"

He whispered into my ear, repeating over and over, "But it feels so good, feels *so* good."

He continued trying to stick his tongue down my throat. I turned my head from side to side to avoid it as much as the device would allow me to move.

After what seemed like an eternity, it finally stopped. He removed the machine from my face and I jumped up, grabbing hold of my phone and purse from the other side of the room.

I turned around to see him sitting in the chair I was just in. I watched in horror as he took the gas and put it on himself.

On the inside, I was screaming in terror, but my only objective right then was to get out of there safely, whatever it took. I stood there frozen, watching in disgust as the dentist began touching himself. The only exit to the room was blocked by the massive anesthesia machine.

I thought about trying to make a run for it. All these thoughts were circling in my head. *If I try and run, he's going to realize he's not getting away with this. Who knows what he'll do to try and stop me? Probably knock me over the head and throw my body in a closet.*

If I run, he's going to chase after me, and I'm only going to get as far as the elevators before he can get to me. I didn't know where the stair-case was, and even though I knew I could fly down those stairs faster than he could, what if I couldn't find the stairwell and got trapped?

I couldn't outrun him, and I couldn't win with force. I had to figure out a way to outsmart him.

I needed to formulate a plan to get out of there so that he wouldn't expect that I was headed straight to the cops and filing a police report the minute I got out. I just had to stay calm and talk my way through it.

You can do this, Ang. Stay calm and keep your composure.

I began walking as slowly and calmly as I could in the direction of the door, hoping that since he had placed himself under anesthesia, I could quietly sneak out. As I came near him, he grabbed my hand and put it on his erect penis.

I immediately pulled my hand away and backed up against the wall.

He started rambling about something, still touching himself. "That picture of you at sunset with the white tank top, the one in the red bathing suit with the ties on it."

Fear and disgust pulsed through my veins. I kept telling myself, *Stay calm, Ang. Just stay calm.*

I needed to figure out a way to get him to let me go will-ingly. Trust me, I'd much rather have clocked him the face at this point, but my only way out was through strategic words.

Keeping a straight look on my face, I began spewing a stream of incoherent bullshit from my mouth.

"I gotta get going," I said, trying to keep my voice from shaking. "My boyfriend is on his way home from San Fran-cisco. His flight lands at LAX soon."

"Oh? You have a boyfriend?" he said.

My heart pounded. "Yes!" I exclaimed. I didn't have a boyfriend, but it was the first thing that came to my mind in the heat of the moment.

Removing the mask from his face, he said, "I didn't know you had a boyfriend."

Oh! Like that would have made it all OK? I kept my thoughts to myself as I pretended to check the time. "I really need to get going," I said, pulling my phone out of my purse so I could be ready in case I needed to dial 911.

He got up from his chair, and I stood there, ready. Ready for whatever was about to happen. I was prepared for the worst.

Inside, I was doubled over in fear, not knowing what was about to happen next. But on the outside, I stood like a statue, stoically standing my ground.

"I'm going to get going now," I said, looking him straight in the eyes. I feared that any sign of emotion at this point would provide an opportunity or reason for him to take further action.

"Let me change out of my scrubs. I'll walk you down," he said, rolling the machine out of the doorway.

I spoke sternly. "I gotta go," I said for the second time.

"All right. Come this way. You can't go through the waiting room now—it's locked."

He led me down a dim hallway to a door. I followed.

When we reached the door, he hesitated for second with his hand on the knob, like he was pondering something.

My mind spiraled with sickening fear.

What is he about to do? I thought. *Where does this door lead to?* This moment of hesitation felt like an eternity. My mind was preparing for the worst.

I told myself, *This is it. I'm trapped, and this man is about to throw me in this storage room and rape me.* I should've run when I had the opportunity to. I looked down at my phone, ready to dial for help.

He opened the closet door and ushered me inside. The room was lined with what looked like a dozen white lab coats. There was a small counter with dental tools laid out on a stained rag. Pliers, scalpels, drills, and blades of every shape and size were spread out in the open.

I closed my eyes and prayed. *Please don't hurt me. Please don't hurt me.*

I heard a door open behind me. When I opened my eyes, I saw a doorway leading into the lobby.

Without a word, I ran. I made it from the elevator down to the lobby and into the garage. This time, the parking garage was an unfamiliar place to me. I was lost in the garage I had parked in a dozen times before.

I started running around the garage from floor to floor, trying to find my car. I burst into tears, thinking the dentist would be down here any minute.

Where is my car? Where the fuck did I park? I set off my alarm and ran toward the noise.

As soon as I got to my car, I called my friend Ali, who was an ER nurse.

Whatever it was I said first made no sense, but she could tell I was hysterical.

"Are you OK? Are you sure you're OK to drive?" she said.

"I have to get out of here!" I responded back.

"You were under anesthesia? Why? Angela, I don't think you should be driving."

"Ali, I *have* to get out of here now!"

"Come straight here to my place," she said.

I drove straight to her home in Venice Beach, and late that evening, we went to the police station and filed the report.

During that twenty-minute drive, I sat in silence, trying to wrap my head around what had just happened and sort my way through these painful memories.

All I wanted to do was bury the entire day deep down and pretend it never happened. I didn't want to believe that it was real. I thought maybe if I didn't report it, it didn't exist.

I even thought for a second, *Maybe I won't go to the police. Maybe it was my fault?*

I was lucky I had a friend, and not just any friend—an ER nurse that was a badass, independent, strong young woman who looked at me and said, "Angela, we are going to the damn police, *tonight*."

We spent hours in that police station, and she stood by me as I relived every memory in elaborate detail for the officer to record. Each time I replayed it in my head, a sense of guilt sank into me.

I started blaming myself for what happened to me. I told myself that it was my fault. I should have known better than go to a dentist appointment at 5:30 in the afternoon on a Friday. I should've gotten up and left the minute things got weird in the waiting room, and I should have never worn that V-neck shirt.

I should've, could've, would've . . . I eventually blamed it on myself for being the "dumb one" or the "provocateur." It consumed me, and I could not let it go. The memories replayed in my head during the day, and at night, they turned into nightmares.

I had been through stuff before. I remember thinking, *I thought I was stronger than this. This has broken me.*

I felt damaged, like I was left defective for having this experience happen to me. I lost trust in others around me and felt unsafe incessantly.

I went over the details again and again in my head, playing out every word, analyzing every memory, even the moments where I have no memories.

In time, I realized something. Everything that happened that day had been meticulously plotted out. It became so obvious. It was *all* premeditated.

Everything from the DM he sent to scheduling the appointment after hours when he knew the nurses would be gone. Even telling me about the girl who wanted the laughing gas in the other exam room. Every time he stepped out of the office to go downstairs to smoke a cigar, and how he locked the door to the lobby when he came back in. It had all been planned out.

I was *not* to blame by any means. I was the victim of a sexual assault and in no way was I at fault in any way, shape, or form. Not me, not my naivete, not my V-neck were to blame.

I knew then that I was *not* the first person this had happened to in that dentist's office. But I was hell-bent on making sure that I would be the last.

I didn't care what I had to do or how many hoops I needed to jump through. I would see to it that I would be the last woman this man laid his hands on. In doing so, I was going to go to every length to make sure of it.

That's just what I did. I didn't sue him. I didn't want a dime of his filthy money, but you damn well better believe that he was pressed with every charge we could.

For the longest time, I asked why this happened to me. And, like I said earlier in this chapter, sometimes bad things happen for a reason too.

For whatever reason, the force that causes these things to happen to us—call it what you want—knew that I was the one strong enough to make it through this horrific experience. I was going to be the one to put an end to this, and I would be the one with the balls to sit in front of a district attorney and tell this story.

This force knew that I was going to be OK living in fear, not knowing when or if this man loses his license to practice, whether he'll try and come looking for me.

I know that the reason this happened to me was because I could handle that load, and I would put a stop to it. The second reason, as I mentioned above, was because I would one day share this story with you. By doing so, my vulnerability would start a chain reaction and give strength for others to follow. I hope that my story will open up a dialogue that *needs* to be had.

One last thing.

I also know for certain that this force had a plan all along to send me what I needed to heal from these wounds and break down the boulders that formed after this event. He was sent to me three months after this traumatic event. His name was Tyler.

Tyler would be the one to come with me to the courthouse, to sit beside me and hold my hand when the time came for me appear before the district attorney.

34

SEPTEMBER 12, 2018

I t was practically undeniable that while there had been an invisible thread between us, pulling on each other ever so slightly, we were unaware of its presence. Or perhaps our rivers had eternally followed the same course, waiting to flow into one another in the perfect divine timing.

Continuously, as our threads wound tighter and our rivers flowed in rhythm, every time I ran away to some new place or his journey changed directions, we had a distant reverberating effect on each other.

When my end of the thread pulled on his or as his river's cadence varied, we changed the course of one another. Out of all beaches he could have chosen to watch over, my thread pulled him to Hilton Head Island.

From Hilton Head, our rivers both flowed from east to west, ending up in southern California, meeting on stage that premiere night. It was like our lives had a butterfly effect on each other's so that we would both ultimately end up right here—right where our journeys were supposed to merge.

When we were emotionally ready, the universe offered us its greatest gift: love.

The place our rivers merged into one, and the moment

that my heart became his, was September 12, 2018, 12:28 a.m.

"What's your secret? Tell me what it is." Tyler said.

It can't possibly be more obvious, I thought. There was nothing "secretive" about it. We (me and every live feeder out there) knew exactly what it was.

I had said it without saying it a thousand times by now. He had to know what it was.

I took a deep breath in, debating whether I would be able to force these words from my lips. These five words had never come out before in this sequence.

Damn, I blew it, I thought. *I tried not to let this happen, I wasn't looking for this, but here it is . . .*

Another deep breath in, and the words came out. "I'm in love with you," I whispered into his ear and rolled back over to my side of the bed.

After I spoke these words, I realized that I wasn't looking for or even expecting to hear it back. I didn't care if he said it back to me or not. I just needed him to know. There was no trepidation, nothing in me that feared getting hurt.

I had always thought the phrases "I love you" and "I am in love with you" were synonymous. I had to experience it before I could understand it.

I interpret "I love you" as an expression of deep emotional gratitude. It's an unconditional feeling that reveals a special place you have designated for someone in your life.

"I am in love with you" starts with the look in your eyes. It roots itself so deeply and fills you so full that it pours out through your eyes, your words, your thoughts, and your actions. It consumes you and makes everything else that once seemed important to you no longer significant. The words "I am *in* love with you" are spoken from your soul when there isn't a doubt the feeling is mutual, without ever needing to hear the words in return. This phrase is the one reserved for who we want to share our lives with.

I had never believed that there was one person meant for each of us. A soulmate, I heard people call it. Not until I found someone who made up for everything I lacked. Who could fill in all the gaps and crevices; who made me feel complete.

I didn't think it was possible for me to care about someone so much that it became the only thing that mattered to me in my world, making everything I once thought important seem so small. The business I'd worked so hard on, the career I'd created for myself—these mountains seemed like grains of sand. Without him in my life, all of it was meaningless.

I do believe now that there is a person out there for each one of us who brings out the very best in us and gives our lives the context they were missing.

He brought out the child hiding in me for so many years. He brought back the drive in me that once strived to be the world's greatest. He showed me I could feel again with my whole heart and love unconditionally without fear of pain. He proved to me that being vulnerable was the only way to let our hearts feel real happiness.

I gave him my heart and he promised to keep it safe, and for that it will be his for eternity.

What I had been searching for all along was right in front of me.

Tyler leaned in close and, kissing me on the forehead, said, "I got a secret. I'm in love with you too."

35

UNBOTHERED PART TWO

Nothing parallels life more than writing a book. The process and even the format mirror each other so perfectly. We sit down at our dark cherry writing desks with our ballpoint pens and stacks of paper—or our MacBook Pros, if that's more your speed. The only thing dissimilar is that in real life there are no erasers or backspace buttons.

In front of me sits my laptop with all twenty-six letters, ten numbers, and punctuation keys whose purpose I'm still unsure of. I have everything right here that I need to form words from these keys, turning them into complete sentences and then into paragraphs.

Both our lives and writing a book start with our thoughts. We sit at our desks, thinking, "What is it I want to write? Where should I begin?" Once we are clear about what it is we want to say, the words begin flowing. The paragraphs soon turn into chapters and just like that, we've created a part of our story.

Life is no different; our thoughts create our reality the same way our thoughts create our chapters. The chapters of our lives are the direct result of the things we've spent so much time thinking about, for better or worse.

It seems so obvious and effortless, so why aren't we all already living the most magnificently fabulous lives?

It really is this simple, but for some reason so many of us are still looking enviously across the street at the Joneses, thinking how unfair it is that their lives are so damn perfect.

First and foremost, you have to be clear about what it is you want before you can begin writing the story of the life you dream about. Without the clarity of your thoughts, you'll begin typing all the subconscious, useless chatter that's full of the lies, misconceptions, and falsities you've come to believe as some sort of truth.

When I started writing this book, believe it or not, I didn't have an outline to follow or really any plan of how everything was going to tie in from chapter to chapter and make logical sense to anyone interested enough to read what I had to say.

I just went for it, the same way I went full speed ahead at every one of my endeavors, only looking back to see how far I'd come—my word count.

My only real plan was knowing that I was going to write a memoir; oddly enough, the idea came to me sitting in the waiting room of my ob-gyn. I know that seems strange. Maybe it was just ironic timing, or perhaps there's some kind of odd energy lingering in gynecologist offices that causes you to start deeply contemplating life.

Whatever it was, the thought hit me out of nowhere: I needed to write a book. It wasn't just one of those thoughts that comes and goes like a cloud on a sunny day, where you barely notice its passing. It was the kind that hit me like a sack of bricks and wouldn't leave my mind until I sat down in front of my computer and had at it.

Instead of writing outlines and chapter summaries, I wrote this book the same way I live my life: no plan, just a clear mind about what it was I wanted to do. With the evidence of my life, I wanted to demonstrate to anyone that picks up this book that they too can be anything and have anything they want in life. I wanted to inspire my readers through my own raw vulnerability that nothing is permanent and you can reinvent yourself as many times as you want. I wanted to show you all that you can have as many chapters in your story as you have dreams. After you've completed one book, you can close it, stash it away in your library, and begin writing the next one.

I hit a roadblock when I came to writing the end of this book. It was my first real writer's block. I couldn't figure out where I would go next or if I would just wrap it all up with a nice bow.

I thought about starting this chapter with my eviction from the BB house and explaining to you all that the woman that walked out of the *Big Brother* house wasn't the same numb, anesthetized girl that entered June twenty-something, 2018. I thought about telling you that neither Tyler nor I won the half-a-million-dollar grand prize, but we walked away with so much more, something that no amount of money could buy. I thought maybe I should explain that it was never about winning the money; it was about going through this journey and coming out a changed person.

I wanted to somehow weave in there that when I watched the season back, I didn't recognize the girl who stood onstage in her Adriano Goldschmied jeans and white linen crop top on premiere night, and that a handful of episodes in, I saw my face change. Like I woke up, and suddenly I could see the life in my eyes again.

Every other time in life when I'd hit a roadblock, I'd google whatever it was I needed to know, and so I did. I opened up my Google Chrome home page on my MacBook and typed out "how to write a conclusion." The very first bullet point read: "Your conclusion wraps up your essay in a tidy package and brings it home for your reader."

Hmm. Well, that seems easy enough, I thought. *That's exactly what I'll do. I'll bring it home for the reader.* I booked a one-way flight from Los Angeles to Hilton Head Island. I was going to literally bring it on home for my readers.

On that familiar four-and-a-half-hour flight from LA to Charlotte, I started thinking about what my definition of the word *unbothered* was.

I started out with what it wasn't. Being unbothered isn't being numb, unemotional, not caring, or the inability to be affected.

It's not even a reaction; it's a feeling. It's the feeling you get when you know your self-worth, when you live your life for yourself first. It's a feeling of empowerment when you know that being *you* is enough. It's being clear about what your passions are and defining yourself by what you love, not what you do. It's being fearless of failure and love while holding nothing back.

It's becoming the role model that your younger self needed.

My journey is still a work in progress, but I no longer see life as just a single book. I see my life as an endless library I can fill with as many books and as many chapters as I damn well please.

But for now, my first novel has come to a close, and my library has its first book to hold and keep safe.

As I sit here at the same desk, in the same room, in the same home I grew up in, writing my last chapter of the story that happened right here, it has come to a complete full circle, quite literally ending where it all began. I realize my purpose of coming home was to complete the circle and for me to see just how far I had come. As I wrap up this book, I'm realizing this story has turned from my memoir to a self-development book to a love story, and now it's ended as a fairytale.

If I'd been handed this manuscript of my book fifteen years ago, when I sat right here at this desk doing my school-work, and had been given an enchanted pen that allowed me to revise any part of my story, I can honestly say that I would not change a single thing. I've made a *lot* of mistakes, I'll be the very first to admit it. But everything that happened—the good, the bad, and the ugly—has led me to where I am right now. It showed me what's really important and the things that are truly fulfilling. Most importantly, it showed me what happiness really feels like. It led me to Tyler, and the rest was happily ever after.

As my last chapter comes to a close, concluding this first book, I leave you with this. As one door closes to another's opening, may each of your chapters be full of happiness and love, and may your protagonist be unapologetically unbothered.

OXOX,
Angela

Angela Rummans is a TV personality, model, and actor. While she is best known for being a contestant on season 20 of *Big Brother*, before her television debut she was a professional pole vaulter and college dropout turned entrepreneur. She is the owner of Paper'd Moments LLC and co-owner of Naut & Chain. She lives in Los Angeles with her boyfriend Tyler Crispen. Together, they own and run the jewelry company Naut & Chain and work as social media influencers and travel bloggers as well as models and actors.

Follow along with their journey: www.TangelaInc.com, @angelarummans, @tylercrispen2.

 facebook.com/angela.rummans.1

 twitter.com/angelarummans2

instagram.com/angelarummans

Community Houses of Prayer

Ministry Manual

reaching others for Christ
through strategic prayer
Revised and Expanded

Stanley D. Gale

Stanley Gale, *Community Houses of Prayer: Ministry Manual*
Original ©2002 by Stanley D. Gale
Revision ©2007 by Stanley D. Gale
Published by: Deo Volente Publishing
                    P.O. Box 119
                    Humboldt, TN 38343

Printed in the United States of America.

ISBN-10: 0-9753446-1-7
ISBN-13: 978-0-9753446-1-3

Community Houses of Prayer Introduction

God is doing a mighty work in our day to bring revitalization to His people for the work of outreach with the gospel of life in Jesus Christ. He is working in them a heart of humility and submission, and is stirring them up to prayer. Community Houses of Prayer (CHOP) is a resource to equip and engage believers in this commission of hope.

CHOP Vision

To see a developing network of committed communities of pray-ers around the world knowing God and seeking God for the souls of those around them

CHOP Mission

To mobilize Christ's disciples around the world where God has providentially placed them to reach others with the gospel through the intimacy and instrumentality of strategic prayer

CHOP Calling

Reaching Others for Christ through Strategic Prayer

Community Houses of Prayer is supported by a website that provides help in starting and leading a house of prayer, as well as other resources. The address is www.CHOPministry.net. Feedback is welcome and encouraged through this website. The author can be contacted at sdgale @chopministry.net.

The basic principles underlying the CHOP approach are laid out in *WARFARE WITNESS: Contending With Spiritual Opposition in Everyday Evangelism* (©2005, Christian Focus Publishing, Geanies House, Fearn, Ross-shire, IV20 1TW, Scotland).

Introduction to the Revised Edition

The second edition of the *CHOP Ministry Manual* reflects feedback gained from those using the first edition as well as general improvements. Some of the changes include: placement of the Basic Training Lessons in the body of the book, inclusion of a fuller presentation of the gospel as a training tool, incorporation of excerpts from *Warfare Witness* as part of the Daily Prayer Guide for introduction and reinforcement of principles and practices inherent in the CHOP approach, thorough revision of the Daily Prayer Guide to aid in strategic prayer, pre-CHOP and post-CHOP guidelines, and a number of stylistic and content changes throughout for ease of use.

What others say about Community Houses of Prayer

I have been humbled in seeing those whom I prayed for respond in a dramatic way to the leading of the Holy Spirit. I had always felt inadequate to be involved in evangelism but the CHOP experience was a blessing to me as I was able to reach out to those around me for Christ. Any Christian can participate in CHOP without having a special vocation for evangelism. **Larry Woodruff, educator and CHOP participant**

Prayer is the most characteristic, and arguably the most important, Christian discipline. No follower of Christ, and no community of His followers, can hope to know full and abundant life, or a bountiful mission and worship, apart from vital prayer together. The pastor who succeeds in leading his congregation to become a praying people has won half the battle in claiming his community for Christ. But the multitude of diversions, distractions, and other worthwhile activities makes getting a whole congregation organized and laboring together in prayer a difficult task. Now Stan Gale shows us how, and why, pastors must make community-wide prayer a major focus of their ministries. The CHOP manual can provide the vision, resources, and step-by-step guidance for any church to begin bathing its community in prayer. And this, in turn, can provide the context and catalyst for revival fires to fall. **T.M. Moore, Principal of The Fellowship of Ailbe and author of *The Psalms for Prayer*, *Celtic Flame* and numerous books on prayer and revival**

In this book Stan Gale guides us into real life evangelism and helps us to more effectively engage our spheres of influence with the gospel message. Herein we see a cord of three stands woven together: confidence that God will answer prayer for the lost; passion for the lost; thoughtful/practical insight as to interacting with the lost. These three strands woven together encourage and facilitate our mandate to be ambassadors for Christ. **Glenn P. Evans, Pastor**

Many evangelism tools speak of the importance of prayer for outreach - CHOP actually taught me to pray evangelistically. CHOP enabled me to develop: *Intimacy* with Christ through its daily devotions and prayer guide; *Strategy* to pray purposefully for unbelievers; *Community* by gath-

ering with fellow believers to pray for the spread of the Kingdom; and *Expectancy* by training me to watch for God's answers to prayer. CHOP will prosper your soul, focus your vision, and empower your outreach!
Dr. Dwight Dunn, PCA Pastor

CHOP is a most practical, teachable, and scriptural tool for personal evangelism. The central emphasis on prayer not only brings petitions before the Lord but also draws the participants into an active and growing community of real support, mutual accountability, and loving encouragement.
Bob Herrmann, Pastor

I've been looking for a way to guide our church into a period of intentional prayer, which would be sound theologically and warm-hearted devotionally, and Community Houses of Prayer meets both those criteria well. As I read through it, my heart was filled with hope at what God will do when the believers in our body begin to pray this way!
Dave Swavely, Pastor and coauthor of *Life in the Father's House.*

The CHOP Ministry is a comprehensive approach to evangelism that helps to make you aware of opportunities that present themselves everyday by treating each individual contact as a person in need of God's grace, instead of as a number to tally into God's kingdom. It's amazing how vested you become in the lives of your friends, family members, colleagues... when you pray for them asking God to reveal himself to them through you.
Jeremy & Olivia Verrillo, CHOP participants

Using the CHOP Ministry Manual as a personal devotion guide really helped establish some of its guiding principles, including the strategic nature of prayer and the primary importance of the gospel being communicated in the context of relationship. It also greatly heightened my anticipation of using the Manual with others in a small group setting.
Steve Gentino, CHOP participant

Community
Houses of Prayer

Table of Contents

Dedication

To Linda, my ever-patient, ever-present wife of my youth

Acknowledgments

I would especially like to express my appreciation to three key figures God has raised up in my life who have contributed to the concept and form of this CHOP ministry tool: **T. M. Moore**, author, pastor and former seminary president for his encouragement and mentoring; **Phil Douglass**, professor at Covenant Theological Seminary, for his direction in exploring a biblically-balanced concept of spiritual warfare in outreach; **Archie Parrish**, founder of Serve, International, for his leadership to the church in understanding prayer as a weapon for outreach and means of spiritual renewal. I am also indebted to **John DeVries** and **Alvin Vander Griend** who planted the conceptual seed of CHOP through their "Neighborhood Houses of Prayer" ministry. I am grateful for the feedback provided by the many who have been involved in CHOP. Their input has contributed greatly to this revised Manual. Lastly, I want to thank **Larry Byars** of Deo Volente Publishing for tremendous help in the production of this manual and for his encouragement to me in the CHOP ministry.

The Author

Stanley D. Gale has been married to his wife, Linda, since 1975. They have four children. He holds Bachelor of Arts and Master of Education degrees from the University of Delaware, a Master of Divinity degree from Westminster Theological Seminary in Philadelphia, and a Doctor of Ministry degree from Covenant Theological Seminary in St. Louis. He is an ordained minister in the Presbyterian Church in America with 20 years of pastoral experience. He is also the author of *WARFARE WITNESS: Contending With Spiritual Opposition in Everyday Evangelism*, and *The Prayer of Jehoshaphat: Seeing Beyond Life's Storms*.

Outreach Orientation

Welcome to Community Houses of Prayer (CHOP), a ministry tool for reaching others for Christ through strategic prayer. As we begin, let's get our bearings. Enter a typical shopping mall and you'll find a large map that gives an overview of the various stores of the mall. On that map will be a little indicator saying, "You are here." As we speak of reaching others for Christ we would do well to step back and survey the bigger picture to identify where we are, how we came to be there and why. These redemptive bearings will orient us to what God has done in history and in our lives, and how He would use us in the lives of others.

Scouting Out the Land
Our Lord Jesus Christ has called us to Himself to belong to Him and to follow Him. He has rescued us from the kingdom of darkness that imprisoned us in sin's mastery, misery and condemnation. He has brought us into His kingdom of light and life, the very ground and reason for our worship (1 Pet. 2:9f.). Through Him we are sons and daughters of the living God, servants of the Most High.

Hope. To us belongs a hope, not a "hope-so" hope of wishful thinking but a hope of confident expectation, assured conviction and vibrant certainty. Ours is not futile hype, but a fertile hope grounded in the historical work of Jesus Christ. As the writer of Hebrews puts it: "We have this as a sure and steadfast anchor of the soul, a hope that enters into the inner place behind the curtain, where Jesus has gone as a forerunner on our behalf." (Heb. 6:19-20a). This hope points to the finished, victorious, redemptive work of Jesus on our behalf that secures our salvation and secures us as heirs of eternal life. The apostle Peter exclaims the praises of such a God who graciously gives us new birth into a living hope (1 Pet. 1:3), in which our inheritance is held for us (1 Pet. 1:4) and we are held in His mighty hand for our inheritance (1 Pet. 1:5). We live out our days in anticipation of the blessed hope, the glorious appearing of our great God and Savior, Jesus Christ (Titus 2:13). Every day of our lives we live as the redeemed of the Lord, children of hope (1 Thess. 5:5), different from those of the world who have no hope (1 Thess. 4:13). As we walk by faith, God fills our lives with faith, hope and love, causing us to overflow with hope by the power of the Holy Spirit (Rom. 15:13).

Kingdom Ambassadors. As part of this new kingdom of hope, joy and peace, we enjoy not only the blessings of heavenly citizenship, we find ourselves as subjects and servants of a new King, workers in His vineyard, soldiers of His kingdom. No longer is this world our home. Rather we are citizens of heaven, aliens and pilgrims in this world, not occupied with building our own kingdoms or enhancing our own reputations but concerned with Christ's kingdom priorities and values, seeking first His kingdom and His righteousness. In this sojourning our Lord calls us to be ambassadors of hope, declaring to those around us without God and without hope (Eph. 2:12), the sure hope of the gospel wherein a perfect righteousness is found in Christ apart from our own efforts at obedience to God's law (Rom 3:19-24).

Our lives bear witness to this God of hope both in word and in deed. The character of our lives is to point others not to how great we are but to how great is our God (1 Pet. 2:11). That our behavior might not point to us or to any notion that salvation is by our good behavior, we are to give *interpretation* to our deeds as the Lord provides opportunity by verbal explanation for the hope we have (1 Pet. 3:15). Our lives are governed by the reality that Christ bore our sins in His body on the tree, so that we might die to sin and live for righteousness; by His wounds we are healed. We were as sheep gone astray, but now by the grace of God we have returned to the Shepherd and Overseer of our souls. (1 Pet. 2: 24f; cf. Is. 53:4-6). Our lives are His and we live for Him.

The Glory of Grace. As we look to embark upon a ministry of reaching others for Christ what bearings are we given? The land we survey gives us a panorama of *grace*, a grace that has swept us up in its current, a grace that oxygenates and invigorates our existence in this world, and a grace that qualifies and empowers our role as ambassadors of Christ. We enjoy the standing we do only by the grace of God. His grace sustains us each and every day, leading us away from self-focus and self-dependence to find our strength and sufficiency in Christ (Titus 2:11-14; 3:4-7). His grace has given us new hope, a new identity and a new home and His grace will lead us home.

With these bearings, as ones who have received every spiritual blessing in Christ because of the grace of God and who are stationed as His witnesses in this world, we turn to how we can be faithful to carry out that role. CHOP is a tool designed to equip, engage and encourage us in faithful service to our Lord as instruments of grace in His hand for the spreading of the sure hope of the gospel.

Operation Outreach

The heart of the Community Houses of Prayer ministry approach to outreach is *prayer*. Our Lord Jesus has given us prayer not only for delight
in fellowship with Him or for bringing our burdens to Him, but also
as a *means* for the extension of His kingdom in this world. Each local
church, as a house of prayer (Luke 19:46), is an outpost of His kingdom,
established by Christ, for the strengthening and extension of His kingdom in the midst of this world. That kingdom is the redemptive rule
of Jesus Christ in the hearts of those formerly without God and without
hope in this world. It is a kingdom that cuts across national borders,
encompassing a people from every tribe, language and nation. It is a
counter-kingdom to that of the fallen world that imprisons its subjects
in darkness, sin and death. This fallen kingdom is ruled over by Satan,
who is called prince, ruler and even a god, as an idolatrous rival to Him
who is the true Prince of peace, the true Ruler promised from the line of
David, the true eternal and incarnate God. As part of His church, we are
all agents of His kingdom, soldiers conscripted by His Spirit. Our Lord
has equipped us with spiritual weapons suitable to carry out our work of
pillaging the kingdom of this world for the cause of Christ. Those basic
weapons are truth and prayer.

CHOP is a ministry tool that directs prayer as a means *to revive* (motivation) our hearts in grace as we draw near to the living God as our loving
Father and *to involve* (participation) us in our everyday lives as active
witnesses for Jesus Christ in dependence and expectation of His working. CHOP looks to cultivate in us a greater *awareness* of the evangelistic
nature of ordinary life in which we find ourselves every day. It kindles
in us an *attitude* of personal involvement and expectation as the witnesses for Christ we are by virtue of being His disciples. It involves us
in the actual *activity* of bearing verbal witness to the glorious gospel of
salvation bound up in Christ alone. We look to draw near to people for
Christ and draw near to Christ for people. And we do it collectively,
united with fellow believers for mutual encouragement in a common
mission.

CHOP weaves together four strands: 1) lifestyle evangelism, 2) strategic
prayer, 3) personal spiritual renewal, and 4) spiritual warfare. Your participation in CHOP will not only *involve* you in these four aspects, but
will also *train* you in them through instruction, reinforcement and practice.

What are these four strands? *Lifestyle evangelism* looks to share the gospel in the context of those relationships at work or at home or wherever God has providentially placed us. *Strategic prayer* is kingdom prayer (i.e., prayer concerned with the matters, priorities and goals of Christ's kingdom) characterized by planning, intention, focus and direction. *Personal spiritual renewal* reaches to matters of motivation as we are invigorated with the scent of God's grace so richly, unexpectedly and undeservedly poured out upon us. It seeks to grow in intimate knowledge of God fueled by His revelation of Himself in His Word. Such prayer draws us near to God, cultivating in us *His* heart for the lost, compelling our witness by love and gratitude and not by sterile duty. *Spiritual warfare* takes into account the biblical data of the reality of spiritual opposition for our work of witness for the extension and strengthening of the kingdom of God against the kingdom of the prince of darkness. It is prayer aware and prayer against. This strand attempts to find firm footing on the foundation of God's written Word, while avoiding the pitfalls stemming from fanciful notions and excesses.

One of our goals will be to learn to use prayer as a *weapon* of the kingdom. We're not all that accustomed to wielding prayer in this way. One of the purposes of CHOP is to train you in *kingdom* prayer, *prayer that seeks God for His purposes and not merely for personal needs or wants.* As with any tool or weapon, the more we become familiar with the way it works the more adept we will become in its use.

CHOP involves a small group of two or more believers committing themselves to a 12-week period of *meeting together weekly* and *praying privately daily.* The mission of the group is the common goal and mutual support of reaching others for Christ, particularly through prayer. This sort of prayer will powerfully affect you as God's instrument and will carry out God's purposes in those around you. God actually uses your prayers to the accomplishment of His providential purposes.

The Community Houses of Prayer ministry approach is based on the following principles and precepts:

These are outstanding!

- ℵ Personal evangelism belongs in some degree to the role of all who would call themselves disciples of Jesus Christ. God has designed it so that those captured by His grace would be called to His service as His instruments for the communication of the gospel.
- ℵ Evangelism belongs to the realm of ordinary life and not only to

those extraordinary opportunities afforded by a special visitation night or in being part of an evangelistic program of some sort.

ꭓ Evangelism is best understood not as an event but as a process, where the role of the witness is to encounter someone for Jesus Christ to the advancement of the person's knowledge, agreement or trust in Christ as the source of spiritual, abundant and eternal life.

ꭓ The gospel is ordinarily communicated in parts and not in totality, or at least developed through a building process. God may use us to sow the seed, weed out error, or nourish through truth. These things are not necessarily all done in a single encounter, nor are they done necessarily just by us. God may raise up others to influence that person for Christ.

ꭓ While the gospel demands a response, a call to response at every encounter is not inherent to faithful evangelism. The presentation of truth in itself demands a response of stance on the part of the hearer. In God's design, it is better to see ourselves as spiritual midwives responding to and cooperating with the work of the Spirit, rather than as spiritual salesmen cajoling conversion.

ꭓ Faithfulness to the evangelistic enterprise is not measured by conversions but by our attitude, intent and activity in obedience to Christ in bearing witness to Him as Savior and Lord. God produces the fruit.

ꭓ The most natural and ordinary way for Christians to communicate the gospel authentically is through the relationships of their lives that serve as the contexts for that communication.

ꭓ God is sovereign and His providence governs all events and contingencies, both means and ends, for His purposes. For that reason it is assumed that we find ourselves in the life-spheres we do at the placement of our God and in service of His kingdom. He has established us as beacons of light in the midst of the darkness of sin and unbelief right where we live.

ꭓ It is only the Spirit of God who opens eyes and changes hearts to understand and embrace the gospel. The effectiveness of evangelism is utterly dependent on the sovereign, gracious working of the Holy Spirit in applying Christ's accomplished work of redemption.

ꭓ By its very character evangelism involves a spiritual dimension in the supernatural working of the Spirit of God for the redemptive kingdom of Christ against the fallen kingdom of darkness ruled by the devil and his demons. This spiritual dimension must be taken into account and dealt with in the wisdom of God's Word and with the weapons of God's provision.

𐤟 Prayer is communication with the living God that will promote intimacy with Him. Prayerfulness is the privilege and responsibility of all Christians, useful for all levels of spiritual maturity.

𐤟 Prayer is a weapon of the kingdom of God ordained by Him as a means for His ends against spiritual opposition.

𐤟 Prayer is intended by God to enfold us into the accomplishment of His purposes for His glory. In the majesty and scope of God's design, in praying we can expect God to do something He would not have done had we not prayed—not to make God dependent on us but to the glory of His unfathomable greatness.

𐤟 Prayer is not merely for therapeutic value in which we unburden ourselves of sins or cares. Rather, prayer is eminently effective for the building and strengthening of the kingdom of God and for the accomplishment of His purposes.

𐤟 God has provided for special benefit and blessing in corporate prayer as opposed to private prayer alone.

Evangelism is a kingdom mission, declaring the glorious redemptive rule of the Savior, calling for the repentant faith of changed kingdom allegiance. It is a spiritual activity, contending with spiritual opposition, relying on God's wisdom and employing the weapons of God's design and with His power. The church is the kingdom's agent, local congregations outposts of the kingdom, the congregation its soldiers.

Community Houses of Prayer seeks to mobilize Christ's disciples for obedience to the Great Commission, emphasizing prayer that would shape us as God's instruments and accomplish His saving purposes in those around us. As soldiers of the cross, we fight not for victory but in victory. Nowadays military missions are dubbed with appropriate identification handles. Perhaps ours could best be captured with the title "Operation Outreach," as we enter the harvest of our worldly surroundings *as witnesses* for Christ intent on *bearing witness* to Him.

OPERATIONS MANUAL

A Community House of Prayer unfolds in three phases: group formation, the weekly meeting and daily private prayer.

Group Formation
From the planning room of prayer that pervades all phases, the first step
in beginning a house of prayer is to gather together a group of two or
more Christians willing to commit to the work of strategic prayer outreach. As with any aspect of discipleship there is cost, particularly cost
of time and effort. A CHOP is very much task-oriented. Certainly, there
are camaraderie and mutual care in Christian fellowship, but particularly
there is a job to do in service to Christ. The work of CHOP is not unlike a
team of people getting together for the common task of building a house.
Workers enjoy one another and support one another in the tie that binds
them together, but the task remains prominent. Only in the case of a
CHOP, the Lord is the one who builds the house; we are His instruments
for the work of kingdom witness.

Once a group is identified, things like time and place for the weekly
meeting will need to be decided upon. The ministry is entitled "Community" Houses of Prayer, because it not only mobilizes the community
of faith and builds community in the body, it takes place in the community of society. While the group can hold its weekly meetings in the
church building, there is much advantage of warmth and worldly presence in meeting in the community, whether it be neighborhood, workplace, dormitory or some other agreed-upon location.

After reading this Outreach Orientation of the *CHOP Ministry Manual* all
participants should complete the "Basic Training Lessons" found in the
next section. These lessons serve to make them familiar with the four
aspects of CHOP (i.e., lifestyle evangelism, strategic prayer, personal
spiritual renewal, and spiritual warfare) and put everyone on the same
page for the nature of the work to be done. Here, participants will complete life-sphere mapping which will provide their core prayer targets for
the weeks ahead.

The actual CHOP takes place over a 12-week period. It involves meeting
together once a week as well as engaging in daily private prayer between
weekly meetings. Meeting weekly is best for continuity, but other group
meeting schedules (e.g. biweekly) can be used as well. Enfolding the
four basic training lessons into four meetings *preliminary* to the actual
CHOP can enhance the time together. Although this stretches the 12-
week commitment to 16 weeks, it does have several advantages, such as
forming solidarity as a team and unity in a sense of mission, promoting
clarity through discussion of basic concepts studied, and steeping the

ministry in expectant corporate prayer. A schedule that includes Pre-
CHOP preparation can be found in Supplement B.

The Weekly Meeting
Each of the 12 group meetings of the CHOP follows the same basic
agenda. The length of the meeting is typically between 60 and 90 minutes. A valuable discipline to establish from the outset is the discipline of
punctuality, in which participants demonstrate good stewardship of time
and respect for others as well as maximize the time together.

After gathering and convening the meeting in prayer, the agenda
involves four basic elements: adoration, debriefing, intercession, and
deployment. Approximate time frames for each are in parentheses in the
box below.

> **CHOP Weekly Meeting Agenda**
> (gathering and opening prayer)
>
> 1. Adoration (10-15 minutes)
>
> 2. Debriefing (10-15 minutes)
>
> 3. Intercession (30-40 minutes)
>
> 4. Deployment (10-20 minutes)

1. **Adoration** (10-15 minutes). Here the group lifts their hearts
    to God in whose name they meet and whose cause they serve.
    Time is spent exalting God for who He is and the great things He
    has done. Something learned about God through the daily devo-
    tions or experiences of the past week may well be fuel for exalta-
    tion. Other stimulants to such adoration could be songs, sung or
    read, or reading and responding to portions of God's Word that
    had a profound impact on those of the group. Stimulated by one
    another in conversational prayer (i.e., brief prayer, building on
    one anothers' prayers), the group can virtually meditate aloud in
    the unity of the Spirit to the praise of His name.
2. **Debriefing** (10-15 minutes). This portion involves reporting

on God's activity since the last meeting. We read of this practice in the book of Acts: "And when they arrived and gathered the church together, they declared all that God had done with them, and how he had opened a door of faith..." (Acts 14:27a). In addition to reports on the handiwork of God, the debriefing could include taking note of God's answers to prayer, in part or in whole. Debriefing provides focus, expectancy and accountability. We sharpen one another as we train our spiritual senses to be alert to God's workings. Other things that might be shared in keeping with the ministry of outreach are personal or circumstantial obstacles (e.g., increased busyness at work) and struggles encountered (e.g., unbelief or a wandering mind) so that the members can support one another in prayer.

3. **Intercession** (30-40 minutes). Depending on the size of the group, here the participants might divide into smaller units for prayer. Sometimes greater openness can result from same-gender groupings. In the prayer cells, updates might be given on those who have been targeted for prayer. After such sharing, intercession can be made for those prayer targets. Often it is easier if a person prays for his or her own prayer targets, but it is certainly appropriate to pray for one another's targets as the Lord leads. Other matters for prayer might be the CHOP ministry in general, the community in which the meeting is taking place, various ministries or needs or outreach events, as well as personal and circumstantial obstacles shared in debriefing. Again, conversational prayer is of great benefit. During this time of prayer, silence should not be seen as something undesirable to be overcome or as a problem to be solved, but as an opportunity to commune privately with the God who is present to receive the prayers of His children and servants. This silent meditation may well overflow into public expression for the benefit of the whole.

4. **Deployment** (10-20 minutes) As the meeting heads toward its conclusion, here the participants reconvene as a whole to lift their eyes to the harvest into which they will be heading in the days ahead as witnesses for Jesus Christ—the workplace, school, the marketplace, the neighborhood. They move from the barracks to the battlefield as soldiers of the cross. Goals for the coming days and expected opportunities in the week to come could be expressed and prayed for. Ideas and encouragement can be shared. Prayer can be offered for upcoming activities in the local church or ministry that seek to have an impact for

Christ. The meeting concludes with a season of prayer for the work and the workers of the vineyard, including prayer aware of and against the opposition of a spiritual enemy that will be faced. Expectant prayer will proceed from prayer rich in recognition of the character of the God we entreat, of the accomplished work of His Christ and of the assurance of His presence with us by His Spirit for His work in which He includes us.

While the daily private prayer can be carried out on an individual basis apart from involvement with others in a CHOP group, the weekly group meeting holds tremendous benefit for encouragement in that daily prayer. It's easier to stay consistent if we are accountable to others. In addition, it is important that the weekly meeting be preserved as a positive thing. Sometimes the enjoyment of one another can take precedence over dedication to the work of God the group has assembled to do. This can lead to shortchanging the time spent in prayer or to meetings that are excessively long or unproductive for the work of prayer at hand, which can discourage regular attendance and reduce expectations that should remain high.

Daily Prayer

In many ways the work of daily prayer is the backbone of the CHOP ministry. With it come the greatest demands of time, priority and effort. Prayer is difficult for a number of reasons, not the least of which is the spiritual opposition of our enemy with whom we contend for the work of outreach. The last place he would have us is on our knees before the throne of grace. He would dissuade us from the labor of prayer, convincing us of its ineffectiveness, in effect disarming us from the very weapon our Lord has placed in our hand as effective for His purposes. We may become easily discouraged in prayer, particularly since it speaks to our lack of ability and competency and to our absolute need for Christ and the work of His Spirit. Prayer is surely an activity of faith that leads away from self to Christ, a position vigorously resisted by pride, the flames of which are stoked by our enemy.

Another discouragement to prayer is that when we rise from our knees we don't have a finished product before us in which to find gratification and encouragement. Or, perhaps we do—a list of prayer items all checked off. But checklist prayer is not what we're after. We want to linger with our Father God in prayer, building intimacy, growing in the grace and knowledge of our Lord, savoring His mercies, seeking His face on behalf of others. Our prayer time is not to be seen as a business meeting. If our hearts would be warmed to the task of evangelism, we must grow to know our God whose work it is and grow to appreciate His amazing grace to us that we would be motivated by humble, loving, sacrificial service.

Our work of prayer is not merely to express our requests. Our challenge and call is to wrestle with God, not as a combatant but in dialog as we seek to conform to His will and take captive every thought to the obedience of Christ. Such prayer is indeed hard work, yet it is a labor of love, both for God and for neighbor. One of our greatest objectives as we would undertake a ministry of prayer is assigning it the importance, seriousness and effort it will require.

On that note, let's walk through a typical day of guided private prayer. You might turn to a page from the Daily Prayer Guide for reference as we review the format.

You'll notice at the top left of the page a reference to the week and day. The Daily Prayer Guide will direct you through 12 weeks of prayer. Your work of prayer will be six days a week, with general prayer guidelines provided for Sundays. So you will find 72 days of prayer spread over 12 weeks, days one through six for each week.

Begin your time in prayer, drawing near to God in delight, thanksgiving and expectation. Remember, you are actually meeting with the true and living God who is Creator and Redeemer, Sovereign Lord and your Heavenly Father by virtue of His adopting grace. Ask Him to help you to pray and to stay focused. Approach your time in a spirit of prayer, looking to commune and converse with your Heavenly Father.

Next, read the text at the top of the page to the right of the week and day. These are excerpts from *Warfare Witness: Contending with Spiritual Opposition in Everyday Evangelism*. These quotes are provided to introduce, reinforce and equip you in the CHOP principles of life-sphere witness, strategic prayer, personal spiritual renewal and spiritual warfare.

Your time of daily prayer is divided into four sections: Drawing Near, Reaching Out, Enemy Profile and Mutual Support. The first section, **Drawing Near**, is intended to help you to grow in intimacy with your Father in heaven. The idea here is to linger with God, to reflect and meditate on His character as He reveals Himself in His Word. He is the God who, as the catechism puts it, is "infinite, eternal and unchangeable in His being, wisdom, power, holiness, justice, goodness and truth." He is a God of mercy, grace and love. These attributes are communicated in His self-revelation, in His mighty works and in His Son, who is the image of the invisible God. That we might be refreshed in His grace and renewed in His service, we want to know Him and to remind ourselves of His astounding, incalculable blessings to us in Christ. For from Him and through Him and to Him are all things; to Him be the glory forever.

God reveals Himself in creation but especially in His Word. We want to learn to approach the text of the Bible attentive to what God is telling us about Himself. It is important that we give God our attention as we read His Word. It is so easy for our eyes to take in the print and even for our minds to grasp the content, but to miss the communication of God.

A Scripture passage is provided for each day's prayer. The selections given expose you to a wide variety of God's attributes. Turn in your Bible and read the full text listed. The bulleted questions following the reading are intended to help draw you into the text, giving ear particularly to the character of the Author, often challenging a response. You can use this Scripture reading *in addition to* or *in place of* your regular devotional reading. Whichever you chose, the key is to *linger* in communion with God and to *listen* to what He is revealing about Himself in the text. Ask yourself, "What is God telling me about Himself and what response does that revelation require of me?"

Following the reading and meditation on God's communication in His Word, you will spend time in prayer *responding* to what He has told you, praising Him, thanking Him, confessing your sin—however the Spirit may lead you. If God's Word is food for our soul, reflective and responsive prayer provides the spiritual digestive juices for assimilation of its nourishment to our growth in grace and strength for service. Our prayer life will be tremendously enriched as we learn to commune with God in response to the communication of His Word.

From communion with your Lord you move to the second section of the work of kingdom prayer, **Reaching Out**. It is here that you engage in strategic prayer for the sake of the kingdom. Your strategic prayer will be particularly concerned with those you have identified for prayer over the 12-week period of the CHOP. These prayer targets will be determined by way of the life-sphere mapping from the first lesson of the Basic Training Lessons. Although you will major on these three persons for strategic prayer, it may well be that over the weeks ahead God will raise up others in your life-spheres for whom you are burdened to pray, particularly as you become more aware of and attentive to those in your life-spheres. Feel free to add them to your list, but be careful not to spread yourself too thin and so overextend yourself, particularly as you look to build relationship with those for whom you are praying.

In this section you look to intercede for those you are praying in respect to *their* relationship to God. You will notice that, though without explicit, biblical textual reference, most of the petitions are scripturally informed, as you employ the truth of God's Word through prayer. Although you will grow to know your contacts as you build relationship with them, God's Word already tells you a great deal about them in their created humanity and fallen condition. This prayer focus takes advantage of this inspired intelligence report.

The next segment leads you in prayer and preparation for God's use of you in the lives of your contacts. Prayer does not *preclude* action, but *presupposes* it to the extent of our opportunity. For example, we pray for our daily bread (Mt. 6:11), yet if we do not work we will not eat (2 Th. 3:10). The book of Nehemiah gives us a concrete picture of such prayer for the sake of the kingdom, emphasizing faith founded on God and flowing out in activity. In the face of opposition to the work, we read: "But we prayed to our God and posted a guard day and night to meet this threat" (Neh. 4:9). As we prayerfully draw near to our contacts, we will look expectantly for God's providence for our involvement in their lives.

Be aware of the *cumulative* character of this segment. Although an item might be specifically mentioned only once as a matter for prayerful involvement in your contacts' lives, they are intended to introduce various ideas to you for involvement and to equip you in their use. For example, early on in the CHOP you might ask God for opportunities to build relationship with your contacts. Later, you might pray that a contact would take initiative to ask you something about your faith. Another time you might be directed to pray for opportunity to perform some act of kingdom kindness or to direct their attention to God through answered prayer. These various items build on one another, training you in the attitude of your mind for loving involvement in your contacts' lives for the sake of Christ. They should not be seen as an assignment for the day at hand but as a repertoire for cultivating a practical mentality of mission in relating to others. Ask God to use you and to show you how you can be used.

In addition, this segment of Reaching Out will lead you in developing and using your personal testimony and will train you in learning a systematic presentation of the gospel for your own edification and for boldness and clarity in sharing the life of Christ with others. You may have worked on these tools for sharing your faith at some other point. In that case, you may want to review what you worked on previously or acquaint yourself with the materials in the supplements section of this manual. The point of these exercises is to equip you to reach out in word, as well as in deed and prayer.

The third section, **Enemy Profile**, brings to the fore the spiritual opposition to which God alerts us in His Word for the work of witness. As you take into account the reconnaissance report of your enemy provided by God in His Word, you can use this information as a basis for prayer on behalf of those contacts for whom you are praying. Bear in mind that your prayer is to your *Advocate*, not to your *adversary*. Scripture does not call us to speak to the devil by reprimand or some other communication. God's Word directs us not to rebuke the devil but to resist him, wielding the weapon of God's Word, through the hand of believing prayer. We resist by standing against our enemy, turning to our Lord Jesus for His protection, strength and working, strong in Him and in the power of His might.

The battle is the Lord's. You are instructed to stand firm in Him and in His mighty power, recognizing who the real enemy is and the conflict of kingdoms that is inherent in evangelism. Prayer that takes into account this spiritual opposition is prayer *aware* and *against* the intentions, activity, tactics, schemes and character of our adversary, as these are exposed to us by God in the pages of Scripture. The portion of the Bible text written out in the Enemy Profile directs our attention to the nature of our enemy through various intelligence data of names, titles, descriptions and tactics provided us by our Lord in His Word. The larger context of the profile entry is found in the Bible reference noted in the parentheses.

Following the Scripture text you will be directed to pray aware of something about the enemy introduced in that text and to pray against the enemy's hold or influence on your contacts in respect to that information.

For example, in taking the information from Ephesians 2:2 (Week One, Day One) into account we might pray for the mercy of God in delivering our contacts from their bondage to sin and the rule of the evil one as they are at home in a fallen world, subjects of his kingdom, and desperately in need of the deliverance of Jesus Christ. As we grow to know our contacts better we will likely see how they are driven by the world's principles and values, given over to gratifying the lust of the eyes, the lust of the flesh and the pride of life, oblivious to the condemnation of God that hangs over their heads. We intercede for them, not as ones better than they but as ones who have been delivered from that fallen kingdom and who know the mercy and power of God, asking that God would be merciful to them and rescue them from the dominion of the evil one.

In the final section, **Mutual Support**, you pray for *yourself* and your *colleagues* in the CHOP ministry. Here general and diverse petitions are provided for you over the 72 days ahead in which to bring yourself and those laboring with you before the throne of grace. In addition to these general petitions you can pray for specific and individual needs of which you become aware over the course of the CHOP. You will learn of these needs through the weekly meeting where you will interact with and come to know your co-workers.

At some point in your daily prayer, devote a few minutes to write in your **Prayer Journal**. You will find this journaling one of the blessings of your time, much like the psalmist must have experienced in putting his struggles, petitions and declarations about God into words. You may want to write out some of your prayers, record observations about yourself, or note something God has impressed on your heart. Dialog with God through your Prayer Journal. Record your responses and thoughts as a personal debriefing with God. Express to Him your doubts and your delights and your desires. Such activity will draw out your heart in a way that just thoughts or verbal prayer cannot.

You might also note requests from your life-sphere targets, your CHOP co-workers, your ministry context and your own needs. Included can be various needs that are shared with you or that you yourself have noticed. Pray not only for the need but for those kingdom concerns and purposes of God that have brought the need to the person's life. This broader perspective is illustrated in Deuteronomy 8:3: "And he humbled you and let you hunger and fed you with manna, which you did not know, nor did your fathers know, that he might make you know that man does not live on bread alone but man lives by every word that comes from the mouth of the Lord."

Keep your eyes open for God's answers to your prayers, both for your own blessing and the group's edification and for sharing with those for whom you are praying. You also want to be vigilant to God's answers so that you can *respond* appropriately to Him, either by praise or thanks or confession or the new obedience of repentance. You might turn back to a previous page of the Prayer Journal and update a request with greater detail or an answer of God. Of course, God's answers may be *in part*, such as provision of a job interview in response to a prayer for a needed car. He may answer "yes," "no" or "not yet" or "not according to the way you have in mind." Surely, God's ways are not our ways; He is the all-wise God.

Don't regard writing in your prayer journal as some formal report to be filed. View it simply as a place to chronicle in believing interaction and expectation your work of prayer in view of the dynamic hand of God who inclines His ear to you and responds to your petitions for the sake of His kingdom.

As you began in prayer at the start of your daily prayer, so wrap up your time in prayer, committing yourself and the day at hand to the end of glorifying and enjoying your God who is with you throughout it. Recognize that as you leave your time of directed prayer you do not leave the personal presence of your God, who is with you throughout the day and with whom you can commune moment by moment.

Approach each day of the Daily Prayer Guide with pen in hand. As you leave each day of prayer, leave the page well marked. Fill in the date at the top. If you're using a portion of Scripture other than the one included in the Manual, make note of it. Mark the page up with prayers and notes and thoughts as you interact with God. Give expression to those things God impresses on your heart. Record the names of your prayer contacts each time before you pray for them. Write out the names of your CHOP co-laborers one by one as you lift them up in prayer. All these are ideas to help you to be active and attentive as you engage in the work of prayer.

As was mentioned above, the Daily Prayer Guide directs your work of prayer six days a week. For Sundays, as you rest from your regular labors of strategic prayer outreach, you might give yourself to more general prayer, looking to the worship of God, the revival of His church and the extension of His kingdom in the world. The following chart gives some suggested items for such prayer.

Sunday Prayer Suggestions

- Pray that God would be glorified through the worship of His people this day.

- Pray that God would renew His people in the joy of their salvation and in awe of His grace and love.

- Pray that God would revive and strengthen His church for service in the world as the agent of His kingdom.

- Pray that God would enfold converts into His church as worshippers of Him in Spirit and truth.

- Pray that God would not allow Satan to rob Him of the glory due His name in the assembly of His saints for worship.

Different people are involved. Different group dynamics are at work. Different circumstances are in play. The Spirit of God is carrying out His purposes. All these mean that no two Community Houses of Prayer will be alike. One constant, however, is the promise of God to be at work in answer to prayer. You will be changed. Your faith will be focused. Your soul will be nourished. God's purposes will be accomplished through your prayers. As you set about your strategic prayer for the work of witness, you can say with the psalmist: "O Lord, in the morning you hear my voice; in the morning I direct my prayer to you *and watch*." (Psalm 5:3, italics added)

One last note to your CHOP experience. You don't want to think that your ministry is limited to the 12 weeks of CHOP or that the effectiveness of what you do in CHOP expires with the end of CHOP. You are cultivating a mentality in yourself, a way of looking at life, a way of looking at God's Word, an expectation of prayer that will serve you in the days ahead. Also, you are preparing soil and sowing seed through what you do in CHOP that may well bear fruit in years to come. I have heard numerous examples of ones who have come to Christ and those praying for them realizing, "Hey, I just realized, those are people I was praying for when I was part of a CHOP."

On the one hand, avoid being outcome-oriented, preoccupied with results in your time. That runs contrary to the very nature of prayer qualified by "Your will be done." On the other hand, do not suppose that your prayers are pointless or ineffective. Faith informs you that you entreat a mighty God who inclines His ear to you and uses what you pray for His perfect purposes. Remember that your labor in the Lord is not in vain.

Basic Training Lessons

Introduction

Woven into the ministry approach of Community Houses of Prayer are four components: life-sphere witness, strategic prayer, personal spiritual renewal and spiritual warfare. The following lessons are designed to lead you in exploration of biblical teaching related to each of these areas. Your study will help to prepare you to participate more meaningfully in CHOP, particularly as you move on to daily prayer.

The study of these components will be enhanced by discussion within the group context. Answers can be shared. Questions raised. While lessons would be completed individually, working through them together will reinforce the concepts. Members can help one another in understanding and application.

As was mentioned in the Outreach Orientation, multiple benefits are gained by spending together time working through these lessons prior to the 12-week CHOP. In addition to promoting clarity through discussion of basic concepts studied, unity and camaraderie in a sense of mission are forged. The time also provides opportunity for steeping the ministry in expectant, corporate prayer. A schedule for this pre-CHOP period of preparation is provided in Supplement B.

One word of direction as you begin the lessons. Often we want to answer questions looking for the "right" answer, usually the one we believe the asker of the question is looking for. While there are correct answers in some cases, in many instances there can be a number of appropriate answers, arrived at from different vantage points. One of the blessings of discussion as a group is hearing those diverse perspectives. Answer each question with your best understanding of both the question and the text.

What you study in these four lessons will be reinforced, amplified and applied through your time working through the Daily Prayer Guide. Through completion of these lessons you are sketching in pencil what will be developed throughout your time in CHOP and throughout your life as a disciple of Jesus Christ.

LESSON ONE
Life-Sphere Witness

The Three Stooges, of American slapstick comedy fame, made us laugh with their antics and by their ignorance. When summoned to another room with the call, "Gentlemen, this way please," they would look at each other wondering where the gentlemen were the butler was addressing. As Christians we can get the same confused expressions on our faces when we hear our Lord say, "You are My witnesses." We look behind us to see whom He is addressing. We wonder if the pastoral staff entered the room without our knowing it or if the Tuesday night evangelism team snuck up behind us. Such ignorance might be funny for the Stooges, but it is not for us as witnesses for Jesus Christ.

If we are to be obedient as the church of Jesus Christ to our risen, reigning and returning Lord, we must recapture the biblical concept that everyone who bears the name of Christ also bears the role of witness for Him. In this lesson we explore some of the biblical precepts to reinstate us to our role and to engage us in our responsibility.

1. As a Christian you are a *disciple* of Jesus Christ. What do the following passages suggest it means for you to be Christ's disciple?

♦ Luke 6:46-49

> *both have heard the same thing, but only one*
> *acts on what's heard*
> *— obedience presupposes knowledge*

♦ Luke 9:23-26

> *· self-sacrifice*
> *· whole of life*
> *· larger perspective needed*
> *· failure to do so results in loss*

♦ Luke 9:57-62

· *following Jesus is the first priority*
· *there is a cost to discipleship*

♦ Luke 18:18-30

· *All belongs to Christ*
· *Again, Jesus is the first priority*
· *you can follow the commandments and still not be a disciple.*

❖ Summarize how being a disciple of Christ is to influence your life.

· *it transforms life and the whole way we see and live every day*
· *other-centered*
· *obedience-driven*

2. What role does Jesus give in Matthew 4:19-20 to those who follow Him? *Fishers of people*

Keeping in mind what we saw in the last question, do we have the option of accepting or rejecting this role? Why or why not?

Can't reject — Following Jesus results necessarily in being changed into this.

What are some descriptions given you as a follower of Jesus?

♦ Matthew 5:13-16

- *salt of the earth - purifying, preservation*
- *light of the world - dispels darkness, shows the way*

♦ Acts 1:8

- *witnesses - μάρτυρες - testifying to what one knows...*

♦ 2 Corinthians 5:20

  - *AmbAssAdors*

♦ 1 Peter 2:9-12

  - *chosen rAce, royAl priesthood, holy nAtion, A people,*
  God's people, foreigners And exiles
  (A distinct people group)

♦ 1 Peter 3:15-16

  · *Apologists*

❖ Why is bearing witness for Christ not an <u>accessory</u> to being His disciple?

  - *because it's pArt And pArcel of being A*
  disciple; it's in the bAse model

❖ Why is it useful that we first see "witness" as a noun (who we are) before we see it as a verb (what we do)?

  - *because what we <u>do</u> must Arise from*
  who we <u>Are</u>; witness is A "life" mAtter,
  And not A mere tAsk now And then.

3. If being a witness is of the essence of discipleship and a statement of identity for followers of Jesus Christ in this world, the next question is *where* are you a witness? To ask the question in this way is to answer it. <u>If being a witness is part of who we are, then we are witnesses wherever we are.</u>

N.B.

  a. The typical translation of our Lord's Great Commission in Matthew 28:19 is to "go and make disciples." Actually, the verb is "make disciples." "Go" is a part of speech that relates to the verb, which can best be expressed, "in your going," or "as you go," make disciples.

What does this understanding of the word "go" suggest about *where* you are a witness?

· it suggests you are a witness all along the way

What does this understanding of the word "go" suggest about *when* you are a witness?

· it suggests you are a witness all the time
i.e. in the whole way one lives, hopes, loves, acts, spends, etc.

b. Jesus says in John 4:35 that "the fields are ripe for harvest." Where are these "fields" to which Jesus wants you to lift your eyes?

– they're everywhere people are

♦ Mark 5:19-20

· At home, among friends and family

♦ Colossians 3:22-24

– At work

♦ Acts 1:8

· here, there, and everywhere

❖ In what specific harvest field has *God* stationed *you* as a worker for Christ? *Police dept., school, Waffle House, Starbucks*

❖ How does this perspective revolutionize your role as a witness
for Christ?

· I am a participant in God's redeeming purposes in the world, right where I am.

4. We have seen that to be a disciple is to be a witness, workers in the
field of harvest around us as God is at work bringing people to a
saving knowledge of Jesus Christ. It is by the providence of God that
we go where we go, know whom we know, work where we work, and
all those other facets of the comings and goings of ordinary life. These
life-spheres are your **spheres of influence**. These spheres are *those
arenas of life in which God has providentially placed you, where you operate
and have contacts, and where you have special opportunity to influence others
for Christ.*

Let's chart your particular spheres of influence. On the diagram below
write your name on the bold line in the center. Then, on the lines at the
end of the arrows write your life spheres (e.g., work, neighborhood, community activities, ministry areas, social settings, extended family, recre-
ational endeavors, marketplace [e.g., bank, restaurant], etc.). Fill in as
many of the lines as you can.

Next, write out the names of two or three people you know under each
of these life spheres. In preparation for your involvement in Community
Houses of Prayer, begin to pray asking God to lay on your heart three
people. These three people can come from one life sphere or a combination of spheres. Once you've decided on three, write their names at the
bottom of your life sphere map. These are the core contacts you will
target for prayer over the next 12 weeks.

If you are planning to establish a CHOP that targets a particular *area* for
prayer (e.g., neighborhood, work place, college dorm), your prayer contacts will all come from the same sphere of influence.

Life-Sphere Mapping

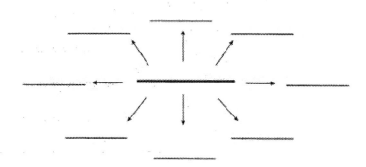

CONTACTS: 1.   **2.**   **3.**

Knowing Satan's efforts to distract us, disgrace us or discredit us, a note of caution is in order. Since these contacts are people with whom you will be working to build a close relationship, it is ordinarily wise to select people of your *own gender*. Family members would be an exception to this principle.

Even now, as God has laid these ones on your heart, you can pray expectantly that He will use you in their lives for His purposes.

5. How can you bear witness to Christ in your life-spheres? What practices does the Apostle Peter identify for us in influencing those around us for our Lord?

- 1 Peter 2:11-12
  - good conduct
  - good deeds

- 1 Peter 2:18-21
  - hard work
  - endure suffering

- 1 Peter 3:15-16
  - be ready ↓ give an answer

- 1 Peter 4:12-15
  - endure hardship + suffering

Why is *verbal* witness necessary and not just witness by our behavior?
- objective content to the Gospel
.

To what does *silent* witness by the way we live our lives point as the way of salvation?
- to Christ and what he has done for us.

6. What do the following passages teach about evangelism in general and your role in particular?

- 1 Corinthians 3:5-9
  - be faithful to what we're called to do, and then trust God; we're in the <u>process</u>
- Luke 10:25-37
  - don't stereotype
  - <u>be</u> a neighbor
- 1 Corinthians 2:1-5

- Proverbs 18:13
  - listen first, before speaking
- Mark 4:13-15
  - sow the word faithfully
  - again, results belong to the Lord
- Matthew 14:14-16
  - meet needs
  - move ahead and trust God with what you have
- Acts 26:4-20
  - personal testimony as an open door
  - God can use anybody.
- 1 John 3:16-18
  - the life of the church as a witness to the world, opening opportunities to proclaim the Gospel
- Ephesians 6:19-20
  - we need prayer

❖ From these passages, summarize how can you have an influence for Christ in the lives of those in your spheres of influence? You might even express this in terms of a personal mission statement.

❖ REFLECTION: What uneasiness or resistance do you find in yourself at the thought of bearing witness to your Lord? Express these to God. Talk through your fears with Him. How would God respond?

LESSON TWO
Strategic Prayer

To have a strategy means you are up to something. You have a goal and you have a way you are going to go about reaching that goal. To be strategic is to be intentional, focused, directed, informed and purposeful. Strategic prayer is to prayer like grocery shopping is to a recipe—it knows what it wants and it goes after it. We submit ourselves to seek our God to serve His purposes.

In this lesson we learn about prayer, prayer as an armament of the kingdom of God placed in our hands as His soldiers for the purpose of the expansion of His kingdom. Such prayer has been likened to a walkie-talkie in the hand of a soldier to his commander, rather than an intercom to the kitchen as is so often the case with prayer. In this lesson, we will explore the role of prayer in evangelism and see how we can wield it as the powerful, strategic weapon that it is.

1. The most basic reason for the necessity of prayer for the work of evangelism is that *evangelism is God's work.* How do the following passages indicate that the work is God's?

 ♦ Psalm 127:1

 ♦ Matthew 19:25-26

 ♦ John 6:44

♦   1 Corinthians 3:6-7

2. What barriers to the gospel are *we* unable to overcome?

♦   Romans 2:28-29

♦   Romans 8:6-8

♦   Ephesians 2:1-4

♦   1 Corinthians 2:14

3. In seeking to reach those in need of Christ, we need not only different strategies; we need a power beyond ourselves. That power comes only from God and prayer is the avenue given us to that power. The power of prayer is not resident in itself or in the strength of our faith but in the God of power who makes it effective for His purposes. Why should this knowledge of God's activity and our inability drive us to prayer?

4. Just as God is sovereign (i.e. in complete control) in salvation, so in His sovereignty He has established prayer as a means for His ends. God has not only told us to pray, His plan enfolds our prayer.

God in His infinite wisdom actually uses our expressions of faith
to bring about His purposes. To say that when we pray God will
do something that He would not have done had we not prayed is
not opposed to the doctrine of God's sovereignty, but included in it.
What does God tell us about prayer in the following passages?

♦   Psalm 5:3

♦   Matthew 21:22

♦   John 16:23-24

♦   James 4:2-3

♦   1 John 5:14-15

5. Prayer is one of the spiritual weapons of the kingdom of God to accomplish His saving purposes in the extension of His kingdom and building of His church. We are to pray, "Your kingdom come." Prayer seeks the face of our King for His subduing work of the kingdom. What are some ways that the *model* prayer our Lord gives us in Matthew 6:9-13 can be seen as a prayer for the work of the kingdom? What points of contrast between believers and unbelievers, between the kingdoms of God and of Satan are reflected in each of the following phrases? Use this contrast to develop a prayer under each phrase. The first is filled in as an example.

> **Our Father in heaven,**
> All humanity is divided into two families, the family of God and the family of the devil. All are naturally born into the family of the devil. In His mercy, God gives new birth to adopt us into His family. Pray that God would rescue those you are praying for from their father, the devil, and bring them into the glorious freedom as His adopted children, making them heirs of eternal life. Pray for the mercy of God in their lives to prepare a heavenly home for them, and grace to call Him, 'Father.'

> **Hallowed be your name.**

> **Your kingdom come.**

> **Your will be done, on earth as it is in heaven.**

> **Give us this day our daily bread.**

And forgive us our debts, as we also have forgiven our debtors.

And lead us not into temptation, but deliver us from evil.

6. Corporate prayer is praying with other believers, in contrast private prayer, which is praying alone. Corporate prayer seems to hold a special place in God's design. Matthew 18:19-20 is a classic passage cited to validate the benefit of corporate prayer. Turn to that text and answer the following.

♦ What is the context for the gathering of believers (Mt. 18:15-18)?

♦ Jesus seems to be applying a general principle (vv. 19-20) to specific situation for the sake of His kingdom. What is that principle?

♦ What benefits for corporate prayer occur to you?

Matthew 18 as a whole shows our Lord's concern for His kingdom, its character and its occupants. The church discipline of verses 15-20 deals with who belongs to the kingdom of light and who do not (at least by their fruits). The church is seen exercising its authority to act on the basis of the revealed Word of God ("binding" = forbidden by Scripture; "loosing" = permitted by Scripture). The King promises to be with His people who bear His name when they are gathered in that name for the work of the kingdom. This would be not only for the specific purpose of church discipline, but for the general work of prayer as well. In other words, Jesus affixes special blessing and purpose to corporate prayer that can be applied to various situations.

The idea of Christ being present to answer prayer where two or three are gathered in His name does not seem to speak of an intensity of power or increased effectiveness in prayer, but to communion with Christ as the risen Lord who holds the keys to death and Hades and who is present in victory over the kingdom of darkness for His church. In view is solidarity with others who bear the name of Christ, as we serve under a common banner for our Lord against His and our enemies. Two or more gathered in the name of Christ is an expression of unity with Christ and community with one another, and an expression of our identity, purpose and dependence upon our King for executing His will on earth as it is in heaven. That which gives corporate prayer its benefit is not numbers but the promise and wisdom of God. The agreement is not simply between those praying but agreement with the Word of God in submission to His purpose and presence.

❖ REFLECTION: What words would you use to describe your own prayer life, both privately and corporately? How do you want to grow in this area?

LESSON THREE
Spiritual Renewal

*[Pray] also for me, that words may be given to me in opening my
mouth boldly to proclaim the mystery of the gospel, for which I am an
ambassador in chains, that I may declare it boldly, as I ought to speak.*
Ephesians 6:19-20

In his request for prayer in Ephesians 6, the Apostle Paul suggests some
obstacles to our communication of the gospel: content, courage, clarity,
circumstances. Certainly, knowledge of the content of the gospel and
how to present it in a coherent, meaningful way is important. Overcom-
ing our inhibitions of what people will think of us, finding the boldness to seize the moment and speak up are hurdles we must overcome.
Speaking with clarity and relevance to an increasingly unconcerned and
biblically illiterate culture offers new challenges. Circumstances themselves can be less than hospitable to the work of evangelism, especially
with hectic schedules, private lives and speech restricted by cultural and
even legal expectations.

But with all these hindrances to gospel proclamation, there is one obstacle that is even closer to home—us. We are inclined to leave our first
love. We so easily distance ourselves from God. We allow the grace of
God to become ordinary instead of amazing. We forget the seriousness
of our sin. We lose our vigor and zeal, our wonder and awe because we
distance ourselves from the God who has treated us with confounding
mercy, incredible grace and amazing love. It's not that we couldn't spout
off the right answers. The obstacle is close fellowship with our God and
Father. Only here will we find the right *motivation* for the work of witness. Only as we return our witness to the realm of glorifying and enjoying God will we be enlivened for the task, compelled by our deep love
for God and for those without Him and without hope in the world.

In this lesson we look to personal spiritual renewal, to rekindling the
flame of heart-based service to Christ. Several elements contribute to
stoke this fire.

1. Basic to spiritual renewal is intimate, experiential knowledge of the
God who has reconciled you to Himself in Jesus Christ. Who is this

God? What does He reveal about Himself to you in His Holy Word?
God reveals Himself to us not merely so that we have our theology
straight, but so that we can know Him—not just know *about* Him. He
wants us to know Him in a real, personal, experiential way, and to continue to grow in that knowledge all our lives. How does God introduce
Himself to you in the following passages?

♦   Job 38:1-41

♦   Psalm 139

♦   Isaiah 40:12-31

♦   Isaiah 42:5-9

♦   Isaiah 55:8-11

♦   Jeremiah 32:16-27

♦   Acts 17:22-28

❖   REFLECTION: God reveals Himself in many other ways through His names, His self-descriptions, and His actions. How would knowledge of the character of God transform your *walk* with Him and *work* for Him in your life?

2. Jesus declared in Luke 7:47 that "he who is forgiven little loves little."
   To put this in positive terms, we might say that the way to increase our
   love is to enlarge our understanding of how great was the debt of our
   sin, how grave was our situation as sinners in the hands of a holy God,
   how much we have been forgiven and its cost, and how much we have
   been given. In other words, we need to grow in our knowledge of the
   grace of God. It is in the grip of grace that we will be energetic instruments for our Lord in loving the lost.

   What do the following passages say about your situation apart from
   Christ?

   ♦   Romans 3:10-20

   ♦   Ephesians 2:1-3

   ♦   Ephesians 2:12

   ♦   Titus 3:3

   ♦   John 3:36b

   ♦   2 Thessalonians 1:5-10

   What happened to alter your situation?

   ♦   Romans 3:21-24

   ♦   Romans 5:6-11

   ♦   Galatians 1:3-5

♦   Ephesians 2:4-10

♦   Ephesians 2:13

♦   Titus 3:4-7

What is your position now?

♦   John 10:7-10

♦   John 5:24

♦   1 Peter 1:3-5

♦   Romans 8:28-31

♦   Galatians 4:4-7

♦   I John 3:1

♦   John 14:7-10

♦   1 Corinthians 15:50-58

❖   REFLECTION: How does knowledge of the extent of your sin, the grace of God, the cost of your redemption, your need for Christ at every moment and in every thing, and God's assurances to you at every point motivate you as a witness for Christ? Write out a prayer confessing your sin, professing your faith and committing yourself to this God who loves you and gave Himself for you.

3. We have life only by grace. We have a hope only by grace. We live life daily only by grace. We constantly fail our God. Our motives are mixed. Our obedience is tainted. Yet with all that sin, we are acceptable to a holy God and accepted by Him. That's grace. Where our sins abound, God's grace super-abounds. No matter where we look in our lives and find sin, God has accounted for it in His manifestation of love for us in Jesus Christ. Fresh apprehension of and appreciation for this amazing gospel of grace is what will be the fuel that will cause the flame of life in our hearts to blaze in an inferno of zeal for Christ and His service.

   What direction from God do you find in the following passages to help you in living in the combustible, invigorating atmosphere of God's grace?

   ◆   2 Chronicles 7:14

   ◆   Nehemiah 9:5-6

   ◆   Isaiah 57:15

   ◆   Daniel 9:17-19

   ◆   Revelation 2:4-5

4. How is our intimacy with God in our reconciled relationship with Him deepened and developed? *The answer is the Word handled with prayer.* The truths of God's revelation are absorbed into our spiritual digestive systems to nourish and energize our beings through prayer.

Prayer is communication with God by which we will strengthen our relationship with Him. God gives us prayer for drawing near to Him. Prayer is what will renew personal zeal for God and His mercy to sinners. Prayer will fan into flame the kindling of God's Word laid up in our hearts as His children and will stir us up to bear witness.

Prayer draws us near to God who is our sufficiency. As we linger in communion with Him who rescued us and subdued us to Himself, delivering us from the kingdom of darkness and death into the kingdom of light and life, our hearts are filled with His love. Our souls are stirred and invigorated with the scent of His grace. We are motivated to His calling as witnesses, not only by a sense of duty, but especially as privilege and delight.

The primary goal of the prayer in view here is not petition, not even praise, but *intimacy*. God is not an abstract concept. He is the God who has reconciled us to Himself in Christ Jesus. Such is the extent of the love He has lavished upon us, that we who were His enemies are now His very own adopted children. Christian service that flows from any other context can degenerate into hollow religion.

We find this illustrated in the prophet Isaiah. Turn to the vision recorded in Isaiah 6:1-8 and answer the following questions

♦ What about God strikes Isaiah as he is escorted to God's throne room? (1-4)

♦ Before the face of this God what strikes Isaiah about himself? (5-

6)

♦   What can Isaiah do to escape or solve his predicament of peril?

♦   What does God do? (6-7)

♦   What is Isaiah's response? (8)

That's the way it works. The better we know God, the more intensely we see our sin and ourselves, and the more we will glory in God's mercy, grace and love to us in doing for us what we could not do for ourselves.

❖   REFLECTION: How would you rate your motivation for mission? How would a fresh awareness of God's grace function to revive you in your walk with God and your work for Him?

LESSON FOUR
Spiritual Warfare

If I told you that a pot of gold was at a particular place and that gold was yours for the taking, you would probably respond with enthusiasm at the prospect. If I told you that the only problem is that the place was crawling with rats and, in order to get the gold, you'd have to deal with the rats, you would probably have some reservations but those concerns wouldn't stop you. However, knowledge of those rats would no doubt prompt you to dress differently, to be on your guard, and to go well equipped to handle the rats as you search for the treasure.

Now imagine God told you that He wants to use you to reach those around you with the gospel of life. But, He warns you, there is an enemy with whom you will have to deal. He alerts you to the enemy—his character, his tactics, his intentions, his power. Can you imagine acknowledging God's description of that enemy, but then turning around and ignoring it for all practical purposes as you venture in to his stomping grounds? Yet that is just what we do when it comes to reaching out with the gospel of Jesus Christ. We don't take seriously God's revealed profile of the enemy we face and the nature of the battle to be waged as we would engage in witness. Obviously, this is our enemy's first victory.

In this lesson we take stock of God's reconnaissance report on our enemy and the nature of the battle we are called to wage. We also see how we can enfold this knowledge into our efforts to reach out with gospel of life in Christ.

1. Evangelism involves a clash of kingdoms, the kingdom of God and His Christ and the kingdom of this world in which Satan is identified as its ruler. How is *the work of Christ* presented in the following passages?

    ♦ Luke 4:1-13

    ♦ Matthew 12:22-29

♦   Galatians 1:3-4

♦   Colossians 1:12-14

♦   Colossians 2:15

♦   Hebrews 2:14-15

♦   1 John 3:8

2. How does the Apostle Paul understand *the work of evangelism*?

♦   2 Corinthians 2:11

♦   2 Corinthians 4:1-6

♦   2 Corinthians 10:3-6

- Ephesians 2:2

- Ephesians 6:10-20

- 1 Thessalonians 2:18

- 1 Thessalonians 3:5

We must not lose sight of the reality of kingdom conflict. The kingdom of God will grow *at the expense* of the kingdom of Satan. The gospel of peace looks not to a truce but a clash of the kingdom of righteousness, joy and peace, ruled by the Prince of Peace, with the kingdom of darkness, decay, division and deception, ruled by the prince of darkness grim. To be ambassadors of a gospel of peace is not to be a broker of peace in some sort of shuttle diplomacy but to announce peace. It is to call people to a change of kingdom allegiances (i.e., repentance and faith).

3. What profile does God give us of our enemy that we need to take into account for ourselves, for our neighbors and for our work of witness?

   Our enemy's titles

- Matthew 13:38

- John 8:44

- John 12:31

- 2 Corinthians 4:4

- 1 Peter 5:8

Our enemy's tactics

- Genesis 3:1-5

- Zechariah 3:1

- 2 Corinthians 4:2-4

- Mark 4:15

- 2 Timothy 2:25-26

♦   1 Peter 5:8

It is for good reason that our God in His written revelation, the Bible, stations us at the tree of the knowledge of good and evil to witness the encounter of the serpent with Adam and Eve, and that He grants us access that Job did not enjoy into the throne room of the Sovereign Lord Almighty to become privy to the celestial conversation. It is for good reason that we are informed that "your adversary the devil prowls around like a roaring lion, seeking someone to devour" and that we are made aware that Satan demanded to sift Peter as wheat, but that Jesus prayed for Peter. It is not without purpose Jesus identifies Satan as the culprit, the thief of the seed of the word sown in the spread of the gospel. In these and numerous other texts, God is giving us a profile of our enemy. He does so not for intrigue or to satisfy idle curiosity. He does so primarily to contextualize and characterize the work of our Redeemer, but also *to equip us* for kingdom living in this world. We will have to contend with this enemy in our spiritual growth and spiritual service. Our introduction to Satan in Genesis 3 already gives us an idea of his intentions and tactics. He poses competing counsel, counsel that will bring death, not life, and distance us from the God who is our refuge and strength. Satan is powerful, active, aggressive, relentless, subtle and insidious. He lies, deceives, accuses, distorts in his efforts to divide and lead astray. But thanks be to God who gives us the victory in Jesus and who is sovereign over all things, including Satan and his minions.

4. What guidance does our Lord give us for contending with such a foe?

♦   2 Corinthians 2:11

♦   Ephesians 6:10

♦   1 Corinthians 2:2-5

- John 17:15-18

- 2 Corinthians 10:3-5

- Ephesians 6:17

- Colossians 2:6-8

- Genesis 4:6-7

- 2 Corinthians 4:5-6

- 2 Thessalonians 3:1-5

- Ephesians 6:18

♦ Hebrews 3:12-13

Our Lord is alerting us, as we would enter the field of darkness as
workers of light, to the fact that we can *expect* opposition. We wield the
weapon of prayer in the knowledge our Commander has given us. Our
prayer can be directed in two ways. It is important, though, to recognize
that our prayer is to God not to Satan. We are to address our Lord to
deal with Satan, not "rebuke" Satan.

The first way we can direct our prayer as we would seek God's face for
those in our life-spheres is against the schemes and devices of Satan to
which we have been alerted. *Prayer that recognizes spiritual warfare must
not only be prayer for, it must be prayer against.* Prayer and the Word of
God are weapons that are to be used in tandem, where the Word directs
prayer and prayer reflects the Word.

The second way we can pray is in light of the evidences of Satan's finger-
prints in the lives of those for whom we are praying. We can take note
of the lies they have bought into, the toeholds the evil one has managed
in their lives, the false counsel they have believed that robs God of His
glory. You can discover these things in the context of the relationship
you are building with them. And you can entreat the Sovereign King on
their behalf.

❖ REFLECTION: How aware are you of your enemy, the devil? What
   difference do you think an awareness of your spiritual enemy would
   make to your Christian life and service, both in theory and in practice?

Daily Prayer Guide

Week **One** ✧ **Day** **One**	God has not left us without instruction on the subject of the spiritual opposition we face and how we are to wage spiritual warfare. In fact, the Bible is full of the counsel of God to equip us for the task. Spiritual conflict forms the backdrop against which we understand life, the work of Christ, and our work of ministry in this present age.

Drawing Near

Read Psalm 115:1-8

"Not to us, O Lord, not to us, but to your name give glory"

- What does verse 3 tell us about the limitations of God?
- How is God contrasted with idols?
- God deserves glory because He is God. But what does the psalmist particularly highlight in v. 1 for praise?

Turn your eyes to your Father in heaven. Review with Him some of the things He has just told you about Himself. Spend time exalting Him for them. Ask God to lead you as you begin this CHOP ministry. Are there areas you see now in your life for confession, areas where you rob God of the glory that belongs to Him?

Reaching Out

Pray by name for those you have targeted for prayer over the weeks ahead that God would: 1) help them to know their relationship to Him as the Creator who is to be forever praised; and 2) start to work in them a distress over their separation from Him in their sinful condition.

Pray that God would give you opportunity to spend time with your contacts so that you can build relationship with them.

Enemy Profile

"...the prince of the power of the air, the spirit that is now at work in the sons of disobedience" (Ephesians 2:2)

Pray aware of who your enemy is and the influence he exerts in your contacts' lives. Pray against his grip on your contacts that Christ might rescue them and by His Spirit make them sons of light and obedience.

Mutual Support

Pray for yourself and your CHOP co-laborers as they begin this ministry with you, that God would fill you with faith and expectation for how He will be at work through your ministry of prayer in the weeks ahead.

Prayer Journal

Week **One** ✧ **Day** **Two**	Scripture leaves us with no doubt about the spiritual conflict inherent in evangelism. The description the Apostle Paul gives us clearly characterizes the work of witness as contending with spiritual opposition. Paul's mission takes place in the same plane as does ours, on this side of the fall, on this side of the cross, on the same field of battle. The enemy is the same. The nature of the conflict is the same. The goal is the same. Our God outfits us with the same weapons.

Drawing Near

Read John 5:19-27
"...the Father raises the dead and gives them life"

- What does it mean for God to be the giver of life?
- The Father is said to "have life in Himself" (v. 26). What does that say about God as God? How is God different from you in that way?
- What attitude do you think Jesus wants to work in us by pointing out this attribute of the Father?

Ask God who has life in Himself to show you how you are absolutely dependent upon Him for your life. Spend time praising Him for this attribute that shows Him to be God and you not to be. Ask God to make you an instrument useful to Him, prepared for every good work. Examine your heart for barriers to this goal.

Reaching Out

Pray for those you have targeted for prayer over the weeks ahead each by name that God would: 1) create in them a thirst for the knowledge of Him; and 2) work in them an awareness that He is a personal, knowable God.

Pray that love for Christ and the love of Christ might be evident in your life in increasing measure as you reach out to others.

Enemy Profile

"...the god of this world has blinded the minds of the unbelievers" (2 Corinthians 4:4)

Pray aware that your enemy is an enemy of God, a rival for His allegiance, and an idolatrous pretender. Pray against his efforts to keep your contacts cloaked in the darkness of sin and unbelief and that the light of the gospel of the glory of Christ might dawn in their hearts.

Mutual Support

Pray for yourself and your CHOP co-laborers that God would protect you and grant you grace to persevere in prayer.

Week **One** ୬ **Day** **Three**	We stand in the prophetic line, proclaiming the message of God with which we have been entrusted. Not that we are vehicles of new revelation, but we are ambassadors of Christ, carrying his message, under his auspices and with his authority. We are called to venture out into an inhospitable, even hostile environment. Our Lord assures us of his presence. He also reminds us that he will use our message to achieve his purposes in the lives of those to whom we carry that word.

Drawing Near

Read Romans 11:33-36
"Oh, the depth of the riches and wisdom and knowledge of God!"

- This doxology follows Paul's discussion of God's sovereign purpose in election. Paul responds not with anger at God's decisions or envy because God has rights he does not. How does Paul respond?
- What does this passage say about how you are different from God?
- How does this passage call us to trust and honor God even when we don't understand events?

Acknowledge to God what He has told you about Himself. Praise Him for your creaturely limitations and for the majesty of His character. Are there times you rebel against God because of your creaturely limitations? Confess those sins to Him that would assert self rather than exalt Him.

Reaching Out

Pray in recognition that each of your contacts is made in the image of God, is separated from Him by sin, and is in desperate need of the reconciliation found in Christ. Pray for them each by name that God would: 1) work in them an awareness that they are empty and orphans in this world; and 2) cause them to begin to see the difference between the idols of this world and Him as the living and true God.

Pray that God would enable you to be a genuine, caring friend to your contacts, and give them a sense of real interest and belonging, sharing yourself first and then your message.

Enemy Profile

"...now will the ruler of this world be cast out" (John 12:31)

Pray aware that the world over which Satan is called a prince will undergo the judgment of God. Pray against this prince's seductions to make the world seem desirable and enduring, a source of hope and life and beauty, thus offering a false sense of security.

Mutual Support

Pray for yourself and your CHOP co-laborers that God would help you to seek first His kingdom and righteousness, laying up treasure in heaven, desiring Him and His priorities.

Prayer Journal

Week **One** ⊷ **Day** **Four**	The command of Matthew 28 is aptly named a 'commission.' Our Lord is giving his disciples marching orders. He has conferred upon each of us who bear his name the authority and responsibility to carry the message of life, liberty, and the pursuit of true happiness to those still held hostage in the bonds of sin. Seeing Christ's command as a military commission is not only warranted by Scripture, it also provides a framework that captures the nature of the mission and cultivates what is necessary to carry it out.

Drawing Near

Read Psalm 90:1-4
"...from everlasting to everlasting you are God"

- What does the psalmist's poetic expression, "from everlasting to everlasting" convey about God that a mere statement of God's being eternal does not?
- Again, how are we as creatures contrasted with God as Creator?
- What stability and security are offered to us in v. 1 as it relates to v. 2?

Give God glory, honor and praise as the One who is from everlasting to everlasting. Give Him glory for this grace that brought you to dwell in Him. How full and rich is your view of God? Confess to God any sin that keeps you from the fullness of relating with Him, by thinking too little of God and too much of self.

Reaching Out

Recognize that each of your contacts is held captive in the darkness of sin and unbelief, with the wrath of God abiding on him or her. Pray for them each by name that God would: 1) work in them a holy despair over the emptiness of life without Him; and 2) bring them to see the foolishness of laying up fleeting treasures in this world, where moth and rust destroy and where thieves break in and steal.

Pray that God would give you opportunity to learn more of your contacts' interests and needs as avenues for conversation and time together.

Enemy Profile

"...the whole world lies in the power of the evil one" (1 John 5:19)

Pray aware of the extent of the grip that the evil one has over your contacts, as they are subjects of his realm. Pray against that hold he has over them and for the deliverance of the Son of God that they might come under the protection of God.

Mutual Support

Pray for yourself and your CHOP co-laborers that you would walk in the freedom of the children of God, delivered forever from the power of the evil one. Pray that God would keep you from idols.

Week **One** ✤ **Day** **Five**	Our salvation is the result of military intervention by our Lord. He subdued us to himself. He leads us in triumphal procession, captives of his grace, in the bonds of his love. When he says that he came to seek and to save those who are lost, he is referring to a military mission of mercy and meekness as the promised Messiah of God. Jesus says that he will build his church. That building is set against the backdrop of spiritual opposition that seeks to overcome. The church operates in enemy territory and contends with enemy opposition. The mission of the church is decidedly militaristic.

Drawing Near
Read Hebrews 1:8-12
"Your throne, O God, is forever and ever..."

- How is this Old Testament description of God applied to Jesus?
- How is God shown to be separate from His creation but also sovereign over it?
- What does this passage say about the confidence you can have in God and His purposes?

Give God glory for His sovereign majesty. Praise Him for His surpassing greatness. Ask Him to strengthen you in your conviction and confidence for daily life, as you trust in Him. Do you see a lack of power in your life? How does that relate to your prayer life that would draw near to know and rest upon God as He has revealed Himself? What do you need to say to God?

Reaching Out
Recognize that each of your contacts is held captive by the devil to do his will. Pray for them each by name that God would: 1) cause them to sense the bondage of their sin and the weight of the yoke of God's righteous law on their backs; and 2) turn their eyes to Him as the loving and kind and perfect Father in heaven who would care for them and their needs.

Pray that God would help you to listen well to your contacts to learn of the things that occupy center stage in their hearts and be able to speak relevantly into their lives.

Enemy Profile
"...the devil has been sinning from the beginning" (1 John 3:8)

Pray aware the devil is the soulmate of sin and that sin is living in his companionship rather than God's. Pray against his efforts in your contacts' lives to promote lawlessness and for the Spirit of God to convict them of sin and need for Christ who came to take away sins.

Mutual Support
Pray for yourself and your CHOP co-laborers that you would know the love that God has lavished upon you that you can be called His children. Pray that God would work in you a greater love for Him and for others, as you have been loved.

Week **One** ❧ **Day** **Six**	Nowadays, we are an invading church as well as an inviting church. The covenant community of the Old Testament stood as a light to the nations. The 'go' of our Lord's Great Commission is the go of invasion. It is not the 'go' of a casual stroll or pointless wandering, but the go of military mission. We go to the nations not as tourists or as terrorists, but as ambassadors of life and hope. The church is not merely situated in the world; it is stationed here at the placement of our King with his orders in hand.

Drawing Near

Read Nehemiah 9:5b-6

"Blessed be your glorious name, which is exalted above all blessing and praise."

- How does Nehemiah address God?
- What is so special about the "name" of God? What does it mean to "bless" His name?
- Why is it good to recite God's character and review His mercies when we pray? How is that in evidence in Nehemiah's prayer?

Bless the Lord. All that is within you, bless His holy name. Praise Him for His mercies to you that inclined your heart to Him. Do you ever find yourself honoring God with your lips but your heart is far from Him? How does your zeal for Him and His work speak to this question? Cry out to God for a spirit of renewal.

Reaching Out

Remember the direction of your life when you were without God and without hope in the world as you pray for your neighbor. Pray for each of your contacts by name that God would: 1) lift the eyes of their hearts beyond the physical confines of this world, to think about spiritual and enduring things; and 2) grant them a desire to be a child of God, an heir of heavenly habitation that they might be where He is.

Listen for caricatures your contacts might have of Christianity, and dialog with them in the direction of truth. Pray for opportunities to speak into their lives for the sake of Christ.

Enemy Profile

"…disarmed the rulers and authorities…" (Colossians 2:15)

Pray aware of that Satan has real power and authority over those under his rule. Pray against his leverage in your contacts' lives and that they might find victory in Christ's work on the cross that canceled the debt of sin and disarmed the accuser.

Mutual Support

Pray for yourself and your CHOP co-laborers that as you received Christ Jesus as Lord you would continue to walk in Him, rooted and built up in Him, established in the faith, filled with gratitude.

Week **Two** ⁓ **Day** **One**	When our Lord appeared to his disciples in the book of Acts, he invests them with an identity. 'You are my witnesses,' he asserted (Acts 1: 8). In the Great Commission and elsewhere disciples are called to 'bear witness.' These two aspects serve as an important reminder for us. We must see witness first as a noun, then as a verb. It is who we are, from which flows what we do. As Paul informs us, we are light; therefore we are to be light (Eph. 5: 8). The indicative grounds and mandates the imperative. Identity directs activity and gives responsibility. Responsibility emerges from a sense of identity. If we see ourselves as customers then we will saunter in to be served. If we see ourselves as soldiers then we will report to serve.

Drawing Near

Read John 8:42-58
"Truly, truly, I say to you, before Abraham was, I am."

- What two families are in evidence in this passage?
- What are some of the telltale traits of each family?
- How does each of these families relate to Jesus?

Address God as your Father. Thank Him for what it means that you have the right to call Him by that name. Acknowledge God's tender mercies that have made you an heir of eternal life. Pray that your heavenly Father would make you more aware and appreciative of the heavenly family into which you have been brought and to which you belong by His grace.

Reaching Out

Pray for those you have identified for prayer that God would: 1) set their minds on things above, giving consideration to Him as eternal, all-knowing, every-where present, and almighty; and 2) begin to work in them a fear of God that knows Him as the Creator God and themselves as created beings.

Pray that God would help you to become more aware of any needs your contacts may have to help you draw near to them in care. Enter their brokenness. Walk with them. Pray with and for them. Listen and guide them to the sufferings of Christ.

Enemy Profile

"…The god of this world has blinded the minds of the unbelievers, to keep them from seeing the light of the gospel…" (2 Cor. 4:2-4)

Pray aware that your enemy looks to be as God, seeking worship for himself. Pray against his efforts to blind your contacts and that the Spirit of truth would expose him in their sight and reveal the true God.

Mutual Support

Pray for yourself and your CHOP co-laborers that you would deal in truth, on guard against manipulation in your contacts' lives, confident in the power and purpose of God.

Week **Two** ~ა **Day** **Two**	In Christ's kingdom there can be no conscientious objectors. In Christ's church, there is no inactive duty. To be a disciple is to be a soldier of the cross. ...There are varying degrees of giftedness, but no one is exempt from military service for the cause of the kingdom. The term of enlistment is a lifetime, beginning with conversion, ending with the discharge papers of transfer to the church triumphant in heavenly rest, where we are eager to hear the words, 'Well done, good and faithful servant.'

Drawing Near

Read Job 36:22-26
"Behold, God is great, and we know him not...."

- How is God described in this passage?
- What differences are in evidence between God and people?
- What attitude should these differences provoke in us?

Exalt the name of the God who is beyond your understanding. Recite to Him some of the things He has taught you about Himself. Spend time praising Him for His character. What barriers do you see in your own heart to prayer? Admit these to God and ask Him for help to overcome them.

Reaching Out

Remember that your contacts are weighed down with the cares of this world and seduced by the glitter of the kingdom of this world. Pray for them each by name that God would: 1) convince them of His transcendent glory that dwarfs the brightest majesty of nature or most brilliant marvel of human ingenuity; and 2) prompt in them a dissatisfaction and restlessness in their inner being with the offerings of this world.

Pray for an opportunity to express kindness and compassion to one of your contacts in some tangible way.

Enemy Profile

"For God, who said, "Let light shine out of darkness," has shone in our hearts to give the light..." (2 Cor. 4:5-6)

Pray aware of the darkness that engulfed you in your unbelief, the same darkness that now grips your contacts. Pray against Satan's efforts to squelch the light of the glory of God in the face of Christ and pray for God's new creating work in their lives.

Mutual Support

Pray for yourself and your CHOP co-laborers that the Spirit of God, who brought you from darkness to light, would renew you in the light of the gospel and the glory and power of God that gave you new birth.

Prayer Journal

Week **Two** ❧ **Day** **Three**	It is in this sense of a world distorted, perverted, and corrupted from God's pristine design that the day in which we live, and every day this side of the fall, is considered evil. Darkness, decay and disintegration appropriately describe the state of the world. When the Bible speaks of 'darkness,' it refers to the moral morass that grips the world and shrouds it in the blindness of unbelief. The evil of this present age particularly refers to the moral evil of sin, its consequences, its capabilities, and its incapacities.

Drawing Near

Read Isaiah 40:18-26
"To whom will you liken God..."

- What strikes you about God in this passage?
- How does this passage convince us that God is greater than we could ever possibly conceive?
- How are we to receive and react to such knowledge?

Ask God to increase your appreciation of His glory and majesty. Focus on one or two of the attributes He has impressed upon you. Spend time praising Him for these attributes, especially in contrast to your creaturely limitations. Cry out to God in confession and repentance, affirming your belief and asking Him to help you in your unbelief.

Reaching Out

As was the case with you, your contacts are ignorant of God's invisible qualities—His eternal power and divine nature, indifferent to them. What knowledge they do have, they suppress in willful rebellion. Pray for them each by name that God would: 1) begin to open their eyes to the glory of His majesty and the consuming awe of His being; and 2) turn their gaze to the dimness of their glory as ones bearing the sin-marred image of God.

Pray for greater sensitivity and compassion in yourself that would incline your attention to needs your contacts may have and that God would give you a genuine interest in others.

Enemy Profile

"...against the rulers, against the authorities, against the cosmic powers over this present darkness, against the spiritual forces of evil in the heavenly places" (Eph. 6:12)

Pray aware of the reality and opposition of the spiritual enemy. Pray against Satan's authority over your contacts, and for the subduing work of the Spirit to bring them to Christ.

Mutual Support

Pray for yourself and your CHOP co-laborers that you not see your contacts as the enemy but see the bondage of the real enemy and both your and their desperate need for Jesus Christ.

	While God characterizes this present, evil age as Satan's territory, does that mean there are territorial spirits with whom we have to contend in mission, demonic landlords over regions or persons? If there are minions of Satan assigned to certain localities, Scripture doesn't emphasize it and certainly does not employ that concept for the spiritual conflict inherent in evangelism. Nowhere are we taught the necessity of identifying a territorial spirit in evangelistic outreach. We do contend, however, with a demonic adversary as we would seek to penetrate the darkness of sin with the light of life. We don't want to minimize or overlook that spiritual reality for the spiritual work given to us. This age presents us with powerful, oppressive, spiritual opposition as we move out in gospel mission.

Week

Two
&

Day

Four

Drawing Near

Read Matthew 11:25-30

"...Father, Lord of heaven and earth...you have hidden these things from the wise and understanding"

- For what does Jesus praise the Father?
- How is the divine prerogative of God in view here?
- What does it mean to be a little child?

Pray that you might grow in the knowledge of God. Ask Him to work those things in you that will make you teachable. What keeps you from lingering in prayer with God, spending time with Him that you might know Him better and enjoy Him more? Confess any pride or neglect or apathy on your part to Him. Pray that you would walk with God as a child with his or her father.

Reaching Out

Your contacts strive to take for themselves the glory that belongs only to God, supposing themselves to be independent of Him and following a role of self-determination rather than submission to Him. Pray for them each by name that God would: 1) graciously and powerfully subdue them to Himself; and 2) cause each to see and admit his or her rebellion against the eternal, invisible, only wise God.

Rather than evangelism, think in terms of 'evangeliving' that seeks genuine, relational witness to the Lord Jesus in actions that serve Him and words that give Him glory.

Enemy Profile

"...the devil prowls around like a roaring lion, seeking someone to devour" (1 Pet. 5:8)

Pray aware that Satan is on the prowl looking to inflict harm. Pray against his evil intent to lure and ensnare your contacts into his lies.

Mutual Support

Pray for yourself and your CHOP co-laborers that you would be self-controlled and alert in your spiritual warfare.

Week **Two** ❧ **Day** **Five**	Since we live in the environment in which our Lord has stationed us, that means we are always on duty and continually to be on guard. The entirety of our life is qualified by our Lord's call as sons and servants, daughters and disciples. In God's infinite wisdom he has not whisked us up to heavenly glory in a chariot of fire at the moment of our salvation. In the wake of his redeeming grace, our God leaves us behind, not by way of abandonment, but by way of deployment. He stations us in enemy territory, for his service.

Drawing Near

Read Isaiah 46:8-11
"I am God, and there is no other; I am God, and there is none like me…"

- What does God say about His purpose?
- On what is God's purpose based?
- Why does God introduce Himself as He does here?

Pray to the God who governs all things according to His good pleasure. Worship Him for the astounding things He has told you about Himself. Pray that God would help you develop a perspective of your being situated in your people environment by His purpose. Examine your heart and confess to God any ways you are resistant to that idea.

Reaching Out

In their darkened understanding, those for whom you are praying do worship, but they worship what they do not know, having formed a god who is in their own image. Pray for them each by name that God would: 1) show them that they are spiritual beings, ones who are worshipers of something; and 2) draw them to Christ as ones who worship the Father in Spirit and truth.

Pray for an opportunity to tell your contacts you are praying about a need they have. Ask if they mind if you pray and follow up.

Enemy Profile

"…Resist the devil, and he will flee from you." (James 4:7-8)

Pray aware of the enemy's presence and that he is a pursuer, a stalker. Pray against his efforts to keep your contacts from Christ and that the Spirit of God would draw them to Christ in His power.

Mutual Support

Pray for yourself and your CHOP co-laborers that you would be faithful in your labors in prayer and be single-minded in seeking God's kingdom and glory and will.

Prayer Journal

Week **Two** *᪥* **Day** **Six**	Not surprisingly, the kingdom of God in the gospels is portrayed as a counter-kingdom to Satan's and as a combative kingdom to his rule over the hearts of his subjects. Jesus shows dominion over the evil one, his minions, and his rule as the prince of this world. This conflict reaches to the heart of Christ's coming and the essence of his saving work. Jesus' parables showed this kingdom in conflict. Satan is identified as the opponent. He snatched the seed of the gospel sown. He sowed the tares among the wheat. Rule over hearts is at stake. The kingdom of God advances at the expense of the kingdom of Satan.

Drawing Near

Read Psalm 135:1-6
"Praise the Lord, for the Lord is good."

- How is the surpassing greatness of God displayed in these verses?
- What does it mean about God and about you for you to be His servant?
- What "gods" in your life or in society might you contrast here?

Humble yourself before the Lord of heaven and earth. Praise His awesome name. Prayerfully and worshipfully and in faith repeat to Him what He has impressed on your heart about Himself. Pray that God would give you a deeper understanding of your prayer as part of His sovereign working. How have you thought too much of yourself and too little of God?

Reaching Out

Pride is the beating heart of your contacts, prompting them to think too highly of themselves, too little of God, too lightly of sin, too superficially of life. Pray for them each by name that God would: 1) open their eyes to Him as the transcendent God whom earth and heaven cannot contain; and 2) open their eyes to God as a good God who cares for people and who dwells with those whose hearts are humble and contrite.

Pray for the need you told your contact you'd pray for and pray for opportunities to follow up with your contact about it.

Enemy Profile

"This is not the wisdom that comes down from above, but is earthy, unspiritual, demonic." (James 3:15)

Pray aware that a tactic of Satan is to impress an appearance of wisdom. Pray against counterfeiting efforts and for the discernment that comes with faith.

Mutual Support

Pray for yourself and your CHOP co-laborers that God would grant you a heart of wisdom and keen discernment between wisdom from above and foolishness from the world.

Prayer Journal

Week **Three** ◈ **Day** **One**	Christ rules now not only in the sense of creation, but of redemption. Just as Christ has always been God, but not man, so he has always been creative king, but not redemptive king, not Messianic king. In the accomplishment of his saving work, Jesus was given rule. The church is where the invisible kingdom of God is most visible, through its community and character of righteousness, joy and peace. The church is the agent of the kingdom of God, charged with proclaiming Christ's redemptive rule.

Drawing Near

Read Ephesians 1:3-14
"Blessed be the God and Father of our Lord Jesus Christ"

- How is the Trinity seen in this passage?
- To what is the faith of v. 13 linked in v. 11?
- What reason for God's saving work is highlighted?

Praise the triune God for His character in evidence in this passage. Thank Him for each of the many blessings spread out for you as a banquet to feast upon. Ascribe to Him the glory due His name. Pray that God would draw you near to Him in utter dependence and in great expectation. Pray that God would help you to see yourself and your prayer targets in light of His sovereign purpose and power.

Reaching Out

Remembering how God, in His love set upon you before the foundation of the world, wrote your name in His Book of Life using the ink of the blood of Christ, pray for your contacts each by name that God would: 1) cause them to desire the Giver over the gifts, and to discover the Creator behind the creation; and 2) be merciful to them as sinners without Him and without hope in this world.

Remind your contacts that you are praying for them. Pray that God would work a spiritual sensibility and sensitivity in them through this. Be open and ready to speak as the Spirit leads you.

Enemy Profile

"...Get behind me, Satan! ...you are not setting your mind on the things of God..."
(Matthew 16:23)

Pray aware of that Satan is opposed to the things of God. Pray against his efforts in your contacts' lives to lead them to do what is right in their own eyes contrary to what God speaks in His Word.

Mutual Support

Pray for yourself and your CHOP co-laborers that Christ would dwell in your hearts through faith with ever-increasing love for Him and His kingdom.

Prayer Journal

Week **Three** ❧ **Day** **Two**	Through his Messianic mission, Jesus established the kingdom of righteousness, joy, and peace. That kingdom grows in the subduing of his subjects to himself as it fills the whole earth, embracing people from every nation, tongue, and tribe. It will continue to grow until all those purchased at the cross are procured by the Spirit, at which time the present age will be done away with and the kingdom of God ushered in in fullness. Jesus in his kingdom ushers in a new rule, a new authority, a new power. His kingdom looks to nothing less than the dawning of a new age that has been liberated from the effects of the fall of man. Christ's kingdom is expressive of the age to come. It speaks of deliverance from this present, evil age.

Drawing Near

Read Colossians 1:15-20
"And he is the head of the body, the church. He is the beginning, the firstborn from the dead, that in everything he might be preeminent"

- How is Jesus Christ described in this passage?
- What is Christ's relationship to His church?
- What would happen to the church without Christ?

Spend time worshipping Jesus, your Lord, your God, your Head. Bow before Him in adoration and submission. Confess your sins of independence and presumption and apathy. Ask God to change you and to revolutionize your prayer life to depend on and submit to Him.

Reaching Out

Any god that your contacts would understand would be one who is a product of the limitations of their finite minds and the fabrications of their depraved desires. Pray for them each by name that God would: 1) cause them to lift their eyes to see Him as holy and set apart from His creation; and 2) cause them to humble themselves as they come to grasp the absolute moral purity of His holiness and the pollution of their own sinfulness.

Communicate a sense of expectation to your contacts by speaking of God hearing and answering prayer. Direct their attention to the wonder and beauty of creation, giving glory to God as the Creator.

Enemy Profile

"...a thorn was given me in flesh, a messenger of Satan to harass me..." (2 Cor. 12:7-9)

Pray aware that Satan ultimately serves the purposes of God. Pray against his efforts to inflame the pride of your contacts.

Mutual Support

Pray for yourself and your CHOP co-laborers that you would learn the sufficiency of God's grace and need for it in your strengths as well as your weaknesses.

Prayer Journal

Week **Three** ⚞ **Day** **Three**	Evangelism is by its very nature power evangelism. But that which will convince someone of the reality of the kingdom of God will not be a demonstration of power by way of signs, wonders and works to the spiritually blind, but the work of kingdom power by the Spirit of God to give spiritual sight. Evangelism is conducted in power, power to open eyes, power to change hearts, power to set free from the bondage of the present, evil age, power to deliver from Satan to God

Drawing Near

Read Exodus 15:1-18
"The Lord is my strength and my song"

- How is God's mighty power displayed?
- In what way is God warrior king on behalf of His people?
- What does God fighting for His people have to do with salvation in Christ?

Praise Him for the way God reveals Himself in respect to salvation. How have you thought too "matter-of-factly" about God's salvation? Pray that God will help you to see yourself as part of His mighty saving plan. Be honest with God about your doubts and struggles. Extol His love and grace that subdued you to Him.

Reaching Out

In their sinful state, those for whom you are laboring in prayer, though they know God, neither glorify Him as God nor give thanks to Him. Pray for them each by name that God would: 1) begin to grant them a God-focus to life, in which God as He reveals Himself comes into focus for them and is brought to be the focus of their lives; and 2) work in them a hunger for the knowledge of God and a thirst for righteousness.

Commend your contacts for their abilities and achievements, looking to give glory to God and direct their thoughts to Him in so doing. Look to follow up with a written note (hard copy or email) assuring of your prayer for them, giving encouragement or reinforcing a biblical truth from a discussion you've had.

Enemy Profile

"Did God actually say…?" (Genesis 3:1-5)

Pray aware that Satan's tactic is to replace the truth of God with a lie. Pray against his efforts to discredit the truth of God and distance your contacts from the God who has spoken.

Mutual Support

Pray for yourself and your CHOP co-laborers that you would be firmly grounded on God's truth and speak the truth in love.

Week Three

Day Four

The call of the gospel is a call to kingdom allegiance, that is, to repentance and faith. The Baptist's message was to repent and believe the gospel because its accomplishment was found in the kingdom of God that had come. The response demanded to the kingdom is the same response demanded by the gospel, the message of the kingdom. The gospel of peace looks not to truce but to a clash of the kingdom of righteousness and peace with the kingdom of darkness and decay. For us to be ambassadors of a gospel of peace is not to be brokers of peace in some sort of shuttle diplomacy, but to announce peace. It is to call people to a change of kingdom allegiances through repentance and faith in Jesus Christ.

Drawing Near

Read Revelation 19:11-16

"...King of kings and Lord of lords"

- What names are ascribed to Christ in this passage, and how do they relate to Him being a warrior?
- Who can stand against Him?
- What does it mean for you to be on the Lord's side?

Look to this Christ, on whose side you find yourself by His grace, and respond to Him in praise and thanksgiving. Pray that God will help you to partner reverently with Him through prayer, not as His equal but as His instrument. Pray that God will help you learn to pray obediently and expectantly and faithfully.

Reaching Out

As part of the kingdom of darkness, your contacts are naturally inclined to rob God of the glory due Him. Pray for your contacts each by name that God would: 1) bring them to submit to Him, saying, "Not to us, O Lord, not to us, but to your name give glory;" and 2) grant them a sense of purpose in life centered on God—to glorify Him and to enjoy Him.

Pray that God would help you to convey the reality and centrality of your personal relationship with the unseen God.

Enemy Profile

"...The Lord said to Satan, "From where have you come?" Satan answered the Lord and said, "From going to and fro on the earth...." (Job 1:6-7)

Pray aware that the devil is on the prowl in search of ways to inflict harm. Pray against his stalking efforts through preying on desires and ignorance that dog your contacts.

Mutual Support

Pray for yourself and your CHOP co-laborers that you would be humble, alert and sober-minded to resist the devil and rest in Christ

Week **Three** ❧ **Day** **Five**	Paul makes it clear that at the heart of it all is a spiritual battle, fought against a spiritual foe, with spiritual weapons and spiritual power, for a spiritual cause (2 Cor. 10:3-5). The picture of the kingdom of God given to us in Scripture is of a rock growing to fill the earth, of a small seed growing and spreading as shade to the nations. The nature of that growth is spiritual conflict. The kingdom of God grows at the expense of the kingdom of Satan.

Drawing Near

Read Psalm 104:1-4, 31-34
"You are clothed with splendor and majesty"

- What does the poetic imagery of the psalm communicate about the character of God?
- How do these images show God working where we cannot and in ways we cannot?
- Why should this description of God fuel our praise?

Spend time praising God for the things He has shown you about Himself in His Word. Take one image and use it to exalt His greatness. Pray that God will help you know that greater is He who is in you than he who is in the world. Confess any sins of fear or doubt to God.

Reaching Out

Your contacts are naturally inclined to separate God from His good gifts to His creatures, attributing them to such things as evolution or chance or "mother nature." Pray for them each by name that God would: 1) help them to see the benefits they enjoy day by day as stemming from God's hand as an outworking of His goodness; and 2) plant in them seeds of appreciation that bear the fruit of gratitude directed to Him.

Pray that God would begin to prepare the minds of your contacts to hear more of Him and be receptive to His truth. Pray that the Holy Spirit would expose them to the Bible and to Christ in a way they never knew.

Enemy Profile

"...Satan went out from the presence of the Lord and struck Job..." (Job 2:6-10)

Pray aware that Satan unwittingly serves the purpose of God. Pray that God would use the efforts of Satan in your contacts' lives to expose their need for Jesus Christ.

Mutual Support

Pray for yourself and your CHOP co-laborers that you would walk by faith, trusting fully in God and content in His ways.

Week **Three** ✦ **Day** **Six**	Being members of the kingdom of God gives us identity, power, and a mandate. It means that we must see ourselves as soldiers of the cross, enlisted for the cause of our King. It means we have a message to bear. It means a power and purpose beyond ourselves is at work in this world, at work in and through us. The command of bearing witness comes from the lips of him who subdued us to himself, conscripted us to his service and is at work through us to complete his work. Considering the nature and the opposition of the kingdom of God and the kingdom of Satan, while the age to come and the present age overlap, we cannot allow ourselves to countenance a peace-time mentality for ourselves or the church. The very nature of the growth of the kingdom of God and its extension through the work of evangelism demands we live life as though we were at war.

Drawing Near

Read 1 Corinthians 8:1-6

"...there is one God, the Father, from whom are all things and for whom we exist..."

- How many Gods are there?
- What are so-called "gods?"
- How are we to express allegiance to the living and true God?

Praise God for His uniqueness. Praise Him for His surpassing greatness. Pray that His glory might be displayed amidst the "gods" of this world. How have you robbed God of His glory by your attitudes or actions? Declare to Him your confidence in His strength and your submission to His purposes.

Reaching Out

As ones separated from God by sin, your contacts seek meaning, identity and purpose in those offerings of the world that can never satisfy. Pray for them each by name that God would: 1) grant them ears to hear His voice, to listen to Him that they might know what is good and what will truly and eternally bring fulfillment; and 2) draw them to Jesus Christ, the living water and the bread of life, that they might partake by faith and find abundant life.

Share with your contacts times God has answered prayer in your life, maybe in ways that had surprised you. Pray for opportunities.

Enemy Profile

"...Satan has demanded to have you that he might sift you as wheat" (Luke 22:31-32)

Pray aware of the pure evil Satan is. Pray against the sights he has set on your contacts and that they might find refuge in Christ.

Mutual Support

Pray for yourself and your CHOP co-laborers that you would find courage and confidence in knowing Jesus intercedes for you.

Prayer Journal

Week	Our enemy, the devil, is strong, savvy, subtle, and relentless.
Four	...while we should have a sober regard for Satan, we don't want to make him larger than life. We need to be on guard against
⋞	glamorizing him or giving him more credit than he deserves. Just
Day	as we can make celebrities larger than life, we can do that with our spiritual foe. The problem with that is we end up ascribing to
One	him attributes he does not have and abilities we don't need to deal with.

Drawing Near

Read Isaiah 45:18-25
"I am the Lord, and there is no other."

- How does God present Himself as the only Creator?
- How does God present Himself as the only Redeemer?
- What attitude does God want us to have as He presents Himself as Creator and Redeemer?

Reflect on the power of God's work of creation and the scope of God's involvement in this world. Exalt Him for the things He impresses upon you. How does the greatness and grandeur of such a God measure up to your conception of Him? Pray that God would renew in you a confidence and expectation and joy as you bear witness for Him.

Reaching Out

Pray for those God has laid it on your heart to pray, remembering that Jesus said that He knows His sheep and He calls them each by name, that God would: 1) penetrate the darkness of their hearts with the light of life in Christ; and 2) call them out of darkness into His wonderful light as part of a people belonging to God.

Convey to your contacts that God is a God to delight in and not just ask things of. Keep Him prominent and personal. Highlight God's providence in their lives, making Him the point of reference.

Enemy Profile

"...the [devil]...said to him, 'All these I will give you, if you will fall down and worship me" (Matt. 4:8-10)

Pray aware that Satan aspires to be God, wanting allegiance and worship. Pray against his efforts to distort the Word of God toward his own ends in the minds of your contacts.

Mutual Support

Pray for yourself and your CHOP co-laborers that God would grant you discernment between the spirit of truth and that of error.

Week	Satan is not God. Satan is not God's equal, the guy in the black

Week

Four

Day

Two

Satan is not God. Satan is not God's equal, the guy in the black hat to God's white hat. Satan is a creature, as in created being. The devil is a counterfeiter as we will see shortly, but he is not God's counterpart. Satan is a created, angelic being who rebelled against God (Jude 6). God permitted this rebellion for his own purposes. We don't want to get the idea that Satan and his fallen angels are autonomous, existing outside the pale of God's providence, which governs all events and entities. Scenes like Satan asking permission to afflict Job or to sift Peter are given to remind us who's in charge.

Drawing Near

Read 1 Timothy 6:11-16
"...the blessed and only Sovereign, the King of kings and Lord of lords"

- How is God described in vv. 15-16?
- What does it mean for God to dwell in "unapproachable light?"
- What are we to give to God because of who He is?

Respond to God for each of the names and qualities He reveals to describe Himself in the passage above. Pray that God would help you to see "witness" as part of your identity as a disciple of Christ and that He would begin to use you to bear witness that others, too, might honor Him. Lay before Him the barriers you see in your heart to His design and desire for you.

Reaching Out

Your contacts are part of a kingdom and under the rule of a king, but the kingdom is that of a fallen world and the king is the prince of the power of the air, the ruler of this dark world. Pray for them each by name that God would: 1) give them a profound awareness of and distaste for the darkness of sin that engulfs them; and 2) enable them to hear the call of the gospel of Christ.

Listen to what your contacts may have against Christianity, noting distortions or even counterfeits. Affirm the error, abuse or hypocrisy they see but assert the truth. Listen in love.

Enemy Profile

"When the devil had ended every temptation, he departed from him until an opportune time." (Luke 4:13)

Pray aware of the relentlessness of Satan in his efforts to lead astray. Pray against his lures in your contacts' lives.

Mutual Support

Pray for yourself and your CHOP co-laborers that you would not be unaware of your enemy and that you would be strong in the Lord and in the power of His might.

Week **Four** ❦ **Day** **Three**	Our foe is fearsome and formidable. But he is a created being nonetheless. Only God is eternal and uncreated. While Satan may be strong, dispatched throughout the earth through his demonic minions, and an adept observer of human weakness and frailty, only God is omnipotent, omnipresent, and omniscient. When we hear him described as a 'god' in God's revealed profile, we are not to think of him as a rival deity in some sort of Greek pantheon. Rather, the devil is an idolatrous created being, who operates with evil intent and insidious tactics, exclusively within the providential confines of the sovereign and true God. The fact that we must encounter and contend with spiritual opposition is itself part of God's overarching and superintending purpose, serving his eternal plan.

Drawing Near

Read Psalm 139:1-18
"...even the darkness is not dark to you"

- What ways does this passage show God's knowledge to be vastly different from yours, both in quantity but in quality?
- How does the psalmist present God's intimate involvement in your life?
- How are you to respond to God for His activity and involvement in every aspect of your life (vv. 14, 17-18)?

Praise God for His divine character that is so vastly different from yours. Submit yourself, with thanksgiving, to His sovereign will that ordains all your days. Pray that God would help you to see how He has positioned you in each of the places He has, and has given you relationships with others in those places. Ask God for His forgiveness in your disengaging yourself from His interests in the lives of those people.

Reaching Out

In buying into the lies of the devil, your contacts have sought to satisfy themselves with his wares and ways. Pray for them each by name that God would: 1) give them a hunger for righteousness, a yearning for joy, and an aching for peace; and 2) deliver them from the kingdom of darkness to the kingdom of the Son He loves, a kingdom of righteousness and joy and peace.

Pray that God would grant you opportunities to testify to your faith and use you as a living epistle of his truth and grace.

Enemy Profile

"...the days are evil" (Ephesians 5:15-16)

Pray aware that the devil is at home in the fallen world of which your contacts are also a part. Pray against his efforts to blind them to the wisdom of God and bring them to delight in evil and folly.

Mutual Support

Pray for yourself and your CHOP co-laborers that you would live cautiously, wisely and opportunistically as good stewards of each day.

Week **Four** ❧ **Day** **Four**	Satan is the accuser who prosecutes the offenses of our sin against those who would stand before the tribunal of God or hold their lives up to the plumb line of God's law. In Christ, however, those offenses are removed from our record. By his sacrificial death, he atones for our sin. He purges our guilt. Though the sin is ours, the guilt becomes his. We are declared 'not guilty,' not because the holy God simply pardons us, but because he pays the debt of our sin in his Son. Satan as the accuser is left without ammunition. All charges against us are satisfied in Christ.

Drawing Near

Read Acts 17:24-31
"...nor is he served by human hands as if he needed anything"

- How is the absolute independence of God described?
- In what ways are we dependent upon God?
- What attitude should this passage give us about God? About ourselves? About our daily lives?

Adore God for His independence and perfect providence that governs all that comes to pass. Think of one place you will be in the day ahead and thank God for what He tells you is true of His presence in that place. Pray that God would help you to sanctify (i.e., set apart for His glory) the spheres of life in which He has placed you. Ask God to use you as an influence for Jesus Christ in your life-spheres. Confess to Him any ways that you keep your light hidden.

Reaching Out

Know that your contacts are weaned on the values of the society in which they live, such as rugged individualism and self-sufficiency. Pray for them each by name that God would: 1) impress upon them their utter hopelessness and help-lessness to escape from the grip of their sin that holds them for the day of judgment; and 2) enlighten their minds in the knowledge of Christ as the only Savior of sinners and Redeemer of His sheep.

Share with your contacts something God taught you in a sermon or your study of the Bible.

Enemy Profile

"...for fear that somehow the tempter had tempted you and our labor would be in vain"
(1 Thess. 3:5)

Pray aware of Satan's tactic of temptation. Pray against his efforts to incite your contacts to sin, to lure them away from the light and to tear up the foundational bricks of truth laid up in their lives.

Mutual Support

Pray for yourself and your CHOP co-laborers that God might strengthen you in the faith and in the knowledge of His Son.

	Our enemy is a deceiver. He tries to get us to believe and act on lies. These
Week	lies are often proffered through the world's system. Hence Paul's warning
	in Colossians 2: 8 that we discriminate between the teaching of the world
Four	that has an appearance of value and wisdom, and the teaching of our Lord
༈	that we are to hear and put into practice. He poses competing counsel to
	God's, counsel that will bring death, not life, and so lure followers away
Day	from the safety and security of God's truth. The devil is a purveyor of lies.
	Those lies are the bait for the jaws of his trap. 'Did God really say?' is the
Five	first line of assault, the initial tear in the fabric from which the cloth is torn
	asunder. Waging warfare witness is waging a war of words, the word of
	truth versus the wayword of error (1 John 4: 1; 2 Cor. 10: 5). Against the
	devil's deceptions, we are to stand firmly with both feet on the given truth
	of God's written Word.

Drawing Near

Read Psalm 8:1-9
"O Lord, our Lord, how majestic is your name in all the earth!"

- What does it mean for the name of God to be "majestic?"
- How is His majesty communicated? To whom is the majesty of God communicated?
- How should an awareness of God's majesty affect your relationship with God? With your neighbor?

Meditate on the majesty of God. Respond to that majesty with reverence and awe. Ask God to give you a profound awareness of His glory. Pray that God would help you to make more of an effort to talk to others and to build relationships. Pray that He would work His love in your heart for those around you. Confess sins of selfishness and hardness of heart.

Reaching Out

God's Word teaches us that flesh and blood cannot inherit the kingdom of God. Pray for each of your contacts by name that God would: 1) grant them new life with its fruit of repentance and faith and new obedience; and 2) grant them the knowledge of Christ unto salvation, working in them a mighty new creating work, enabling them to rest in Christ so that they might be children of the living God, heirs with Christ of eternal life.

Have your contacts tell you the story of their religious background and how it impacted their lives. Listen for the tinder of truth that you can gather for the Spirit's flame. Note areas for future dialog.

Enemy Profile

"...but Satan hindered us" (1 Thess. 2:18)

Pray aware that Satan is a powerful foe. Pray against his efforts to impede the gospel.

Pray for yourself and your CHOP co-laborers that God would work in your heart a compelling love for those without hope and without God.

Prayer Journal

Week **Four** ✋ **Day** **Six**	Satan is the siren who would lure us to the rocks of spiritual ruin and ministerial impotency. He tempts us, playing on the sin that remains in us—the lust of the eyes, the lust of the flesh, and the pride of life. He plays on the lust of the eyes that sees and yearns after the world's trinkets. He plays on the lust of the flesh that indulges in anger and sexual impurity. He plays on the pride of life that is more concerned for pleasing men than God, more concerned for exalting self than God. We seek first our kingdom and our righteousness. Against the devil's temptations, we are to be ever vigilant. We are to hold fast to our Lord, finding our strength in him, girding our minds for action as obedient children in pursuit of holiness, out of love for God.

Drawing Near

Read Ephesians 3:14-21

"...to know the love of Christ that surpasses knowledge..."

- How is the love of God prominent in this passage?
- Why would God even call us to try to know a love that surpasses knowedge?
- What role does power play in this passage? Why do you suppose it is emphasized?

Tell God what is on your heart. Praise Him for His surpassing greatness, for His unbounded power, and for His immeasurable love. Pray that God would draw you closer to His heart, that you may be filled with His love and compelled by that love. Confess your lack of love for God, for neighbor, for the brethren, for your enemies, for the unsaved.

Reaching Out

Saving faith, faith that rests and trusts in Christ, is the avenue by which anyone enters the kingdom of God. Pray for each of your contacts by name that God would: 1) qualify them to share in the inheritance of the saints in the kingdom of light, working faith in their hearts; and 2) rescue them from the dominion of darkness and bring them into the kingdom of the Son He loves, in whom is redemption, the forgiveness of sins.

Draw your contacts out to see the view they have of the person and work of Jesus. Show Jesus to be more than a moral mentor but a suffering Savior. What is their view of the cross?

Enemy Profile

"...Satan immediately comes and takes away the word that is sown in them" (Mark 4: 15)

Pray aware of Satan's active opposition to Christ and the gospel. Pray against the ways he takes away the word sown in your contacts.

Mutual Support

Pray for yourself and your CHOP co-laborers that you would entrust yourself to God and His purposes as you seek to witness for Christ, knowing the power and wisdom and glory are all of Him.

Prayer Journal

Week **Five** ✑ **Day** **One**	Satan is also described as 'the ruler of this world,' 'the prince of the power of the air,' and 'the god of this age.' He is Beelzebub, lord of the flies. He is leader over the angelic demons. He is also ruler over human beings who by their fallen nature are part of his fallen realm. It is in this sense that Jesus says to those who are against him, 'You belong to your father, the devil, and you want to carry out your father's desire.' There may well be an angelic hierarchy of military rank in this spiritual realm as some suggest. Jude 9 calls the elect angel Michael an 'archangel.' Ephesians 6: 12 may indeed describe 'hell's corporate headquarters....' The authority structure, however, is not made clear by God in his Word and is never sorted out for separate and varying approaches in our dealing with spiritual opposition.

Drawing Near

Read Psalm 18:1-6
"The Lord is my rock and my fortress and my deliverer, my God"

- What names or descriptions of God are used in these verses?
- How is each of these names and descriptions to impact us?
- What terms of intimacy do you find?

Express your love to God. Think through some of the ways He has shown Himself your rock and strength. Thank Him for His providence over your circumstances and His provision for you. Pray that God would create in you a thirst for Him that can be satisfied only by intimate, intense prayer. Pray that He would teach you to pray.

Reaching Out

Pray for each of your prayer targets—real people, with real needs, each with only one real Hope—that God would: 1) remove their foolishness and grant them a heart of wisdom; and 2) give them ears to hear the gospel that is the wisdom of God unto salvation for all who believe.

Listen for ways your contacts have confused and tangled biblical Christianity with secular and religious notions, especially related to their concepts of God, Christ, sin, righteousness and faith.

Enemy Profile

"...that Satan might not tempt you..." (1 Cor. 7:5)

Pray aware that Satan uses natural desires, as well as the lust of the flesh, the lust of the eyes and the pride of life as allies to temptation. Pray that the Spirit would deliver your contacts from a desire-driven life and work in them a love for Jesus Christ.

Mutual Support

Pray for yourself and your CHOP co-laborers that God would stir your heart to know the love He has lavished on you that you should be called children of God.

Week	It's not a matter that our enemy 'might' oppose us, he does. God's Word cautions us to be constantly on guard and continually prepared. Our
Five	enemy the devil prowls about looking for someone to devour. In the environment of the age in which we live, sin is continually crouching at our
✍	door, ready to pounce, and it desires to have us. The Apostle Paul cautions us not to be unaware of Satan's schemes. Why?—'lest he outwit us.' We
Day	live and serve our risen King in a fallen world, facing spiritual opposition.
Two	That spiritual adversary is real. The spiritual conflict is real. The key to our battle is threefold: 1) that we beware of the real and present danger, 2) be aware of our enemy's character and tactics, and 3) bear the weapons and methods suitable for the task given to us by God.

Drawing Near

Read 1 Samuel 2:1-10
"There is none holy like the Lord"

- What about God amazes Hannah?
- In what ways is God involved in this world?
- How is humility before God in evidence? What is the source of such humility?

Reflect on all that God has done for you in Jesus Christ—from where He brought you, to where He brought you, and why. How does your heart instruct you to respond? Now tell God. Pray that God would fan into flame the embers of His truth and grace in your heart. Pray that He would restore you in the joy of your salvation, including an awe of His amazing love.

Reaching Out

From the beginning, Satan was portrayed as one who brought competing counsel to bear against the expressed will of God. Pray for each of your contacts by name that God would: 1) cause them to be open to His revealed will, the Bible; and 2) grant them His Holy Spirit that they might have the spiritual capacity to discern the things of God, and to recognize them as wisdom.

Be alert to the spiritual stirring in your contacts by the work of the Spirit to convict them of their sin and need for Christ, and be ready to respond in step with the Spirit.

Enemy Profile

"...so that we would not be outwitted by Satan; for we are not ignorant of his designs" (2 Corinthians 2:11)

Pray aware of Satan as a conniver. Pray against efforts to darken the minds of your contacts and draw them into his web.

Mutual Support

Pray for yourself and your CHOP co-laborers that you would take every thought captive to the obedience of Christ.

Prayer Journal

Week	Satan works through deception, temptation and accusation. His
Five	primary leverage over us has been broken. He has been cast down from his position of accusation before the judgment seat of God by
❧	the redeeming work of our Advocate, Jesus Christ. ...We have not
Day	only been freed from sin's condemnation, we have been liberated from sin's power. Our hero is Jesus Christ. In him, by his Spirit,
Three	we prevail against our enemy's deceptions, temptations and accusations. In Christ, we are empowered and greatly encouraged for the evangelistic mission he gives us.

Drawing Near

Read Jeremiah 32:17-27
"I am the Lord, the God of all flesh. Is anything too hard for me?"

- How is God's almighty power shown?
- What is an example of how God's power is displayed directly? Indirectly?
- Why does God tell us two times in this passage that nothing is too hard for Him?

Praise God whose might is greater than yours. Praise Him that He is the God of the impossible. Ponder in your heart the position this puts you in before Him— and exalt His glorious name for it. Pray that God would convince you of His power, power that is at work in you and through you. Examine your heart and see how you try to find strength in yourself instead of in God, for whom nothing is too hard. Confess your sin of self-sufficiency.

Reaching Out

Blinded by sin and unbelief, held captive by the devil to do his will, your unbelieving contacts follow the way that seems right in their own eyes. Pray for each of your contacts by name that God would: 1) work in them a respect for His revealed Word, the Bible; and 2) open their eyes that they might see wonderful things in God's Word, especially the wonderful salvation of God in Jesus.

Don't force but fit, working in tandem with the Holy Spirit. Be attentive as a spiritual midwife and not as a spiritual salesman.

Enemy Profile

"...they may escape from the snare of the devil, after being captured by him to do his will" (2 Timothy 2:25-26)

Pray aware of Satan's tactics to bind through error and foolishness. Pray against his blinding to the truth that sets one free.

Mutual Support

Pray for yourself and your CHOP co-laborers that God might grant you the courage of faith that trusts and obeys.

Week **Five** ⌇ **Day** **Four**	The Scriptures characterize the incarnation and mission of Jesus Christ in military terms. He came to destroy the works of the devil. He rescued us from this age, liberated us from the kingdom of darkness, and established us in the kingdom of life and light. Just as the power of the kingdom of God resides in the resurrection of Jesus as the Christ, so the effectiveness of the mission resides in our weapons imbued with the redemptive purpose and power of Christ's work. That's part of what it means to find our strength in the Lord and his mighty power—power of the new life and the age to come at work in this age, through us in the weapons we wield.

Drawing Near

Read James 4:4-10
"God opposes the proud, but gives grace to the humble."

- What ways do we distance ourselves from God?
- What does it mean for God to be jealous?
- What attitude or posture does God want us to grow in that we might draw nearer to Him?

Praise God as the God who is far above all He has made, yet near to all who draw near to Him in proper recognition of who He is and who they are. Spend time dialoging with God in what He has told you of Himself and His dealings. Pray that God would cause you to grow in the knowledge of His glorious grace. Pray that He would work in you the qualities of humility and submission.

Reaching Out

The Bible teaches that the sinful mind is hostile to God; it does not submit to God's law, nor can it do so. Pray for each of your contacts by name that God would: 1) release them from the bondage of the flesh and bring them into the glorious freedom of the children of God; and 2) incline their will to His for their obedience in faith toward the gospel.

Pray that your contacts would take initiative in asking you about your faith and relationship with God.

Enemy Profile

"'You will not surely die,' the serpent said to the woman. "For God knows that when you eat of it your eyes will be opened, and you will be like God..." (Gen. 3:2-5)

Pray aware that Satan has been a liar from the beginning. Pray against his efforts to deceive and that God would open the eyes of your contacts to grant them a thirst for truth.

Mutual Support

Pray for yourself and your contacts that God would work in you a greater fear of the Lord that is the beginning of wisdom, and that recognizes, regards and responds to God for who He is.

Prayer Journal

The method our Lord describes in his binding of the strong man does not give us a method for conducting spiritual warfare in the work of evangelism. No, his description gives a picture of his unique work as the Messiah of God. Our work of witness operates on the basis of binding Satan, but not as something we do: it is what Christ has done to bring life and liberty to his sheep ready for slaughter. Christ's binding of Satan is not our model, but our motivation for reaching others with the gospel of freedom from sin's tyranny. It is true that those 'others' we seek to reach are held captive by sin and are part of Satan's fallen realm. But nowhere in Scripture are we given instruction in binding for our efforts at reaching others for Christ.

Drawing Near

Read Isaiah 6:1-8
"Holy, holy, holy is the Lord of hosts"

- What attribute of God dominates this scene?
- How does this attribute impact Isaiah as he finds himself face-to-face with this awesome God?
- What does this passage suggest will give us an enhanced awareness of our sin, our situation, and our salvation?

Ascribe to the Lord the glory due His name and worship Him in the splendor of His holiness. Reflect on what it means for God to be holy and for you to draw near to Him as a holy God. Pray that God will increase your awareness of His holiness and consequently of your sin and correspondingly of His grace. Pray that He would work in you a spirit of repentance that draws near to Him.

Reaching Out

God's will is both secret, holding His perfect purposes in all things, and revealed, written down in the Bible for us and our children to obey. Pray for each of your contacts by name that God would: 1) subdue the rebelliousness of their hearts to the God whose ways are greater than their ways and whose thoughts are higher than theirs; and 2) subdue their wills to His as He has expressed that will in His Holy Word.

Pray that God would provide ways you can express the love of Christ to your contacts. As a child of God, look to 'show and tell' grace.

Enemy Profile

"The great dragon was thrown down, that ancient serpent who is called the devil and Satan, the deceiver of the whole world" (Rev. 12:9)

Pray aware that Satan is a formidable foe and that he is at work now as he has been from the Garden of Eden. Pray against his cunning and deceit to keep your contacts from the light and life of the gospel.

Mutual Support

Pray for yourself and your CHOP co-laborers that you would not fear, for God is with you and for you, and given you victory in the Lamb.

Prayer Journal

Week **Five** ✎ **Day** **Six**	We are not liberators. Christ is. We are heralds of that liberation. Christ's work is our confidence. His work says that we have something to say. We don't proclaim the possibility of salvation in Christ. We proclaim the success of his mission for his sheep. The gospel as it focuses on Christ does not offer a King who made people redeemable, but a Lord who actually redeemed his people, accomplishing their liberation. When we approach someone to share the glorious news of the kingdom of God by sharing the gospel of life and liberty in Jesus Christ, do we face demonic opposition? Most assuredly, we do. But we do not face it as did Christ. We don't face the opposition of evil as a foe to be defeated. We encounter a defeated foe. We don't fight for victory. We fight in victory, in the Lord and the strength of his might—not the might of mere divine power, but the might of redemptive power.

Drawing Near

Read Revelation 4:1-11
"Worthy are you, our Lord and God..."

- What words would you use to capture this heavenly portrait of God?
- Who is responding to God as He is revealed? What is their response?
- How does v. 11 help you to understand what it means to lay your "crown" before the throne of God (v. 10)?

Give glory, honor and thanks to God. Lay your crown before His throne in acknowledgment of who He is and in deference to Him. How has your heart grown cold toward God? How have the glories of His salvation become ordinary to you? Search your heart and confess these to God, asking Him to fan into flame the embers of your faith.

Reaching Out

It is Jesus Christ who will build His church. It is the Spirit of God who convinces and converts sinners and so expands the redemptive rule of Christ in the hearts of sinners. Pray for each of your contacts by name that God would: 1) accomplish His will for His purposes on earth as His will is accomplished perfectly for His purposes in heaven; and 2) remove their spiritual blindness, hardness of heart and deadness of spirit so that they might come to Christ and live.

As a living epistle, bring the reality of your relationship with God and your heart for Jesus Christ to the fore of your conversation. Freely talk about what is important to you and the sum of your life.

Enemy Profile

"The Spirit expressly says that in later times some will depart from the faith by devoting themselves to deceitful spirits and teachings of demons" (1 Tim. 4:1)

Pray aware that the world's false teaching can be traced to the evil one. Pray against his efforts to lull people to a false sense of security and lure them to eternal ruin.

Mutual Support

Pray for yourself and your CHOP co-laborers that God would help you to be devoted to the truth and to discipline yourselves for godliness.

Prayer Journal

Week **Six** ❧ **Day** **One**	Our enemy the devil would try to disarm us of the weapons our Lord says are suitable for the task. In his usual tactics, Satan sows seeds of doubt and tries to undermine our confidence by saying, 'Will that really work? Isn't there something better or quicker or flashier or more fun that you could use? Isn't there a better way to use that weapon?' The irony rests in the idea that our enemy is the one who attempts to convince us what will work against him. Although we live in the world, we do not wage war as the world does. The weapons we fight with are not the weapons of the world. On the contrary, they have divine power to demolish strongholds.

Drawing Near

Read Psalm Jeremiah 10:10-16
"...who established the world by his wisdom"

- How is God contrasted with idols?
- What does it mean that God founded the world 'by His wisdom'?
- What should be our response to the wisdom of God?

Praise Him for His wisdom and His ways. Praise God in whom all wisdom dwells. How are you wise in your own eyes? To what do you give ear that has an appearance of wisdom? Confess your sins of rebellion and waywardness. Ask God to help you to rest in His wisdom rather than what seems right in your own eyes.

Reaching Out

Pray for your prayer targets, giving thought that each one is likely to have a family and friends who will be in the glow of the light of the gospel were that prayer target to come to a saving knowledge of Christ, that God would: 1) deliver them from the kingdom of darkness and bring them into the kingdom of His marvelous light; and 2) show Himself powerful and gracious and wise by the demonstration of the riches of His glory to the objects of His mercy.

Read Paul's testimony in Acts 26:9-23 and pray that God would help you in developing or refining your personal testimony as a tool for sharing your faith in Christ.

Enemy Profile

"The devil....said, 'For it is written...'" (Luke 4:9-11)

Pray aware that Satan twists and distorts the truth of God for his own ends, appealing to selfish desires. Pray against his efforts to lure your contacts in with a grain of truth encrusted with lies.

Mutual Support

Pray for yourself and your CHOP co-laborers that you stand firm on the Word of God, able to discern between truth and error.

Prayer Journal

Week **Six** ✧ **Day** **Two**	No one can be delivered from the kingdom of this world and be established into the kingdom of God apart from the work of the Holy Spirit. Just as we did not come to Christ on a whim, but because of the direct operation of the Spirit in our hearts to convince and convert us, so the Spirit must work in those we seek to reach for them to come to Christ. Only the Spirit of God has the power to make effective the weapons we employ, giving them power to deal with the spiritual opposition we face. The weapon of kingdom warfare is the Spirit of the risen Christ. But we don't want to get the idea that we wield the weapon of the Spirit. Rather, he wields us. He makes our efforts effective. He accomplishes his purposes through us. The Spirit is the one who infuses the weapons issued to us with the divine power for doing what he wants to accomplish.

Drawing Near

Read 1 Corinthians 1:18-31

"...the foolishness of God is wiser than men"

- How is God's wisdom displayed?
- How is God's wisdom contrasted with that of man's?
- In what way is Christ the wisdom of God?

Praise God in whom all wisdom dwells. Praise Him for His wisdom and His ways that are greater than yours. Praise God for His wisdom manifested in Jesus Christ. Pray that God would work in you a confidence in His wisdom and expectation as you step out in faith, doing things God's way. Pray that God would nourish your faith with His truth and help you to grow in the knowledge of Him.

Reaching Out

As Christ builds His Church, the gates of hell will not prevail and the purposes of God in salvation will not fail. Pray for each of your prayer contacts by name that God would: 1) accomplish His good and perfect will in their lives to the glory of His name; and 2) thwart the devices of Satan as he would contend against God and His kingdom.

Read the theology behind Paul's testimony and yours in Ephesians 2:1-10, praying that you would see God at the center and not self.

Enemy Profile

"...deliver this man to Satan for the destruction of the flesh, so that his spirit may be saved..." (2 Corinthians 4:4-6)

Pray aware that Satan is a destroyer. Pray against his efforts to destroy and that God may use Satan to bring your contacts to an end of themselves that they might repent and turn to the Author of life.

Mutual Support

Pray for yourself and your CHOP co-laborers that you would walk in the light as the children of light you are in Christ.

Prayer Journal

Week **Six** ❦ **Day** **Three**	Satan aims his darts at our heart. As the father of lies, he touts our self-reliance. As the accuser, he posts our transgressions. As the enemy of Christ, he promotes our rival lordship. When we look at our lives we see sin. Doubts may plague us, guilt overwhelm us, or despair sideline us, but God outfits us with the breastplate of righteousness and the helmet of salvation. We are clothed in the righteousness of our Lord Jesus Christ. Our salvation is secure in him, bound up in his accomplished work on our behalf.

Drawing Near

Read Colossians 2:1-8
"...Christ, in whom are hidden all the treasures of wisdom and knowledge"

- What does it mean for Jesus to be the repository of 'all the treasures of wisdom and knowledge'?
- What battle lines are drawn for your allegiance?
- If Christ is the wisdom of God, how does God want you to follow Him?

Praise God for His wisdom revealed in His written Word and in the Word Incarnate. Praise Him for the truth and understanding and practicality of His wisdom to everyday life. What barriers of foolishness, of unbelief, of sin are preventing your heart from drawing nearer to Christ? Cry out to God, asking Him to give you a greater heart-acquaintance with Christ as well as a head-acquaintance.

Reaching Out

God sends His rain on the just and the unjust; all people enjoy the fruit of His goodness shed upon all His creation. Pray for each of your prayer contacts by name that God would: 1) open their eyes to see the many blessings God has bestowed upon them and His mercies that are new with each day; and 2) enable them to see the good gifts of God coming to them in spite of what they deserve.

Turn to the Personal Testimony Worksheet in Supplement A and list elements of your life for Chapter 1, "Estranged from Christ."

Enemy Profile

"...that you may be able to stand against the schemes of the devil" (Ephesians 6:10-11)

Pray aware that Satan is a schemer. Pray against his plots to trap and ensnare your contacts to keep them from Christ and mire them in sin.

Mutual Support

Pray for yourself and your CHOP co-laborers that the Spirit of God would help you to be strong in the Lord and in His mighty power rather than your own wits and strength.

Prayer Journal

Week **Six** ❧ **Day** **Four**	As we seek first the kingdom of God and his righteousness as the governing principle of our lives, we will live counter-kingdom lives. Such lives will be God-centered, Christ-serving, and Spirit-empowered. We will be zealous for the glory of God in all things present and future, public and private, secular and sacred. His righteousness will be our garment and our goal. We will desire to live such good lives before others that those of the kingdom of this world will see our distinctive behavior and glorify our Father in heaven.

Drawing Near

Read Psalm John 3:25-36
"...God is true"

- What does it mean for God to be a God of truth?
- How is the true hope of the gospel seen coming from the hand of God?
- What attitudes and goals does God want you to develop and pursue as you seek to be His instrument?

Praise God for sending His Son. Praise God for giving His Spirit. Praise God that He deals in truth. Pray that you would decrease and that Christ would increase in your life and ministry. Pray that you would seek Him more, lean on Him to a greater degree and increasingly yield to Him in all things. Confess your sins of pride and self-sufficiency and self-service.

Reaching Out

What is the season of the year in which you find yourself right now? God sustains the rhythmical order of life and displays a progression of design as the seed of spring becomes the harvest of fall. Pray for each of your prayer contacts by name that God would: 1) sow or grow the seed of the gospel in their hearts through you, that He would raise up others to feed and to weed that soil; and 2) begin a good work in them and see it to the day of Christ Jesus.

Turn to the Personal Testimony Worksheet in Supplement A and list elements of your life for Chapter 2, "Encounter with Christ."

Enemy Profile

"...we do not wrestle against flesh and blood" (Ephesians 6:12)

Pray aware that Satan is the adversary, not your contacts. Pray against his grip on their hearts and for the liberating grace of God to release that grip.

Mutual Support

Pray for yourself and your CHOP co-laborers that God would work in your heart a greater love for Him and neighbor.

Week	Our deeds of kindness can testify to the kingdom of God we seek and serve. We try to make others' lives easier, giving them relief from the harshness of existence in a fallen world, a cup of cold water to their parched throats, a helping hand to their oppressive burdens. Those acts of kindness can also serve as doors into a person's life, by which we might have opportunity to give verbal witness to the good news of the kingdom. While there is benefit in the act of kingdom kindness itself, our goal is always to direct people to Jesus Christ, as the Lord provides opportunity. There are those who say that they bear witness by their lives. But righteous deeds unqualified by verbal comment only communicate to others how great we are or that salvation is by works. Deeds of kindness can point to us. We want people to see Christ in us, the hope of glory.
Six	
﹌	
Day	
Five	

Drawing Near

Read Isaiah 45:18-25
"I the Lord speak the truth"

- Where do you see reference to God's truth in this passage?
- What does it mean for God to be trustworthy?
- If all that God says is true, how are we to respond to what He says?

Praise God for who He is as the God of all truth. Thank Him that He has not spoken in secret, but in our hearing, recorded for us in His Word. Select one declaration of God from the passage above and spend time adoring Him for it. Pray that God would give you a heart receptive to His truth and responsive to His desires. Pray that the Spirit of God would work in you a broken spirit, a broken and contrite heart.

Reaching Out

The Bible teaches that not only is the spiritual dimension of life good, but so is the material world. God's plan is for the body as well as the soul, as the promised bodily resurrection of believers attests. Pray for each of your prayer contacts by name that God would: 1) use the material blessings He has bestowed upon them to prompt them to reflect also on the spiritual blessings He provides in Christ; and 2) direct their thoughts to Him from whom all blessings flow and to take steps in responding in heart-felt thanks.

Turn to the Personal Testimony Worksheet in Supplement A and list elements of your life for Chapter 3, "Enslaved to Christ."

Enemy Profile

"...extinguish all the flaming darts of the evil one" (Eph. 6:16-18)

Pray aware of that Satan is a warrior, waging battle with spiritual weapons. Pray for protection against his assaults to keep your contacts imprisoned in unbelief and for their deliverance.

Mutual Support

Pray for yourself and your CHOP co-laborers that God would strengthen your faith in Christ Jesus.

Week **Six** ⚜ **Day** **Six**	The world and its satanic system will try to lure us away and lead us astray, seeking to make us prisoners of war. The expression Paul uses is 'take us captive.' Those are fighting words. We live in constant conflict in this world that is trying to lead us astray, capture us with the net of deception and bind us with the cords of a lie. This is true both for our sanctification and service in the face of spiritual opposition. The Word of God, properly divided and not deceitfully twisted, as Satan is prone to do, is our weapon against the enslavement of error. The Scriptures have divine power to demolish arguments and every pretension that opposes the knowledge of God. The power is not magical, but through communication, correction, and cultivation of truth in response to error.

Drawing Near

Read John 14:6-14

"I am the way, and the truth and the life."

- Where in this passage do you see Jesus as both the truth and as the speaker of truth?
- What confidence does Jesus want us to have in our service for Him?
- What relationship is there between truth and faith?

Praise the name of Jesus, who not only speaks truth but is Himself truth. Praise God for the faith He has worked in your heart that you might have ears to hear that truth. Confess your sin of prayerlessness. Ask God to pour out upon you a spirit of grace and supplication. Ask God for power and resolve to pray without ceasing.

Reaching Out

While the kingdom of God and the kingdom of this fallen world co-exist at the moment, the day will come when the kingdom of this world will be destroyed and the kingdom of God ushered in in fullness. Pray for each of your prayer contacts by name that God would: 1) cause them to stop and think about where they are laying up their treasures; and 2) capture their hearts for Himself and convince them of the beauty and permanency of His everlasting kingdom.

Prayerfully review each of the chapters of your personal testimony from Supplement A to see what you might change or add.

Enemy Profile

"…may be delivered from wicked and evil men…and the Lord will establish you and guard you against the evil one" (2 Thess. 3:1-3)

Pray aware that Satan uses those who are part of his kingdom as his tools. Pray against his efforts in your contacts' lives to seduce and persecute them by the world.

Mutual Support

Pray for yourself and your CHOP co-laborers that God would strengthen and protect you from the evil one, the flesh and the world.

Week **Seven** *❧* **Day** **One**	God has not sent us into battle as mavericks or mercenaries. He has enfolded us into an army, a company of fellow soldiers, fighting under the banner of the kingdom of God and his Christ. God's provision for us in the work of witness means that we are not alone. Our Lord and King accompanies us. He is with us always until the end of this age for the carrying out of his mission, entrusted to us, to make disciples of the nations. We also have fellowship with one another, participation in a common salvation and for a common cause. We desperately need one another. Our enemy the devil continually exerts his efforts to make us deserters. We need the community of the company to watch our backs, to encourage us in the fray, to maintain *esprit de corps* with a proper focus on Christ lest we grow weary and lose heart.

Drawing Near

Read Psalm 33
"Let your steadfast love be upon us…"

- How is God's love displayed so brightly in this psalm?
- How does our hope relate to God's steadfast love?
- What many things does the psalmist cite on which we can pin our hope as we trust in God?

Praise God for His abounding, abiding, amazing love. Praise Him for the love He set upon you, though you did not deserve it. Praise God for those things that His love has brought you. Pray that God would cause your heart to blaze with His love and ignite those around you. Confess and repent of ways you have left your first love.

Reaching Out

Pray for your prayer targets by name, aware that they are people in dire need and that God's gracious provision for that need is Jesus Christ, that God would: 1) help them to recognize that all their possessions and talents and capacities are theirs because they have received them, and are not reason for boasting in self; and 2) begin to open their hearts to God's gift of love in Jesus Christ.

Write the items you listed in Chapter One of your personal testimony in narrative and conversational form.

Enemy Profile

"…he is a liar and the father of lies" (John 8:44-47)

Pray aware that Satan is liar. Pray against his seductions in the lives of your contacts as he leads them to shipwreck on the rocks of error and false hope. Pray they would hear the truth of God's Word.

Mutual Support

Pray for yourself and your CHOP co-laborers that you would stand firm on the Word of Truth, unmovable in the hope of the gospel.

Prayer Journal

Week **Seven** ✒ **Day** **Two**	Prayer seems to touch everything in the Christian life. It affects us as God's instruments, touching everything from our motivation to our vitality to our stance in the work of witness. Prayer has been so designed by God that he uses it even to accomplish his purposes and to effect change. Prayer can be directed to self, others, present, future, hearts, circumstances, preventative and remedial, and the list goes on. Prayer is prominent and pervasive in the Christian's life and ministry. Prayer is a weapon of the kingdom of God, suitable not only for the infirmary but for the field of battle. As a spiritual weapon, prayer is particularly powerful and indispensable to the spiritual combat inherent in the nature of kingdom conflict.

Drawing Near

Read Romans 5:1-11

"God shows his love for us in that while we still sinners, Christ died for us."

- How is God's love displayed so gloriously in this passage?
- What blessings have been poured out upon us from the fountain of God's love?
- For what response does the Apostle call to the love of God?

Spend time counting your blessings, thanking God for each one, praising Him for His incredible love. Pray that the love of God and love for God would be the inspiration and compelling reason for your service to Him. Pray that God would work in you His heart for the lost. Plead with God to give you a love for Christ from the depths of your heart.

Reaching Out

A perspective of the kingdom of God is that man does not live on bread alone but on every word that proceeds from the mouth of God. Pray for each of your contacts by name that God would: 1) work in them a hunger for righteousness; and 2) create in them a hunger for the living bread and a recognition that that bread is provided by God in Christ.

Write the items you listed in Chapter Two of your personal testimony in narrative and conversational form.

Enemy Profile

"...the devil who had deceived them..." (Rev. 20:10)

Pray aware that Satan works to lead astray. Pray against counterfeiting activity that offers a false hope and horrific future.

Mutual Support

Pray for yourself and your CHOP co-laborers that you would rejoice in God's gracious deliverance of you from the bonds of death.

Week **Seven** ∽ **Day** **Three**	Prayer is one of those basics of the Christian life, a staple for sanctification and service in relationship with God and dependence upon him. Prayer is also the most basic weapon against the spiritual warfare inherent in those aspects of the Christian life in a fallen world. Prayer can be defined any number of ways, from any number of perspectives. For our purposes we can define prayer as 'personal, conscious awareness of and communication with the living and true God.' Prayer is the created capacity to commune with the Creator.

Drawing Near

Read Romans 8:28-39

"...will be able to separate us from the love of God in Christ..."

- Where in this passage do you see the love of God the Creator and Redeemer holding you in its grip?
- Why does verse 39 speak of God's love holding us rather than His power?
- How does this passage give you security and stability?

Thank God for His love for you. Praise Him for His love that He set upon sinners—you and others He has called according to His purpose. Pray that God will grant you a greater awareness of His love that holds you in His kingdom and protects you from the kingdom of Satan. Pray that He will open your eyes to the power of His love that is at work in you who believe.

Reaching Out

It is the poor in spirit to whom the kingdom of heaven belongs, those who recognize their spiritual poverty and bankruptcy before a holy God. Pray for each of your contacts by name that God would: 1) open their eyes to the grace of the Lord Jesus Christ, that though He was rich, yet for the sake of His sheep He became poor, so that they through His poverty might become rich; and 2) incline their hearts to true riches, to the pearl of great price.

Write the items you listed in Chapter Three of your personal testimony in narrative and conversational form.

Enemy Profile

"...Satan standing at his right hand to accuse him" (Zech. 3:1)

Pray aware that Satan is the accuser, prosecuting people's sins against them. Pray against his tactics to keep people in the bondage of sin's guilt and power, and for God to lead them to the Advocate.

Mutual Support

Pray for yourself and your CHOP co-laborers that you would rest in the truth that your sin is nailed to the cross and you bear it no more, freed from sin's guilt and power.

Week **Seven** *&* **Day** **Four**	Prayer as a weapon requires intentionality. We need to be deliberate and purposeful as we feel the grip of prayer in our hand. The prayer we want to get a grip on for the work of witness is decidedly active communication of purpose, not passive communication of presence. When it comes to prayer as a weapon of the kingdom, we might think of our Lord commanding us to 'present arms,' to wield the weapon of prayer. A basic reason to pray rests on the orders of our Commander.

Drawing Near

Read 2 Chronicles 7:1-14
"...he is good, for his steadfast love endures forever"

- What is the significance of God dwelling among His people?
- How do the people respond to the glory of the Lord?
- What promises does God extend to the prayer of His people? What qualifications does He affix to their prayer?

Declare to God His goodness. For what expressions of His goodness do you especially want to thank Him? Praise Him for His goodness to all people as Creator and to His people as Redeemer. Pray that God will grant you a "kingdom-consciousness" that makes you aware of His deliverance of you from the kingdom of darkness and of that kingdom as your battlefield, and your access to Him in that light.

Reaching Out

No one can serve two masters; we cannot belong to both the kingdom of darkness following its ruler and to the kingdom of light and follow its Ruler. Pray for each of your contacts by name that God would: 1) help them to see the difference between wants and needs; and 2) lift their eyes from the mundane to see Him who supplies seed to the sower and bread for food, who provides in many ways so that His children will be made rich in every way so that they can be generous on every occasion, resulting in gratitude to God.

Read your entire personal testimony and revise it for clarity, accuracy and flow.

Enemy Profile

"Satan said, 'Does Job fear God for no reason?'" (Job 1:9-11)

Pray aware that Satan's agenda is to turn people against God. Pray against his efforts to lead your contacts to love the gifts over the Giver.

Mutual Support

Pray for yourself and your CHOP co-laborers that God would keep you faithful and that you would hold loosely the things of this world.

Week **Seven** ∽ **Day** **Five**	Prayer is a spiritual weapon invested with divine power, entrusted to us by God for the nature of the battle we face in the work of witness. How can we possibly break the grip of Satan on the lives of those who are part of his kingdom of this age? That's the case whether I am concerned for my next-door neighbor or a missionary's neighbor in Senegal. Prayer reaches where we are not and accomplishes what we cannot. Prayer is an instrument of impotence, ours not God's. The power necessary for the work of witness is exclusively the power of God himself, divine power.

Drawing Near

Read Psalm 145:1-13
"The Lord is gracious and merciful, slow to anger and abounding in steadfast love."

- What expressions are there in these verses of God as King?
- What benefits does God as King bestow upon His subjects?
- What direction does the psalmist give us for giving God glory?

Praise and thank God for each blessing listed in the passage above. Pray that God will work in your heart a greater appreciation for His deliverance of you. Pray that God's grace, mercy, goodness and love to you would fuel your interaction with others.

Reaching Out

The kingdom of God is not a matter of eating and drinking, but of righteousness, joy and peace. Pray for each of your contacts by name that God would: 1) convict them of sin, righteousness and judgment; and 2) grant them a budding knowledge of something more to life and of their great need for forgiveness of their sin.

Re-read your testimony in narrative form and use it as springboard to respond to God's grace and mercy. Begin to commit it to memory. Pray for how God might be pleased to use it as a witnessing tool.

Enemy Profile

"...give no opportunity to the devil" (Eph. 4:27)

Pray aware that Satan is opportunistic. Pray for the protection and deliverance of your contacts against the relentless efforts of the evil one to entangle them in the bonds of sin and blind them to that sin through pride and self-righteousness.

Mutual Support

Pray for yourself and your CHOP co-laborers that the Spirit would keep you firm in the faith, abounding in every good work.

Week **Seven** ✺ **Day** **Six**	Paul also recognized what was necessary for light to break though the darkened heart, something he was impotent to do. God had to intervene with creating power of the new life. God has to make the spiritually dead spiritually alive if our witness would find receptivity. When we remember that the effectiveness of evangelism is entirely dependent on the enlivening and illuminating work of God, we are driven to our knees. We can speak to people dead in sin all we want, but no matter how loud, how eloquent or how persistent we are, the only way the dead will hear the voice of the Son of God is by the immediate work of God in their lives to enable them. So we pray. Prayer is our avenue to the power of God necessary for the success of the gospel in our exercise of the mission given to us by our Lord Jesus Christ.

Drawing Near

Read Lamentations 3:19-26
"Great is your faithfulness"

- How is the faithfulness of God on display in Jeremiah's lament?
- What spokes do you see in vv. 22-25 emanating from the hub of God's faithfulness?
- How have you seen God's faithfulness in your life, even in adversity and afflictions?

Review the many expressions of God's faithfulness to you. Praise Him that in His faithful love you are not consumed. Ask God to open your eyes to just how big and how grand and how powerful is His saving work through Jesus Christ. Ask Him to help you to see your role anew as an ambassador of His kingdom, recognizing His faithfulness to you.

Reaching Out

Those who belong to the kingdom of darkness are at home in this world because of their fallen natures. Pray for each of your contacts by name that God would: 1) help them to see that not only do they sin, but that they are sinners; and 2) open their eyes to see how their sin ravages their lives and separates them from a holy God.

Practice sharing your personal testimony with a Christian friend, feeling free to have the narrative you prepared in front of you.

Enemy Profile

"…the tempter came and said to him …" (Matt. 4:3)

Pray aware that Satan is a talker, offering counsel counter to God's. Pray that God would expose Satan's lies with the truth of the gospel and the wisdom of His Word.

Mutual Support

Pray for yourself and your CHOP co-laborers that God would help you to hold fast to His Word and walk in the whole counsel of God.

Prayer Journal

Week **Eight** ᪗ **Day** **One**	In one respect all prayer is kingdom prayer. Prayer is a privilege of the kingdom. It is a right of a child of the King. Kingdom prayer, however, looks not to context but to content, not to right of access but to what we pray for. Kingdom prayer is prayer that seeks first the kingdom of God and his righteousness. There is a difference between what we might call therapeutic prayer and kingdom prayer. Therapeutic prayer is prayer that unburdens. Kingdom prayer seeks not only relief, but relief for a reason. Kingdom prayer deals with the essential and not just the peripheral, looking to seek and serve the purposes of God in those who serve in his army.

Drawing Near

Read Psalm 100
"The Lord is good"

- What responses from His people does the psalmist call for to such a great God?
- Why is it important for us to know the Lord is "God"?
- How is God shown as our Creator? As our Redeemer?

Worship God for each of His attributes listed in the psalm. Thank Him for His mercies. Respond joyfully to such a great God! Ask God to develop in you sensitivity to the spiritual battle that rages for the minds and hearts of men and women around you. Pray that God would give you an ever-deepening awareness that He is God. Draw near to Christ as your King in whom alone victory and strength are found.

Reaching Out

Pray for each of your contacts, recognizing that, as is the case with all subjects of the kingdom of this world, they have incurred a massive debt of sin, that God would: 1) begin to convince them they owe a tremendous debt of sin, the wages of which is death; and 2) begin to help them to understand their predicament and peril as sinners in the hands of a God whose anger is against the unrighteous, among whom they must count themselves.

Pray for opportunity to share your testimony with one of your contacts. Also, browse through the gospel presentation in Supplement E, noting the content and logical flow.

Enemy Profile

"Your adversary the devil prowls around..." (1 Peter 5:8)

Pray aware that Satan is active in seeking to devour with lies and false hope. Pray against his destructive efforts.

Mutual Support

Pray for yourself and your CHOP co-laborers that God would help you to be humble, self-controlled and alert.

Week **Eight** ✧ **Day** **Two**	God's glory, God's goals, God's righteousness, the strengthening and lengthening of God's kingdom in the hearts of others—these are the parameters of kingdom prayer. Inherent in such prayer is an awareness of the spiritual struggle and opposition we face in this present, evil age. Kingdom prayer seeks the advancement of the kingdom of God, looking at self and life and needs in that light, toward that end. When we pray, 'Your kingdom come,' we seek our God for the subduing work of his kingdom. We pray, 'Lead us not into temptation, but deliver us from evil.' This prayer escorts us into battle against the spiritual forces of evil that are at work to oppose us in mission.

Drawing Near

Read 1 Thessalonians 5:12-25
"He who calls you is faithful…"

- What does Paul look to incite in us as he cites God's faithfulness?
- How does God's faithfulness give us confidence for our sanctification and service, our walk and our work?
- How have you seen God's faithfulness in your life over the past week?

Thank God for the evidence of His faithfulness you have seen in your life over the past week. Praise Him that He is a faithful God who does not change like shifting shadows. Pray that God would give you a greater awareness and confidence of the presence of Christ with you as your King. Pray that God would grant you increasing dependence upon Him and submission to Him.

Reaching Out

The righteousness of the subjects of the kingdom of God must exceed the righteousness of even the most religiously disciplined. Pray for each of your contacts by name that God would: 1) broaden their view of sin, extending it to sins of omission as well as commission, to sins of the heart as well as sins of behavior; and 2) deepen their view of sin, seeing how it pollutes even their very best of intentions, contaminating the entirety of their being, leaving them bankrupt in respect to righteousness.

Carefully read the introduction and 'Creation' portions of the gospel outline in Supplement E, noting the focus and flow.

Enemy Profile

"…who were oppressed by the devil" (Acts 10:36-38)

Pray aware of the oppression of the devil through the sin and miseries of this life. Pray for the mercy and resurrection power of Christ who alone can prevail against him and deliver from the devil's tyranny.

Mutual Support

Pray for yourself and your CHOP co-laborers that God might strengthen you with power through His Spirit in your inner beings, that Christ may dwell in your hearts through faith.

Prayer Journal

Week **Eight** & **Day** **Three**	Prayer is a means by which God enfolds us into the outworking of his eternal plan. Prayer is God's means for God's ends. God executes his plan and accomplishes his purposes through the mediation of our prayers as his people. Prayer is intended by God to engage us in the accomplishment of his purposes for his own glory and goals. We can put it this way: in the majesty and scope of God's design, in praying we can expect God to do something he would not have done had we not prayed.

Drawing Near

Read Daniel 9:4-19
"O Lord, the great and awesome God, who keeps covenant..."

- What are some of the terms Daniel uses to describe God?
- How much is your prayer punctuated with terms that reflect the multi-faceted glory of God?
- On what basis does Daniel beseech God to act in vv. 17-19?

Identify some of your sins and the sins of your church or ministry group. Contrast these with God's character and confess those sins. Claim forgiveness through Jesus, praising God that He is a forgiving God. Ask God to give you a greater sense of solidarity and mission with those in your church. Ask Him to give you greater solidarity and purpose as an outpost of His kingdom.

Reaching Out

The kingdom of God is a kingdom whose animating feature is faith, seeing and living by that spiritual capacity given by God. Pray for each of your contacts by name that God would: 1) open their eyes to the difference between faith and works, between saving faith that rests on Christ for salvation and faith that is mere knowledge and agreement; and 2) lay the planks for an understanding of the gospel, the righteousness of God unto salvation for all who believe.

Carefully read the 'Alienation' portion of the gospel outline in Supplement E, noting the focus and flow.

Enemy Profile

"...the accuser of our brothers..." (Rev. 12:10)

Pray aware that Satan prosecutes people's sin against them. Pray for deliverance of your contacts through the kingdom power of Jesus.

Mutual Support

Pray for yourself and your CHOP co-laborers that you would believe that all authority has been given to the risen Christ, and act on it.

Week **Eight** *❧* **Day** **Four**	We can say that in praying we can expect God to do something he would not have done had we not prayed, not to limit God, but to exalt the glory of his unfathomable providence that governs all causes, mediate and immediate. In other words, to suggest God waits on our prayers does not make God smaller. It makes him bigger than we could possibly fathom. Who is like God, governing means and ends, including the acts and prayers of his creatures, without violating their free agency and still maintaining their responsibility and culpability? Yet that is exactly the way God works and the way he shows us he works both in history and in his use of prayer—our prayers. We can take it a step further: God's sovereign plan not only does not invalidate responsible action, it establishes it because that is the way God has designed things. Prayer does work, not as an outside influence but in purposed congruence in God's eternal plan.

Drawing Near

Read Luke 1:46-55
"My soul magnifies the Lord"

- How is God's abiding faithfulness in evidence in Mary's song?
- How is God's faithfulness shown to be practical?
- What promises have you seen God keep in your life?

To 'magnify' means to make big. In your inmost being magnify the greatness of the Lord. Rejoice in God your Savior. As He fills your gaze, ask Him to clothe you with compassion, kindness, humility, gentleness and patience, to bear with others and to forgive them as the Lord forgave you.

Reaching Out

The garments of all those in the kingdom of God are hand-me-downs in that they are the clothes of the alien righteousness of Jesus Christ. Pray for each of your contacts by name that God would: 1) help them to see that their very best works are as filthy rags; and 2) lead them to evaluate their righteousness in respect to Him and not in respect to their neighbor.

Carefully read the 'Initiation' portion of the gospel outline in Supplement E, noting the focus and flow.

Enemy Profile

"He was a murderer from the beginning" (John 8:44)

Pray aware that Satan desires death and kills through lies and folly. Pray that Christ would rescue your contacts from the bonds of death.

Mutual Support

Pray for yourself and your CHOP co-laborers that you would rejoice in love the Father has lavished on you to make you His adopted children, heirs of everlasting life and heavenly glory, secure in His arms.

Prayer Journal

	Where does the power of prayer reside? The effectiveness of prayer is not
Week	found in numbers, frequency or fervency of those praying. Prayer finds its
	potency in the hidden will of God, his perfect plan that governs all things,
Eight	for his own glory. That's why our prayers are always qualified by, 'Your
∽	will be done.' We submit our will to God's and trust that he will use what
	we have brought to act in accordance with his good pleasure and purpose.
Day	That's what we want. We want our prayers presented by the Spirit in
	complete and uncompromised conformity to the will of God to which we
Five	submit ourselves. We know full well that we do not know all. Only God
	sees the beginning from the end. Father knows best. The power of prayer
	is not resident in the prayer itself or in those praying, but in the eternal
	purpose of God himself. We don't need to somehow discern that purpose.
	Ours is but to trust and to pray. His will, will be done.

Drawing Near

Read 2 Samuel 22:45-51
"The Lord lives, and blessed be my rock..."

- What does it mean for God to be a rock? For Him to be *your* rock?
- How is the stability and security found in God expressed in this passage?
- How can these qualities of God affect your life, especially in the spiritual opposition you face in your Christian walk and service?

Worship God according to each of His names or titles in the passage above. Thank Him for what these mean to you for daily life. Pray that God would open your eyes to the harvest around you. Pray that you would see yourself positioned in the hand of God to bring others to the firm foundation of Christ. Pray also that He would sensitize you to the spiritual struggle and your absolute need for Him in the work set before you.

Reaching Out

Those in the kingdom of God, not only have the peace *of* God, but also have peace *with* God through the reconciling work of Christ. Pray for each of your contacts by name that God would: 1) bring them to know that if they claim to be without sin they make God out to be a liar and that they are distancing themselves from His Word; and 2) draw them to Jesus Christ as the Righteous One, the only provision of God for their sin by which the peace of God can be theirs.

Carefully read the 'Reconciliation' portion of the gospel outline in Supplement E, noting the focus and flow.

Enemy Profile

"...the ruler of this world..." (John 12:31)

Pray aware that Satan is the prince of darkness. Pray to the Prince of peace against his rule in your contacts' hearts.

Mutual Support

Pray for yourself and your CHOP co-laborers that God would teach you what it means to abide in Christ for life, vitality and fruit.

Week **Eight** ∽ **Day** **Six**	Faith rests, receives, believes, submits, trusts, waits, and defers. In other words, praying in faith is praying with the conviction of God's hearing, the expectation of God's answering and the confidence that no matter how great is the thing we ask for, God is able to do immeasurably more than we could ask or think. What a tremendous encouragement to us for the effectiveness of the God-given weapon of prayer. The God for whom nothing is impossible is at work through our prayers for the accomplishment of his purposes. That's what faith knows and how it functions in prayer. We pray with faith's focus on God.

Drawing Near

Read Isaiah 54:1-8

"...with everlasting love I will have compassion on you"

- How is God's perseverance in view in this passage?
- What names of God does Isaiah mention in vv. 5-6? Why would he build one name upon another?
- How can God's revelation of Himself and His purposes through us seen in this passage encourage us for His use?

Worship God according to each of His names or titles in the passage above. Praise Him for the ways He has worked and is working through you. Pray that God would grant you courage and expectation in the knowledge that Christ is with you for the battle. Ask Him to help you make Him your focus. Pray that His love would banish fear from your heart.

Reaching Out

The One who commands our attention in the kingdom of God is the King, Jesus Christ, and He is our Commander. Pray for each of your contacts by name that God would: 1) cause them to recognize Jesus Christ as the only Savior of sinners; and 2) cause them to bow the knee before Jesus Christ as Lord of life.

Carefully read the 'Obligation' portion of the gospel outline in Supplement E, noting the focus and flow.

Enemy Profile

"...sin is crouching at the door..." (Gen 4:6-7)

Pray aware that Satan is evil, vigilant, relentless, powerful, oppressive and aggressive, lurking and looking to inflict spiritual harm. Pray against his intentions and that your contacts might find refuge and safety by grace through faith in Jesus Christ.

Mutual Support

Pray for yourself and your CHOP co-laborers that you would delight in God's power and grace that made you alive and secure in Christ.

Prayer Journal

	Faith infuses prayer with great expectancy, because it knows God and
Week	knows that God has ordained prayer as his means to his ends. Such prayer
	identifies with the psalmist: 'In the morning, O Lord, you hear my voice; in
Nine	the morning I lay my requests before you and wait in expectation' (Ps. 5: 3).
☙	God will answer: yes, no, not now, in this way, in this time. Faith expects
	God to work and so looks for his working, accepting of his answers, in sub-
Day	mission to his purposes. Another way we could express the effectiveness
	of prayer in the hand of the God who has given it to us as a weapon is that
One	it never misfires, nor does it ever miss. It always works. It always finds its
	target. The coordinates of our prayer originate in the heavenly realms and
	will find its mark under the guidance of God's infallible providence. There
	will be no collateral damage, no extraneous benefit or unexpected result
	outside of the perfect plan of God.

Drawing Near

Read Jeremiah 9:23-24
"...I am the Lord who practices steadfast love..."

- In what does God say He delights?
- How do these lead us to boast only in Jesus Christ?
- To what does our God direct our attention that we might have joy and confidence in Him?

Spend time worshipping God as He reveals himself. Praise Him for how He has touched your life. To what degree has Satan, your enemy and Christ's, been successful in withering your prayer life? Confess your sin of self-reliance to the degree of your neglect of prayer. Ask God to grant you a heart of wisdom, humility and love.

Reaching Out

The ones you are remembering in prayer are dazzled and deceived by the lure of Vanity Fair, where much is promised but nothing is received. As you pray for each of your contacts let your heart be moved by compassion in seeing them being led by a false shepherd and pray that God would: 1) lead them to the Shepherd of souls, who leads in the way of righteousness for His name's sake; and 2) enable them to hear the voice of the Good Shepherd, that they might follow Him and find goodness and mercy all the days of their lives and dwell in the house of the Lord forever.

Read the "What happens next?" and "FAQs about sin" pages of the gospel presentation in Supplement E.

Enemy Profile

"...the angel of the bottomless pit..." (Rev. 9:11)

Pray aware that Satan's home is ultimately destruction. Pray against his grip on your contacts that would carry them with him.

Mutual Support

Pray for yourself and your CHOP co-laborers that you would exult in Him who has the keys of death and Hades for your deliverance.

Prayer Journal

Week **Nine** ∾ **Day** **Two**	Our prayer is to our King, not to the prince of this world. We are not called to address Satan to bind him or command him to go away, to let go, or to do anything. Our petition is to our King who has promised to be with us and in whom is our strength. Our Lord Jesus does not stay at headquarters when he dispatches us to engage in evangelism. No, he is with us. He lives in us by his Spirit. When we face spiritual opposition we look to him, asking him for strength. We turn to him for protection. We trust in him for provision.

Drawing Near

Read 1 Timothy 1:12-17
"To the King of ages, immortal, invisible, the only God..."

- How is the patience of God so wonderfully displayed in this passage?
- How can you identify with Paul's self-description in a way that magnifies the grace of God?
- What prompts the Apostle to erupt into the doxology of v. 17?

Praise God from whom all blessings flow. Reflect on who you were and what you were like when the grace of God dawned in your heart. Pour out the overflow of your heart in worship of God. Pray that Jesus would draw you closer to Himself as you set your sights on the enemy to which He alerts you as you seek to serve Him and advance His kingdom. Recognize your need for other believers, fellow sinners saved by grace, fellow sojourners in the race, fellow soldiers of the cross.

Reaching Out

The kingdom of God is a kingdom of people reconciled not only to God but also to one another as the peace of Christ reigns in their hearts. Pray for each of your contacts by name that God would: 1) break down any notion that they exist in society as independent individuals, without need of others; and 2) open their eyes to the sin that runs rampant in their relationships with other people, dividing and destroying relationships.

Commit to memory the boxed summary statement, the bold-faced points and a key Scripture text of 'Creation' in Supplement E.

Enemy Profile

"The weeds are the sons of the evil one." (Matt. 13:38)

Pray aware of the families of light and darkness, and the nature and future of each. Pray that Christ would bring your contacts into the glorious freedom of the children of God.

Mutual Support

Pray for yourself and your CHOP co-laborers that you would be faithful and expectant in God's work through you to wrest others from the hand of the devil.

Prayer Journal

Week **Nine** ⤚ **Day** **Three**	As best we can, we want to aim the weapon of prayer and not to discharge it indiscriminately. In no way does this suggest that we have a limited supply of ammunition or a cut off to our requests. Rather, the idea is simply to pray intelligently. We pray as we think best, in keeping with the revealed will of God. We don't need to seek some secret knowledge. If we believe Jerry is making a foolish decision, we pray what we think appropriate, in view of that information. God will receive and use our prayers as he sees fits. Our job is to content ourselves with his answer. Prayer as a weapon of the kingdom of God is prayer conducted in knowledge—knowledge of our Savior, of ourselves, of Satan and of situations. Such prayer knows the times and takes into account what it sees, bringing it to our Lord.

Drawing Near
Read Nehemiah 9:29-35
"...the awesome God, who keeps covenant and steadfast love"

- How is the patience of God highlighted in this passage?
- What ways do you see God pursuing His people even in their unfaithfulness and rebellion?
- Recognizing your own sin, to what does this passage attribute your standing before God?

Praise God for His abiding love. Reflect on God's mercies to you in the face of your waywardness. Pour out the overflow of your heart in worship of God. Pray that God would alert you and train you for the spiritual struggle you face in your Christian walk and service to Christ. Confess any sins of apathy or laziness. Ask God to restore to you the wonder of His mercy and grace.

Reaching Out
A hallmark of the kingdom of God is a peace that exists through forgiveness of transgression against God. Pray for each of your contacts by name that God would: 1) teach them the nature of His forgiveness that He might establish them in the community of saints as ones who forgive as they have been forgiven; and 2) impress on their hearts the immensity and graciousness of His incredible forgiveness as the One against whom they have sinned.

Commit to memory the boxed summary statement, the bold-faced points and a key Scripture text of 'Alienation' in Supplement E.

Enemy Profile
"The god of this world..." (2 Corinthians 4:4)

Pray aware that Satan is described as a rival for the glory of God. Pray against His de-creating and desecrating efforts to blind your contacts and rob God of his glory.

Mutual Support
Pray for yourself and your CHOP co-laborers that God would grant you grace to know and serve Him as the living and true God.

Prayer Journal

Week **Nine** ⤲ **Day** **Four**	Praying in the Spirit is a simple reminder to us of the ground and power for our prayer. Prayer is spiritual activity. We pray as ones indwelt and enlivened by the Spirit. We pray in communion with the Spirit. Our prayers are brought to the Father and conformed to his will through the Spirit. To pray in the Spirit is to pray in profound awareness of our redemptive relationship with God, in deep dependence upon him, and in perfect submission to his desires. Praying in the Spirit means one other thing for wielding the weapon of prayer. We must pray along the contours of God's Word. Of the three persons of the Triune God, the Spirit is the one identified as the author of the Bible. Our prayers are to be structured by Scripture and saturated in Scripture.

Drawing Near

Read Romans 3:19-26

"....so that he might be just and the justifier..."

- How does this passage show the patience and justice and love of God working together?
- How is God shown to be both the one who requires perfect righteousness and the one who provides that righteousness?
- Why should this passage leave us dumbfounded and astounded?

Thank God for each of the things He has done for you in Christ. Give Him glory by describing the song of your heart tuned by His grace. Pray that God would empty you of self and fill you with Christ. Pray that God would impress upon you the reality of spiritual battle, the intensity of it, and your absolute need for Jesus Christ at all points.

Reaching Out

The kingdom of God is for the healing of the nations and the church is to be a healing agent, manifesting the unity in love that is a fruit of God's grace. Pray for each of your contacts by name that God would: 1) convict them of their pride in protecting an unforgiving spirit that alienates them from others; and 2) bring them to see the log in their own eye instead of the speck in others', that they might see their need for Christ.

Commit to memory the boxed summary statement, the bold-faced points and a key Scripture text of 'Initiation' in Supplement E.

Enemy Profile

"...Satan disguises himself as an angel of light" (2 Cor. 11:14)

Pray aware that Satan is masquerader. Pray against his efforts to lure your contacts to ruin, and for God to expose his deceptions by His Word and Spirit.

Mutual Support

Pray for yourself and your CHOP co-laborers that you would hear the words of your Lord and put them into practice.

Prayer Journal

Week **Nine** ⤚ **Day** **Five**	How did Paul wield the weapon of truth? He sought to dislodge the error with the truth. In our kingdom building, we can try to raze the error and raise the truth in their minds. Or, we can look to push out the error with the truth as the dead leaves of an oak are discarded through the new sprouts of spring. In our interactions with others, we want to attend, to listen, to discern deviation from the truth of God's Word. Key areas for inspection are their views of God, the person of Christ, and the way of salvation. Try to communicate the corrective of God's truth. Communication is not just talking; it's getting through, at least to the degree of knowledge, not necessarily their agreement with it.

Drawing Near

Read Deuteronomy 32:1-4
"...for all his ways are justice"

- For what is God magnified in this song of Moses?
- How can this knowledge be to our souls as "gentle rain upon the tender grass"?
- How does such knowledge prompt proclaiming the name of the Lord?

Exalt God as a God of justice. Praise Him for the perfection of His being and His fairness in dealing with men. Pray that God would lead you to a more detailed and more intimate knowledge of Him. Pray that He would work in you a greater trust in Him, dependence upon Him and desire to see His name exalted.

Reaching Out

All things in heaven and on earth submit to God as Sovereign Lord, including the fallen angels. Pray for each of your contacts by name that God would: 1) work in them a fear of the Lord, an awe of the splendor of His majesty; and 2) open their eyes to see Him as the living God, who endures forever, and whose kingdom will never end, who rules over all.

Commit to memory the boxed summary statement, the bold-faced points and a key Scripture text of 'Reconciliation' in Supplement E.

Enemy Profile

"...some have already strayed after Satan" (1 Tim. 5:14-15)

Pray aware that Satan is a seducer, enticing to sin and ruin. Pray against his lies, counterfeits, perversions and distortions, and that the Spirit might bring your contacts to a saving knowledge of the truth.

Mutual Support

Pray for yourself and your CHOP co-laborers that you would seek to be holy as your Heavenly Father is holy, and that you would desire truth in the inmost parts of your being.

Prayer Journal

Week	Descriptions of our enemy from God's Word can be a springboard
	for our prayer in the face of the enemy's efforts, evident in the lives
Nine	of others we engage for Christ. Other portions of Scripture can be
∽	brought to the service of prayer. In every case, however, we want
	to remember that we are opposed in this age by the spirit of the
Day	antichrist, whose tactics are lies and deceptions, distortions of that
Six	truth, offering a contrary and counterfeit hope. Warfare witness is
	communication of God's truth, particularly his Messiah as the way,
	the truth and the life, in the face of spiritual opposition with the
	weapons God has issued to us suitable for the task, wielded in the
	way of his design.

Drawing Near

Read Psalm 99
"Holy is he!"

- What characteristic of God dominates this psalm?
- How are God's justice and holiness related?
- Why is the holiness of God a stimulus to our worship?

Praise God as a holy God, who hates sin. Praise Him as a gracious and forgiving God who hears and answers prayer. Ask God to search you and know your heart, to try you and know your anxious thoughts, to see if there is any offensive way in you, and to lead you in the way everlasting. Take to Him your doubts and fears in witnessing for Him.

Reaching Out

God and Satan are not equals. God is Sovereign Lord and Satan is a created being, whose activity is not unrestrained but serves the purposes of God for His own glory. Pray for each of your contacts by name that God would: 1) lift their eyes to see Him as Lord of lords and King of kings, who sustains the humble but casts the wicked to the ground; and 2) thwart the efforts of the evil one in their lives to take them captive to do his will.

Commit to memory the boxed summary statement, the bold-faced points and a key Scripture text of 'Obligation' in Supplement E.

Enemy Profile

"...the deceiver of the whole world" (Rev. 12:9)

Pray aware that Satan is not just evil but that he ensnares others. Pray against his competing counsel, false hopes and empty promises that come to your contacts through the world.

Mutual Support

Pray for yourself and your CHOP co-laborers that God would help you to be strengthened in Christ, rooted and built up in Him, and overflowing with thankfulness for His love, mercy and grace to you.

Prayer Journal

Week	Our God is sovereign. He is infinitely wise. Just as churches are

Week

Ten

Day

One

Our God is sovereign. He is infinitely wise. Just as churches are outposts of the kingdom of God, providentially stationed by him for the work of the kingdom, so are we strategically positioned by our Commander in this world for the campaign of his kingdom. I know we are the ones who decide what houses to buy and what gym we go to. But ultimately, it is by the providence of God that we go where we go and know whom we know. His guiding hand leads not only in the way of righteousness for his name's sake, it leads us for the way of righteousness, positioned for the good news of kingdom proclamation.

Drawing Near

Read Isaiah 51:1-8
"...my salvation will be forever"

- How comprehensive is the justice of God?
- How do the law, justice, righteousness and salvation relate to one another?
- What confidence does God impress upon us in vv. 6 & 8?

Praise God for the good news of His salvation in Christ. Praise Him for the steadfastness of His salvation. Praise Him that greater is He who is in you than he who is in the world. Ask God to remove from you any fear of men and to give you instead a genuine love for people that listens biblically and compassionately.

Reaching Out

Jesus Christ will build His church and the gates of hell will not prevail against it. The building blocks of Christ's church are the living stones such as those for whom you are praying. Pray for each of your contacts by name that God would: 1) redeem them from eternal calamity, sanctify them to Himself, and install them in the secure confines of His community of saints; and 2) use you and others to shine in them the light of Christ and dispel the darkness, leading to eternal life.

Practice sharing the 'Creation' portion of the gospel presentation in Supplement E with yourself.

Enemy Profile

"...Satan filled your heart..." (Acts 5:3)

Pray aware that Satan's base of operations in your contacts' lives is their heart. Pray for the regenerating work of the Holy Spirit, who alone can change the heart and take them captive for Christ.

Mutual Support

Pray for yourself and your CHOP co-laborers that you would deal in truth, not distorting or manipulating the word of God you seek to share with others.

Week **Ten** ⤚∾ **Day** **Two**	Not only do we live in the theatre of operations for the kingdom of heaven, we have been strategically stationed there by the wise providence of God. He has established us on the high ground in which we are beacons of light. Our engagement for the cause of Christ is not extraordinary to life, but part of ordinary, everyday life. Those encounters and relationships in ordinary life, 'in our going,' provide us the forums for engaging others for Christ. God has planned it that way. He has put us in their way.

Drawing Near

Read Jeremiah 23:1-6
"The Lord is our righteousness."

- What does God do in the face of the failure and unfaithfulness of people?
- How is God's tender compassion communicated?
- Why is righteousness emphasized in God's promised provision?

Thank God for His sending His Son to be the Shepherd of His sheep, the righteous Branch in the line of David. Reflect on the breadth and focus of God's plan of redemption and give Him glory. Pray that God will grant you a deeper awareness that you belong to Jesus. Confess your sins of trying to find identity and direction outside of Him.

Reaching Out

God is the one who rescues from the dominion of darkness and brings His own into the kingdom of life and light. Pray for each of your contacts by name that God would: 1) exert the power of His glorious might in their lives to deliver them from the bondage of Satan and establish them in Christ's hand; and 2) lead them to Jesus Christ in the power of the Holy Spirit in order to qualify them for the inheritance of the saints in the kingdom of light.

Practice sharing the 'Alienation' portion of the gospel presentation in Supplement E with yourself.

Enemy Profile

"...by the activity of Satan..." (2 Thess. 2:9-12)

Pray aware that Satan is the driving force behind all that stands against God. Pray against his work to lead your contacts astray.

Mutual Support

Pray for yourself and your CHOP co-laborers that your sovereign God and Father would not lead you into temptation but would protect and deliver you from the evil one.

Prayer Journal

Week	Every area of your ordinary life is a forum for impacting others for
Ten	the cause of the kingdom of life and light. We might call these your
✍	life-spheres—areas of activity and relationship that make up your
Day	life. Examples of life-spheres are our family, our neighborhood, our
Three	workplace, our activities, our recreation, the marketplace. Each of

Week

Ten

✍

Day

Three

Every area of your ordinary life is a forum for impacting others for the cause of the kingdom of life and light. We might call these your life-spheres—areas of activity and relationship that make up your life. Examples of life-spheres are our family, our neighborhood, our workplace, our activities, our recreation, the marketplace. Each of these is a sphere of influence for us. Spheres of influence are those arenas of life in which God has providentially placed you, where you operate and have contacts, and where you have special opportunity to influence others for Christ.

Drawing Near

Read Psalm 7:10-17
"God is a righteous judge..."

- What provokes the wrath of God's judgment?
- How do verses 10 and 17 speak of what God has done for you?
- What responses does the psalmist highlight to such wonders?

Express to God your gratitude for all that He has done for you. Reflect on and praise Him not only for His attribute of love but also for His attribute of righteousness. Praise Him that His love and justice collide at the cross—for you. Ask God to work in you a heart for prayer and a sense of urgency for you to labor in prayer for those without Him and without hope.

Reaching Out

God is commander of His hosts and a fortress and stronghold for His people. Pray for each of your contacts by name that God would: 1) prompt them to be still and know that He is God, that He is exalted among the nations, that He is exalted over the earth; and 2) lead them to the Rock of refuge for safety and security from their foes, the spiritual forces of evil that operate as part of the kingdom of this world.

Practice sharing the 'Initiation' portion of the gospel presentation in Supplement E with yourself.

Enemy Profile

"...powers, false signs and wonders..." (2 Thess. 2:9-12)

Pray aware that Satan is not a creator but a counterfeiter, passing off evil as good and presumption as hope. Pray that the Spirit would open your contacts' eyes to discern truth from error and to see the precipice to the pit of hell that lies ahead.

Mutual Support

Pray for yourself and your CHOP co-laborers that you would walk in the Word of God that is a lamp unto your feet and a light unto your path in a dark and dangerous world.

Prayer Journal

Week **Ten** ✎ **Day** **Four**	When we speak with others about the truth, we want to exercise great patience with them. We want to take our time. We don't want to shake the dust off our feet in exasperation at the first glimmer of rejection or unreceptivity. We don't want to allow a raised eyebrow or furled brow to deter us. We want to be tolerant of resistance, allowing room for the Spirit. We don't just talk at people. We talk with them. We engage in dialog, the give and take of communication. We don't want it to degenerate into point-counterpoint, but to foster understanding. This goal is pursued through presentation of the truth of the Word in great patience and careful instruction.

Drawing Near

Read Romans 1:18-25
"...the Creator, who is blessed forever"

- What provokes the wrath of God?
- What tactic might the devil use to blind people to their sin, against which we can pray?
- What response does God desire and deserve of His creatures?

Praise God that He has sought you and brought you to be a true worshipper, one who will acknowledge Him and worship Him in Spirit and truth. Praise Him who redirected His rightful wrath from you to Jesus Christ. Ask God to enlarge your faith and broaden your perspective for His work of redemption through you as you turn to Him in prayer. Ask Him to help you to pray fervently and expectantly.

Reaching Out

Jesus Christ is the firstborn from the dead and the ruler of the kings of the earth who has freed His people from their sins by His blood. Pray for each of your contacts by name that God would: 1) free them from the bondage of their sin through the risen and reigning Christ, who holds the keys of death and Hades; and 2) work in them a fear of Him who can destroy both soul and body in hell and not those who can merely kill the body.

Practice sharing the 'Reconciliation' portion of the gospel presentation in Supplement E with yourself.

Enemy Profile

"...with all wicked deception..." (2 Thess. 2:9-12)

Pray aware that Satan deals in the currency of evil intended to lure to ruin. Pray against the grip he has on your contacts by virtue of their being spiritually dead in sin by beseeching Christ to make them alive by His Spirit, established in the hollow of His loving hand.

Mutual Support

Pray for yourself and your CHOP co-laborers that God would grant you a heart of wisdom that begins with the fear of the Lord.

Week **Ten** ⁓ **Day** **Five**	Respect is a by-product of love. It employs the Golden Rule of doing unto others as you have would them do unto you. Respect is ready to listen. Respect is the eye contact of loving communication. Respect is the willingness to become all things to all people for the sake of the gospel. Gentleness, respect, patience, instruction—these are the elements of the delivery system that God gives for launching those spiritual weapons capable of destroying strongholds.

Drawing Near

Read Job 1:6-12
"The Lord said to Satan..."

- How extensive is the sovereign rule of God?
- What else do we learn about God in this passage?
- How should we respond to God amidst any questions and confusion we might have about this scene?

Worship God as Sovereign Lord over all His creation, events and created beings. Cover your mouth in submission and praise Him for who He is and for the wonder of His ways. Pray that God would help you to pray. Humble yourself before the Lord that He might lift you up and that you might find your sufficiency and certainty in Him.

Reaching Out

Jesus Christ gave Himself for the sins of His people to rescue them from the present evil age, according to the will of our God and Father in heaven. Pray for each of your contacts by name that God would: 1) enlighten their minds in the knowledge of Christ; and 2) grant them newness of life and participation in the age to come when the old order of things is done away with and there will be no more death or mourning or crying or pain.

Practice sharing the 'Obligation' portion of the gospel presentation in Supplement E with yourself.

Enemy Profile

"...refused to love the truth and so be saved..." (2 Thess. 2:9-12)

Pray aware that Satan stimulates fallen taste buds to savor error and find truth repugnant. Pray that God would work in your contacts a love for the truth, a hunger for righteousness and a thirst for the knowledge of God.

Mutual Support

Pray for yourself and your CHOP co-laborers that you would revel in the grace of God that has brought you salvation and redeemed you from all wickedness and taken you as His very own.

Prayer Journal

Week **Ten** ✤ **Day** **Six**	A related means of assault on the kingdom of this age are planned efforts to do good to others. By deeds of kindness, we want to ease burdens of life in a fallen world. Our good deeds are to be not only active in our lives and so seen by others, not only reactive in response to persecution and suffering, but proactive in an agenda of deeds of unmerited, unexpected, undeserved kindness. Try offering to mow your neighbor's lawn because he hurt his back and see if that doesn't shake him up. In other words, the righteous obedience of our lives is not only defensive; it is offensive as well. Just as signs, wonders and works of power that reversed the effects of the fall evidenced the inaugurated presence of the redemptive kingdom, so our deeds of kindness demonstrate that reality and bring relief to those of the kingdom of this age.

Drawwung Near

Read Zechariah 3:1-5
"The Lord rebuke you, O Satan!"

- Before whose throne does Satan act as accuser?
- How are Joshua's best efforts at righteousness characterized?
- How is this a picture of gospel, in respect to God, to sinners and to the provision of God?

Ascribe to the Lord the glory of those attributes He has made beautiful in your eyes. Pour out your heart to Him in wonder, praise and thanks. Pray that God would lift your eyes to the harvest around you, those still subject to Satan's accusations. Pray that He would help you to see the work of His power and purpose in their lives. Ask God to help you converse with people in the awareness of His working.

Reaching Out

Jesus drove out demons from people, showing that the redemptive kingdom of God had arrived with the presence of the King. Pray for each of your contacts by name that God would: 1) capture them by His Spirit for Jesus Christ that they might be for Him instead of against Him; and 2) protect them from blasphemy against the Holy Spirit that would reject the Christ to whom the Spirit bears witness.

Practice sharing the introduction and 'What happens next?' portions of the gospel presentation in Supplement E with yourself.

Enemy Profile

"...a snare of the devil" (1 Timothy 3:7)

Pray aware that Satan is devious. Pray against his plots to ensnare your contacts by his deceptions and temptations.

Mutual Support

Pray for yourself and your CHOP co-laborers that you would have a good reputation that adorns the gospel in your lives.

Week **Eleven** ❧ **Day** **One**	To what do good deeds point? They can announce what a great guy I am. They draw people's attention to me—my character, my values, my lifestyle preference. Or, good deeds can point to a salvation by works. I'm obeying God so that I can earn my way into heaven. My efforts at law keeping are what merit salvation for me. In other words, deeds unqualified by words have the potential of pointing people to us instead of Christ, and to works instead of grace. Deeds validate. Words verify. Authenticating deeds beg opportunity for interpretive word giving the deeds their position in mission. We need to be prepared to give an answer for the hope we have, a hope explained by Peter in the opening verses of his letter. That hope is salvation rooted in the triune God. The idea is for the light of our lives penetrating the darkness to draw attention so that people will ask questions. And we need to be prepared to give an answer.

Drawing Near

Read Nahum 1:2-8
"The Lord is a jealous and avenging God"

- How is God different from the popular conception of Him?
- What would it be like to be an enemy of God?
- What contrast is seen for those who take refuge in Him?

Praise God as a jealous God, who will not share His glory with another. Praise Him for His mercy and faithfulness in the face of your fickleness. Reflect on what it means to pray that God's will would be done. Pray that God would use you to the accomplishment of His will and the extension of His redemptive kingdom in the hearts of those around you.

Reaching Out

As you pray for your contacts, know that they are not angels but human beings; with such Christ identified in His incarnation and for such He died. Pray for each of your contacts that God would: 1) free them who all their lives have been held in slavery by fear of death, bringing them into Christ's victory over the devil by His death; and 2) turn their hearts to Jesus as a merciful and faithful high priest, who is the atonement for the sins of God's people.

Role-play sharing the gospel with one of your CHOP coworkers.

Enemy Profile

"...destroy the one who has the power of death, that is, the devil" (Hebrews 2:14-15)

Pray aware that Satan holds the power of death. Pray that Jesus would free your contacts from the power and fear of death.

Mutual Support

Pray for yourself and your CHOP co-laborers that you would know that by the power of the risen Christ death has lost its hold and sting for you.

Prayer Journal

Week **Eleven** ✑ **Day** **Two**	The rule of engagement is that prayer does not preclude action; it presupposes it. We don't just pray for someone's salvation. We pray and act in light of that prayer as we have ability and opportunity, expectant of God's working for his purposes. We want to talk to God for people and we want to talk to people for God. Both cases involve prayer. The first rule shows the necessity of prayer and participation in tandem. The second rule for the use of prayer as a weapon has to do with the essential conflict between the kingdom of God and the kingdom of Satan. The antagonistic and adversarial nature of the kingdoms suggests that our prayer must be not only prayer *for* but also prayer *against*.

Drawing Near

Read Isaiah 26:1-12
"O Lord, …you have done for us all our works."

• How does God present Himself as one who is to be trusted?
• What does verse 12 inform us about what we accomplish?
• What fruit of such trust can we expect in our hearts?

Worship God for the splendor of His glory and for the mystery of His ways. Ask God to help you to know the hindrances of your heart to prayer, even ways you are riddled with unbelief. Are there ways in which you think you don't need God? Confess your sins to Him.

Reaching Out

Christ has provided weapons of the kingdom that have divine power to demolish strongholds and arguments and every pretension that sets itself up against the knowledge of God. Pray for each of your contacts by name that God would: 1) take their every thought captive to the obedience of Christ; and 2) do an extraordinary work of power and grace in their lives to subdue them to Himself and bring them to bow the knee in submission to Christ.

Share the gospel presentation with a Christian friend.

Enemy Profile

"…the keys of Death and Hades" (Rev. 1:17-18)

Pray aware that Satan is a warden of the prison of sin, death and the grave. Pray that by God's grace your contacts might find victory and liberation through faith in Jesus Christ.

Mutual Support

Pray for yourself and your CHOP co-laborers that you would grow in the grace and the knowledge of Jesus Christ and in gratitude for His deliverance of you from sin, death and the grave.

Prayer Journal

Week **Eleven** ⪡ **Day** **Three**	In presenting the gospel, the good news of freedom in Jesus Christ, all of us as Christ's ambassadors need to be prepared to explain it. We need to be able to lay out a logical outline, ready with supporting Scripture, perhaps buttressed with examples and illustrations. The gospel is logical. The reason for the gospel is not logical in that God set his love on the unlovable. God's grace is illogical. There is a disconnect between what we deserve in our sin at the hands of God's justice and the outpouring of his grace. In his mercy, God does not give us what we deserve. In his grace, he gives us what we do not deserve. While grace is gloriously illogical, the gospel is thoroughly logical, flowing from one truth to another, each 'since' leading to a 'therefore.' Our responsibility as soldiers of Christ is to unfurl that gospel in its logical framework.

Drawing Near

Read Ephesians 2:1-10
"....God, being rich in mercy, because of the great love..."

- Why did God grant you salvation?
- How is the power of God displayed in this passage for your life?
- How is the grace of God magnified in this passage?

Reflect on the fact that you were a child of wrath, entrapped in the kingdom of darkness—ignorant, senseless, and disobedient—when the light of the gospel shone forth in your heart. For what will you give God praise and thanks? As a child of God, created to glorify and enjoy God as your Father, how is life reshaped and refocused by your relationship with Him. What place does prayer play in your life?

Reaching Out

The kingdom of Satan is characterized by reigning sin, by blind unbelief and by rebellion against God. Pray for each of your contacts by name that God would: 1) cause His light to shine in the darkness of their hearts to give them the light of the knowledge of the glory of God in the face of Christ; and 2) open their blinded eyes so that they can see the light of the gospel of the glory of Christ, who is the image of God.

Pray that God would give you opportunities to share some aspect of the gospel with one of your contacts.

Enemy Profile

"...canceling the record of debt that stood against us..." (Col. 2:13-15)

Pray aware your contacts' sin provides legitimate opportunity for Satan's accusations. Pray that the Spirit of God would make them alive in Christ, forgive their sins, and make them glory in the cross.

Mutual Support

Pray for yourself and your CHOP co-laborers that you find your standing before God solely in the gospel and not your own efforts.

Prayer Journal

Week	There can be a variety of ways to approach and explain the gospel. The centerpiece is always Jesus Christ and his saving work. We are to tell His-story. For us, the point is that we need to be able to lay the message of the way, the truth, and the life out on the table. We relate what God has done in Christ. The second way we see in Acts of communicating the gospel is through my story in Christ, my testimony of God's work of grace in my life. A personal testimony speaks to what God did in my heart to bring the salvation of his Son home to roost, where by his Spirit God claims me as his own, having been purchased for him by the Son.
Eleven	
✎	
Day	
Four	

Drawing Near

Read Titus 3:3-7

"...when the goodness and loving kindness of God our Savior..."

- What qualities of God in our salvation are highlighted in this passage?
- According to this passage, why did God grant you salvation?
- What does God's mercy spare us? What does His grace give us instead?

Praise God as the God of grace who called you to His eternal glory in Christ Jesus. Meditate on what He has done for you, punctuating your meditation with expressions of praise and thanks. Ask God for the wisdom to see where you are allowing obstacles to hinder you in your witness for Christ. Beseech Him for the grace and strength to overcome them through Christ, purposing this very day to new obedience.

Reaching Out

The power of the kingdom of God is that of a new creation, a resurrection power through which God is reconciling the world to Himself in Christ, not counting men's sins against them. Pray for each of your contacts by name that God would: 1) open their ears to the witness of His ambassadors as they direct them to Jesus Christ who is the life that is the light of men; and 2) enable them to be drawn to the glory of Jesus Christ, as the only Begotten of the Father, full of grace and truth.

Pray that one of your contacts would ask you to give a reason for the hope you have.

Enemy Profile

"...to deliver us from the present evil age" (Gal. 1:3-4)

Pray aware that your contacts are at home in the world in which Satan prowls. Pray for God's grace and peace in their lives.

Mutual Support

Pray for yourself and your CHOP co-laborers that you would know both peace with God and the peace of God in your hearts.

Prayer Journal

Week	The gospel, which speaks of Jesus Christ and him crucified, is the force
	undergirding the arsenal of the church against the forces of spiritual dark-
Eleven	ness. The gospel testifies to the finished, victorious, liberating work of Jesus
	Christ. It is not a blueprint. It is not a battle plan. The gospel is a record of
~∽	Christ's work to provide all that is necessary for liberation from the bond-
	age of this age and is a receipt of those for whom Christ died, whose entire
Day	debt of sin is paid in full. The gospel is the proclamation of Jesus Christ
Five	as the way, the truth and the life—a message of assault on the kingdom of
	Satan and all that it stands for. For us to fly the colors is to hold aloft for the
	world to see the finished work of Jesus Christ and the promise of deliver-
	ance it holds for all who will believe.

Drawing Near

Read Titus 2:11-14
"...our great God and Savior Jesus Christ"

- What purposes of God are emphasized in this passage?
- How does grace function in your life?
- What is your sure and certain hope as an object of God's love?

Praise God that you belong to Him and that, although you are in the world, you are not of it. Give praise to Jesus, your Lord and your God, for His giving His life to redeem you. Pray that God will teach you to pray expectantly. Ask Him to give you a greater sense of fellowship with Him in your prayers and a greater awareness of the power of prayer as it looks to Him who is able to do all things.

Reaching Out

As His Redeemer King, God has placed all things under Christ's feet and appointed Him as head over everything for the church, which is His body, the fullness of Him who fills everything in every way. Pray for each of your contacts by name that God would: 1) enlighten the eyes of their hearts in order to know the hope of His calling and the riches of His glorious inheritance in the saints and His incomparably great power in those who believe; and 2) grant them a Spirit of wisdom and revelation that they might come to know Him whom to know is life eternal.

Review the 'Conversational Transitions' in Supplement C to see ways you can transition to spiritual discussion. Add your own.

Enemy Profile

"...one stronger than he attacks him and overcomes him" (Lk. 11:20-23)

Pray aware that Satan is powerful and too strong for you. Pray for the kingdom power of Christ in the lives of your contacts.

Mutual Support

Pray for yourself and your CHOP co-laborers that you would know yourselves as the precious spoils of Christ's redeeming work.

Prayer Journal

Week **Eleven** ❧ **Day** **Six**	The Prince of peace came to bring peace and usher in a kingdom of righteousness and peace. That peace is the fruit of a restored relationship with God and a peace that runs contrary to the present, evil age. Those in Christ have peace with God and the peace of God rules in our hearts, giving us comfort and confidence in the conflict of the day and bright hope for tomorrow. To be ambassadors of the gospel of peace is not to be brokers of peace in some sort of shuttle diplomacy. It is to announce peace. It is to call people to a change of kingdom allegiances. That change of allegiance is effected by God's Spirit and expressed in repentance and faith.

Drawing Near

Read 2 Timothy 1:3-14
"…because of his own purpose and grace…"

- How is God established at the heart of salvation in this passage?
- What brushstrokes of your salvation can you sort out from this passage?
- How should this spur us on to witness?

Praise God who set His love upon you from the beginning of time, sent His Son in the fullness of time, brought new life to you in His time, and saved you as His own child for all time. Unleash the thoughts and emotions these facts provoke in a wellspring of glory to your Father who is in heaven. How have you divorced prayer from such a glorious and gracious God, making prayer an end in itself rather than a means to God's ends and communion with Him?

Reaching Out

The presence of the kingdom of God speaks to the victory of Christ and the validity of the message of the kingdom to repent and believe upon Him who reigns now and forever. Pray for each of your contacts by name that God would: 1) give them the Holy Spirit that they might understand the things of God, accept the truth of God, and embrace the Christ of God; and 2) deliver them from the lies and lures of the devil who would keep them from Christ.

Pray for your contacts that the Holy Spirit would convince them of their sin and misery, enlighten their minds in the knowledge of Christ, renew their wills, and persuade and enable them to believe.

Enemy Profile

"The God of peace will soon crush Satan…" (Rom. 16:20)

Pray aware that Satan and his kingdom will not endure. Pray for your contacts that they might know the victory of the Seed of the woman, that they might escape the coming wrath.

Mutual Support

Pray for yourself and your CHOP co-laborers that you would take refuge in Christ as your security, stability and strength.

Prayer Journal

Week **Twelve** ᭥ **Day** **One**	For our morale nothing is more vital for us to keep in view than the gospel of our salvation. It is the gospel that will revive us in our complacency, refresh us in our weariness, and restore us in our mission. Looking to the gospel will introduce us anew to the love of our God and the sacrifice of our Lord. The gospel can become encrusted with the dust of self-glory and the corrosion of self-righteousness. We forget the extent of our sin. We forget the degree of our despair. The cost of God's love and the sacrifice of our Savior are reduced to mere facts, dry doctrine. The grace of God becomes ordinary. It becomes something owed us as a right, instead of unexpected and undeserved as it really is.

Drawing Near

Read Acts 17:22-31
"God...has fixed a day on which he will judge the world..."

- How does the Apostle introduce God to his audience?
- How would this God run counter to their polytheistic notions?
- For what response does the Apostle call?

Praise God for His opening up of your eyes to the gospel of Jesus Christ and for His turning your heart from idols to know and serve Him, the living and true God. Exalt Him as the only true God. Ask God to expand your grasp of prayer as communication ordained by Him to do great things. Ask Him to give you greater vision for who He is, what He's done, what He's doing and how He is doing it.

Reaching Out

Pray for each of your contacts, keeping in mind that they will one day bow the knee before Him whom God exalted to the highest place and gave the name that is above every name, that at the name of Jesus every knee will bow, in heaven and on earth and under the earth, and every tongue confess that He is Lord—to the glory of the Father, that God would: 1) thwart the activity of the evil one to discredit Christ in your contacts' eyes; and 2) grant them a spirit of humility and repentance that turns from their sinful rebellion to bow the knee before the risen Christ.

Pray for God's gracious nourishing of the seeds you and others have sown in the lives of your contacts.

Enemy Profile

"See to it that no one takes you captive..." (Col. 2:6-8)

Pray aware that Satan uses that which seems right to a man to hold others captive in unbelief. Pray that God would work faith in the hearts of your contacts that looks to Christ and rests in Him.

Mutual Support

Pray for yourself and your CHOP co-laborers that as you have received Christ Jesus as Lord you would continue to live in Him.

Prayer Journal

Week

Twelve

⚜

Day

Two

Satan draws our attention to our sin to drive us to despair. God directs our attention to our sin to drive us to Christ and to delight in his grace. The wonder of the gospel that embraces us is that no matter where we look in our lives and find sin, that sin has been accounted for and charged to the account of our Lord Jesus Christ, who paid for it in full. On the day of judgment, there will be no sin tucked away with which Satan will surprise us and find leverage to accuse us. In Christ, our sin is paid for fully and finally. Reflection on these truths of the gospel oxygenates our blood with the amazing love and unfathomable grace of our God. We become animated for the activity of the kingdom of God in which we grow and serve. If repentance drives us to our knees in contrition, awareness of God's grace drives us to our faces in humility and submission—the posture of a soldier of the cross.

Drawing Near

Read Revelation 1:4-8

"To him who loves us and has freed us from our sins…"

- How is the name of Jesus magnified?
- What blessings are directed to us as believers?
- What does it mean for us to be a kingdom and priests?

Recount to God each of the benefits He has lavished upon you. Tell Him what each of these means to you. Adore Him. Ask God to teach you to pray to seek first His kingdom and His righteousness. Confess your sin of seeking to build your own kingdom and to enhance your own reputation, rather than Christ's, in the eyes of men.

Reaching Out

Christ is on the throne. He is worthy to receive glory and honor and power, both as Creator and as Redeemer. Pray for each of your contacts by name that God would: 1) work in them an intense longing for Him; and 2) turn them from their rebellion to give glory to God.

Pray that God would raise up others in the lives of your contacts to influence them for Christ.

Enemy Profile

"…neither angels nor rulers…" (Rom. 8:37-39)

Pray aware that Satan desires to obscure the love of God in Christ through his accusations, deceptions and temptations. Pray that God would convince your contacts of His love that overcomes.

Mutual Support

Pray for yourself and your CHOP co-laborers that you would not look to be served but to serve and to give your life for Christ.

Prayer Journal

Week	The primary goal of prayer is drawing near to God in our relation-
Twelve	ship of redemption. In view here is not petition, not even praise, but intimacy. God is not some sort of abstract concept. He is the
∽	God who set his love upon us and sent his Son to redeem us and reconcile us to himself. Prayer is fellowship with the living God in
Day	the context of a reconciled relationship. We were his enemies. He
Three	had something against us in our rebellion and sinfulness. But now we are his children, adopted in love. As we linger in communion with this God who rescued us, our hearts are refreshed in his love and renewed in his presence. Our souls are stirred and invigorated with the scent of his grace.

Drawing Near

Read Revelation 7:9-17
"Salvation belongs to our God...and to the Lamb."

- Who is participating in this scene of heavenly worship?
- What words would you use to describe the tone of the worship?
- How will God use you to recruit true worshippers for His glory?

Join in the perpetual heavenly worship right now. Use the inspired words to declare the praises of God and to devote yourself to His service. Speak God's Word back to Him, praying the truths of His Word. Respond in humble adoration to the scene unfolded.

Reaching Out

Christ purchased men and women for God and made them to be a kingdom and priests to serve Him. Pray for each of your contacts by name that God would: 1) change their hearts from hearts of stone to hearts of flesh and so write the law on their hearts and lead them to Christ; and 2) convince them of the glory of undeserving love demonstrated in Christ.

Pray that God would grant you opportunity beyond CHOP to be an influence for Christ in the lives of your contacts, as well as others.

Enemy Profile

"...to present you holy and blameless and above reproach before him..." (Colossians 1: 21-23)

Pray aware that Satan is the accuser who prosecutes people's sins before the tribunal of a holy God. Pray for the power of the gospel in the lives of your contacts to remove the guilt of their sin and to provide a righteousness from God received by faith.

Mutual Support

Pray for yourself and your CHOP co-laborers that God would grant you grace to continue in the faith and make you a faithful servant of His gospel of life and hope in Jesus Christ.

Week	Against Satan's tactic of accusation, we preach the gospel to ourselves, reminding ourselves of the grace in Jesus Christ that rose to
Twelve	bring the light of the new creation to dawn in our dark world and
✦	that will erupt in the brilliance of heavenly glory. There we will
Day	appear before God, without fault and with great joy, all because of the gospel that brings us forgiveness of sin and a perfect righ-
Four	teousness before a holy God. Our enemy's accusations are groundless in Christ.

Drawing Near

Read Revelation 12:1-11

"...the salvation and the power and the kingdom of our God and the authority of his Christ have come..."

- What position has Satan lost by virtue of the death and resurrection of Jesus Christ?
- How is Satan to be overcome?
- How is allegiance to Christ and His kingdom expressed?

Praise God that the victory is His. Praise Jesus who loved us and freed us from our sins by His blood. Thank God for the assurance He gives us. How have you not continued in Christ as Lord of your life, being rooted and built up in Him, strengthened in the faith and overflowing with thankfulness? How have you allowed yourself to be taken captive by hollow and deceptive philosophy that depends on the world rather than on Christ? Confess any sin the Spirit shows you and flee to Christ your only righteousness.

Reaching Out

Salvation belongs to our God, who sits on the throne and to the Lamb. Pray for each of your contacts by name that God would: 1) put a new song in their hearts that proclaims "praise and glory and wisdom and thanks and honor and power and strength be to God for ever and ever"; and 2) enfold them into the great congregation of His people that will recite His praises for ever and ever.

Review the 'Post-CHOP Follow Up' in Supplement D for ideas to continue what God has begun. Add your own ideas to the list.

Enemy Profile

"All authority in heaven and on earth..." (Matthew 28:18-20)

Pray aware that Satan has power and authority over the subjects of his kingdom. Pray for the mighty working of the kingdom of God and His Christ to deliver your contacts from Satan's rule.

Mutual Support

Pray for yourself and your CHOP co-laborers that God would grant you great courage and confidence in the accomplished redemption of Jesus Christ and His reign on high for His church.

Prayer Journal

Week	Against Satan's tactic of temptation, grace leads us to walk by the Spirit so that we will not carry out the deeds of the flesh. The Spirit

Week

Twelve

&

Day

Five

Against Satan's tactic of temptation, grace leads us to walk by the Spirit so that we will not carry out the deeds of the flesh. The Spirit who turned our hearts from idols to know and serve the true and living God continues at work in our lives causing us to die more and more to sin and live more and more to righteousness. As children of the living God, we enjoy the full rights of sons and daughters. Our Father in heaven is disciplining us, directing and protecting us, working all things for our good that we might grow into the image of his Son in knowledge, righteousness, and holiness.

Drawing Near

Read Revelation 19:1-10
"Salvation and glory and power belong to our God..."

- For what is God exalted in this heavenly scene?
- What picture are we given of those gathered around God?
- How would you describe the atmosphere of worship?

Walk through these various snapshots of heavenly worship, lingering, rejoicing and joining in the chorus of praise. Pray that God will give you a greater awareness of the schemes and intentions of the devil who would rob God of His glory. Pray that God will strengthen you to stand firm against the lure of the kingdom from which you have been delivered.

Reaching Out

The Lord God of hosts reigns in power and victory for His people and against His foes. Pray for each of your contacts by name that God would: 1) cause them to fear Him and so to praise Him, to rejoice in Him, to be glad and to give Him glory; and 2) grant to them in His great mercy and grace the reward of Christ.

List three ways you can keep the fire of love burning for God and neighbor that has been stoked in your time in CHOP.

Enemy Profile

"...from darkness to light and from the power of Satan to God" (Acts 26:15-18)

Pray aware that Satan acts in the power of the darkness of sin and unbelief. Pray against efforts to obscure the glory of God, to dim the light of truth, and to blind them to their need for Christ.

Mutual Support

Pray for yourself and your CHOP co-laborers that you will move out in witness confident of the reality and power of the gospel.

Prayer Journal

Week	Against Satan's tactic of deception, God gives us his Word and Spirit that we might discern between truth and error. By the standard of that Word, which is truth, the devil's lies are exposed. Instead of being dispirited in the struggle and frustrations of the fight, we are filled with the Spirit, bringing the Word of God to dwell in us richly. We have solid ground on which to stand and firm footing from which to fight. And so readied for battle by the energy of his grace, we move out in the valor of humility that knows, trusts and depends on the God who is at work in and through us for his mission of salvation.
Twelve	
∽	
Day	
Six	

Drawing Near

Read Revelation 21:1-8
"I will be his God and he will be my son."

- How is a reconciled relationship with God prominent in this vision of the new heaven and the new earth?
- What promises does the future hold for you as God's child?
- With the prospect of the day of suffering and toil being over forever, what should that prompt in you as long it is still today—the day of salvation?

Respond from your heart to this picture painted by God that has you by His side—forever. Pray that God will use you, even you, just as He will and when and where, until His blessed face you see, His rest, His joy, His glory share. ('Be Still My Soul' by Katharine von Schlegel)

Reaching Out

In the kingdom of God the curse has been removed and blessings have been poured out by the King on all His subjects, who will reign with Him forever and ever. Pray for each of your contacts by name that God would: 1) work in them a spiritual thirst that longs after God and that leads to Jesus Christ, that they might take of the free gift of the water of life; and 2) display to their souls Jesus Christ, who redeemed His people from the curse of the law by becoming a curse for them, that all of the blessings of God might come to them, and they shall dwell in the house of the Lord forever.

Pray that God would incline your heart to others around you, bringing Christ to them in word and deed and bringing them to Christ in prayer.

Enemy Profile

"...the devil who had deceived them was thrown into the lack of fire..." (Rev. 20:10-15)

Pray aware that Satan will receive punishment from God, as will his followers. Pray for the mercy of God to snatch your contacts from the flames and bring them into the kingdom of the Son He loves.

Mutual Support

Pray for yourself and your CHOP co-laborers as you conclude your time together that God would continue the work He has begun in you, making you an instrument prepared for the work of witness.

Supplements

Supplement A

Introduction to a Personal Testimony

A personal testimony speaks to what God did in your heart to bring the salvation of His Son home to roost, where by His Spirit God claims you as His own, having been purchased for Him by the Son. A personal testimony is one way we can communicate the gospel in a real and relevant way to our hearers.

Paul provides us with the example of his personal testimony when he appeared before King Agrippa in Acts 26. Paul's story of conversion falls into three sections: 1) his life before Christ, 2) his encounter with Christ, and 3) his new life in service to Christ. Each section of Paul's testimony expresses the theology he lays out in Ephesians 2:1–10, and can be paralleled with one another.

First, in Acts 26:9–11 Paul describes something of his life before his conversion, when he was still dead in sin (cf. Eph. 2: 1–3). He speaks of his zeal as a persecutor of the faith and his efforts in keeping with that zeal. For us, we might ask questions like: How did I live for self rather than for Christ? What fulfilled and motivated me in life?

Paul didn't get into gruesome details as he might have. He didn't try to sensationalize his life before Christ or try to glamorize sin. But he did give the king a good feel for his life in rebellion against the lordship of Christ, in keeping with his bondage to sin.

Perhaps you were raised in a Christian home. You can never remember a day when you did not know and trust Jesus Christ for your salvation. The first section of your story might seem rather anemic to you. What can you say? You can praise God for his early mercies to you. You might describe what it was like to be raised in a covenant home where your parents taught and did things differently than those of your friends. Or, you might describe what you saw in the world around you or wrong ideas to which God alerted you. Even a believer as long as you can remember, you know the struggles of sin that remains in you, much as the Apostle Paul describes in Romans 7. You might express some of these temptations that were particularly strong for you, and for which you give God praise for Christ's imputed righteousness to you.

Remember, that salvation is not by socialization. As with every believer, God worked immediately in your heart. You were born dead in sin and you are alive because of the work of the Holy Spirit to unite you to Jesus Christ. Your testimony may be filled in more by what God your Father tells you in His Word about the days before He caught you up in His grace and adopted you, just as an adopted child might not remember the orphanage from which she was rescued. She would need to be told about it by her father and would relate that to others.

Next, Paul relates the time when he met Jesus Christ on the road to Damascus. In Acts 26:12–18, he tells of how he was going about business as usual, carrying out the agenda of his religious zeal, when Christ came to him. Here he provides some of the details about his encounter with Christ.

What details might you include? If you were knocked to the ground in a dramatic conversion, you would tell the story. For most of us, however, we grow to know. Over time, through different situations and a variety of people we learn more. The sin that seemed delightful becomes repugnant. The guilt of our sin becomes oppressive. The Christ who was only an historical figure starts to become real and beautiful. For this section, we might ask ourselves questions like: What people, events and factors did God use to change my thinking and my opinion about Christ? In what ways did the Spirit convince me of my need for Christ? Was there one thing that I particularly became convicted of against the backdrop of my life before Christ? All this expresses the theology of Ephesians 2:4–9, where by God's grace and power, death gave way to life, darkness to light, works to faith.

The final section of Paul's testimony points to new life in Christ. What does it look like now that I am a citizen of heaven and am seeking first the kingdom of God and His righteousness? Paul in Acts 26:19–23 pointed out that now, instead of fighting against the kingdom of God, he fought for it. He became an advocate for Christ and held a radically new interpretation of Scripture from what he did previously.

Ephesians 2:10 informs us that there will be fruit of salvation by grace through faith. A new lifestyle will characterize us because of the power of the new life at work in us. Here we might ask ourselves: How does my everyday life now reflect God's changing work of grace? How am I different now that I am a child of God? How do I think differently? How are your goals changed?

We want to be careful here not to communicate any sort of contribution we make to our salvation, as though my reformed life contributes to Christ saving work. But at the same time, we want people to know the handiwork of God's grace. Saving faith is fruitful faith and we want people to taste and savor the Savior, to whom belongs all the glory. Faith rooted in God's grace will grow and manifest itself in the fruit of God's grace. The call of discipleship for those with ears to hear is to come and follow Christ.

I can't tell you how many times I have heard people lament their dull or tame testimony of salvation in Christ. They almost would rather have lived a more wretched life so that their testimony would shine brighter and be a more worthy witness. We want to understand that there is no dull testimony. Every account of personal conversion testifies to the resurrection power of God to bring life from death. It speaks of one dead in sin, supernaturally being made alive in Jesus Christ. Every testimony magnifies the grace of God to the undeserving and the love of God to the unlovable. The brightness of a personal testimony is the glory of God in the face of Christ against the blackness of a sinful heart and the bleakness of eternal damnation.

(Adapted from *Warfare Witness*, pages 187-189)

PERSONAL TESTIMONY WORKSHEET
(based on the example of Acts 26:9-23 and the theology of Ephesians 2:1-10)

Chapter 1 "Estranged From Christ" (the backdrop for grace; Acts 26:9-11; Eph. 2:1-3)

- *How did I live for self rather than for Christ?*
- *What fulfilled and motivated me in life?*
- *What did my life look like apart from Christ?*

Chapter 2 "Encounter With Christ" (the blossom of grace; Acts 26:12-18; Eph. 2:4-9)

- *What people, events and factors did God use to bring me to Himself and change my way of thinking?*
- *In what ways did the Spirit convince me of my need for Christ?*
- *What did I learn about Jesus?*

Chapter 3 "Enslaved to Christ" (the willing bondage to grace; Acts 26:19-23; Eph. 2:10)

- *How does my life now reflect God's changing work of grace?*
- *How is my everyday life different now that I belong to God?*
- *How do I think and see things differently?*

Supplement B

Pre-CHOP Preparation

◆ Read through the Outreach Orientation (pages 9-28) and complete the four Basic Training Lessons (pages 29-61).
◆ Partner with one or two others to pray about getting a CHOP started.
◆ Recruit other participants.
◆ Hold an organizational meeting to (1) decide on a meeting place and time and (2) provide a *Community Houses of Prayer Ministry Manual* for each participant. Give assignment for pre-CHOP #1 (see below).
◆ Conduct pre-CHOP group meetings
  ❏ Pre-CHOP #1
     ■ Opening prayer
     ■ Discuss Lesson One, "Life-Sphere Witness" (pp. 32-40)
     ■ Discuss Outreach Orientation, pp. 11-14 (up to the bulleted 'Principles and Precepts')
     ■ Season of prayer for the CHOP ministry and items related to reading and lesson.
     ■ Give lesson and reading for next meeting.
  ❏ Pre-CHOP #2
     ■ Opening prayer
     ■ Discuss Lesson Two, "Strategic Prayer" (pp. 41-46)
     ■ Discuss Outreach Orientation, pp. 14-18 (up to 'Weekly Meeting')
     ■ Season of prayer the CHOP ministry and items related to reading and lesson.
     ■ Give lesson and reading for next meeting.
  ❏ Pre-CHOP #3
     ■ Opening prayer
     ■ Discuss Lesson Three, "Spiritual Renewal" (pp. 47-54)
     ■ Discuss Outreach Orientation, pp. 18-20 (up to 'Daily Prayer')
     ■ Season of prayer the CHOP ministry and items related to reading and lesson.

- ■ Give lesson and reading for next meeting.
- ❏ Pre-CHOP #4
    - ■ Opening prayer
    - ■ Discuss Lesson Four, "Spiritual Warfare" (pp. 55-61)
    - ■ Discuss Outreach Orientation, pp. 20-28
    - ■ Season of prayer the CHOP ministry and items related to reading and lesson.
    - ■ Begin Week One, Day One of the Daily Prayer Guide the next day and continuing until next week's meeting.
- ♦ First meeting of the 12-week CHOP. Follow the weekly meeting agenda on page 18. For review, it is useful in the first regular meeting to read aloud the description of each agenda segment before beginning that segment in the meeting. For example, before beginning the agenda segment of adoration, you would read the description of adoration on page 18 and provide additional instruction or answer any questions the group may have. The same would be done for each of the agenda segments for this first meeting.

Supplement C

Conversational Transitions

- "What do you believe about God?"
- "Who do you think Jesus was?"
- Share a Scripture from a sermon or study and discuss.
- "Do you think there's more to life?"
- Share an example of God working in your own life.
- Share an answer to prayer.
- "Do you ever read the Bible? How does it affect you?"
- Ask them to read a passage of the Bible and discuss it together.
- Speak Scripture into their lives. E.g., If you see worry, share Matt. 6: 34.
- Talk about God, sin, Jesus, salvation.
- "What does it mean that God is love? Do you think there's more to God?"
- "What is your religious background? What effect does it have on your life today?"
- "Do you ever pray? What about? How do you think God uses prayer?"
- "What's your biggest objection to religion?"
- "How is sin different from making mistakes?"
- "When you think of God what comes to mind?"
- Turn to a passage of the Bible and ask, 'Why do you think God says...?' (e.g., Ps. 51:4; John 3:16; Acts 17:29; Is. 55:1-3; Prov. 14:12; Prov. 1:6; Rom. 9:22-23; John 14:6)
- "Why do you think God gave the Ten Commandments?"
- "Why do you think Jesus had to die?"
- Ask permission: 'Could we sit down for a few minutes and I can share a summary of the Bible's main message?'
- Give a God-oriented description of your occupation or hobby instead of just a title or name. E.g., 'I study God's world' vs. 'scientist.'
- Discuss Christian terms and fill with biblical definition.
- "Why do you think the Bible says efforts to reform ourselves don't help in restoring our relationship with God?"

- "What do you think happens when you die?"
- Select a psalm for them to turn to in distress as entry to the Bible.
- Offer to pray for people. Be quick to listen, slow to speak, quick to pray.
- Look at a film or current event from a Christian perspective, not just in moral terms but also in respect to a biblical worldview.
- "What does it mean to be a 'Christian'?"

Supplement D

Post-CHOP Follow Up

- Pray for your contacts using the pattern of the Lord's Prayer from Matthew 6:9-13.
- Follow up with them periodically to explore for evidences of God's handiwork of grace and to offer encouragement and prayer.
- Partner with one of your CHOP group members to pray for you and to hold each other accountable in outreach.
- Make witness for Christ part of your daily prayer life and agenda.
- Use the *CHOP Ministry Manual* on your own.
- Transfer your devotional practices learned in CHOP to your regular devotional times.
- Redraw your life-sphere map every month or two.
- Pull together and lead another CHOP group.
- Think more about 'evangeliving' versus evangelism.
- Continue to review and practice your personal testimony and presentation of the gospel.
- Keep the fires of witness stoked through reading books on the subject.

As you read your Bible with an eye to how God has blessed you so abundantly in Christ, give thought and prayer to how you can 'pass it on,' comforting others with the comfort of the gospel you received from the grace of God.

Supplement E

Introduction to a Gospel Presentation

In presenting the gospel, the good news of freedom in Jesus Christ, all of us as Christ's ambassadors need to be prepared to explain it. We need to be able to lay out a logical outline, ready with supporting Scripture, perhaps buttressed with examples and illustrations. The gospel is logical. The *reason* for the gospel is not logical in that God set his love on the unlovable. God's grace is illogical. There is a disconnect between what we deserve in our sin at the hands of God's justice and the outpouring of his grace. In his mercy, God does not give us what we deserve. In his grace, he gives us what we do not deserve. While grace is gloriously illogical, the gospel is thoroughly logical, flowing from one truth to another, each 'since' leading to a 'therefore.' Our responsibility as ambassadors of Christ is to unfurl that gospel in its logical framework. (Adapted from *Warfare Witness*, page 185)

It is not enough and borders on evangelistic malpractice simply to say to someone, 'You just need to believe in Jesus.' Why should that person believe in Jesus? What is their need? What's so special about Jesus? Isn't the world filled with concession stands offering all sort of religious options, among which is Jesus? Why should anyone pay special attention to the booth you've chosen? What does it mean to 'believe' in Jesus?

We must be prepared to unfold the gospel in relevance and reasonableness. The barrage of questions above is fair and deserves an answer. More than that, the integrity of the gospel demands an answer. The faith to which we call people must rest on a firm foundation. We don't want to shortchange biblical teaching in order to rush to a 'decision for Christ.' Our goal is communication not conversion.

Learning a systematic presentation of the gospel will help you to be confident, even bold, in sharing with others what God has done in Christ. You will be ready to give an explanation for the hope you have.

Although you will be prepared to do so, your goal in learning a formal presentation of the gospel is not necessarily to lay it all out at one sitting or to share it in some formal, stilted manner. Your goal is to be prepared to present, discuss and explain. The amount of information you convey and the rate at which you do so is contingent on the receptivity of the person. Communicate by dialog not diatribe. As we learned earlier, interact with gentleness, respect, patience and careful instruction, in prayerful dependence on the Holy Spirit. Listen intently and compassionately. Feed them to the degree of the opportunity afforded by the Spirit. Pay attention to non-verbal cues to let it go for the time being.

GOD's good news is but one presentation of the gospel. There are many arrangements and approaches out there. It does what any systematic presentation does; it provides an ordered, logical outline of the gospel for sharing with others. The acronym C-A-I-R-O guides you in the logic, as well as associates the message with the Old Testament Exodus from Egypt in which God redeemed His people from the bondage by the blood of the Passover lamb.

You'll note that *GOD's good news* begins with creation. Creation speaks to God's claim on us and His design for us in relation to Him. It also gives a backdrop for the fall, apart from which sin and separation make no sense. The Bible itself gives this backdrop, with the first three chapters of Genesis forming the backdrop for the gracious history of redemption to follow.

GOD's good news also emphasizes repentance. In one sense, a call to faith implies repentance. A person turns from something to follow something else. But repentance is useful in that it makes explicit the need to reject one's own saviorship in deference to Christ and one's one lordship in submission to Christ. It communicates a divesting of self and investing of all salvation capital in the righteousness of Christ alone.

There's also a visual element to *GOD's good news*, if desired. We live in a day where people are accustomed to looking at images dancing on a screen. The six symbols of the presentation can be written on a napkin as you go along, serving as a focal point, or they can be visual markers in your own mind for what you want to communicate.

G O D ' S
good news
a summary of the Bible's message of life

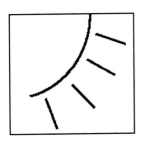
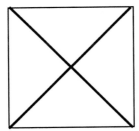
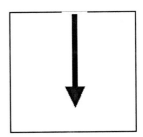

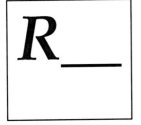

> *"O Lord, you awaken us to delight in your praise,*
> *for you made us for yourself,*
> *and our heart is restless,*
> *until it rests in you."*

That's a quote from Augustine, Bishop of Hippo (A. D. 401) in his book, Confessions. He hits on something basic to being a human being. It involves a relationship with God and a restlessness without Him.

That relationship is what the Bible talks about. It's a subject that reaches to the very core of life.

This little booklet traces the broad strokes of the Bible's message. It addresses the issue of the restlessness, discontentment, loneliness, out-of-whackness, ill-at-easeness, wondering-what-it's-all-aboutness we all face in life.

Please find a quiet spot and spend some time reading what follows. You might even offer a prayer, asking God to help you think through these things. The Bible passages from which these thoughts are drawn are listed in the back.

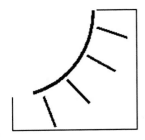

CREATION
(krē-āt, *to bring into being from nothing; to cause to exist*)

God created us for relationship with himself.

The opening chapters of the Bible make one thing abundantly clear: life has everything to do with God. We were created by the eternal God to know and enjoy him. The book of Genesis tells us God made us in his image.

> **God created man in his own image, in the image of God he created him; male and female he created them.[1]**

Being made in the image of God has to do with relationship with God and our very existence in this world. As image bearers of God:

→ *Of all living creatures, we alone have the **ability** for spiritual relationship with God. God has endowed us with a rational intellect and a spiritual capacity to know and relate to him as God. Animals don't pray. We can and do.[2] Prayer reminds us of this ability for relationship.*

→ *Like a reflection in a mirror, an image finds its true **identity** in the one whose image is reflected.[3] As ones created in God's image, we can answer the question, "Who am I?" only in relationship to God.[4]*

→ ***Meaning** in life for us is found in respect to God. He gives direction and purpose in life.[5] The image of God gives us understanding of why we are here and what life is all about.*

The image of God we bear says that we belong to God and that our lives are understood and lived in reference to him[6]. The psalmist declares:

> **Know that the Lord, he is God. It is he who made us and we are his.[7]**

God's design in creation paints a picture of fullness and delight[8] in knowing, loving and serving our Creator.

But something happened…

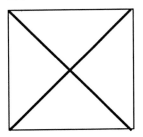

ALIENATION
(ā´-lē-´-ənāt, *to estrange; to make unfriendly or hostile where a relationship formerly existed*)

That relationship with God was broken by sinful rebellion.

The same opening chapters of the Bible that describe personal and intimate relationship of people with their Creator also tell of the tragedy of that relationship being broken by sin.[9] This account is not only an event of history, it the story of every ordinary human being since.[10] Because of those events every one of us is a sinner, in rebellion against God, in violation of his moral law, in danger of eternal punishment, in desperate need of salvation, and deprived of true life. The Bible declares in sweeping terms:

All have sinned and fall short of the glory of God.[11]

Your iniquities have made a separation between you and your God; your sins have hidden his face from you.[12]

This broken relationship with God has left all of us lacking and looking—lacking in the joy and meaning of lives lived with God and looking for some way to fill that void. The image of God in us is now deformed and defaced.

→ Now our lives are characterized by **hollowness**. We have lost that meaning, purpose, and identity that were part of God's design in relationship with him. A void exists in the very center of our beings in our separation from God by sin. Of course, voids seek to be filled; they motivate us to fill them.[13] And so we try to find satisfaction in all sorts of things—career, material possessions, money, educational degrees, appearance, athletics, religious practices and involvement, and the list goes on.

→ We are **helpless** to deal with this sin that grips us. God is holy.[14] He is perfectly and morally pure and cannot tolerate sin.[15] Our predicament is not just our sin but our sinfulness. We sin because we are sinners.[16] We break God's law by what we do[17] and what we fail to do,[18] not only in action,[19] but even in our thoughts.[20] There is nothing we can do, either to make up for the guilt of our past sin or to measure *up to God's unchanging standard of perfection*[21] *that he requires.*

→   *We are left* **hopeless.** *Incapable of dealing with the condition of sin in our lives, we can only expect the punishment of God upon us for our sin.*[22] *Not only are we without God and without hope in this life,*[23] *the gavel of God's judgment on us as violators of his moral law is poised to fall at our physical death.*[24] *God's pronouncement of "guilty" hangs over our heads and his sentence of eternal separation looms before us.*[25]

What a tragic and terrifying predicament! In our separation from God we live an awkward and anemic life in this world, trying to make the best of things, satisfying ourselves with temporary and illusory measures.[26] *We are impotent to deal with the guilt of sin that condemns*[27] *us and the power of sin that enslaves*[28] *us. (What's sin all about? See sin FAQs on page 239)*

But God

Cause for Pause

Do I find emptiness in my own heart and restlessness in my life?

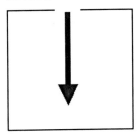

INITIATION

(in-ish´-ē-āt, *to start, to cause the beginning of, take the first step*)

> ## *God took initiative to restore that relationship.*

What is extraordinary is that while we were without God and without hope in the world, separated from our Creator God in our sinfulness, unable to do anything to save ourselves from the judgment of God and consequences of our sinful rebellion, God took initiative. God, the Holy One who was wronged, set his undeserved, unexpected and unmerited love on sinners to save them.[29] Notice God's initiative in saving his people from their sins:

But God shows his love for us in that while we were still sinners...[30]

We... were by nature children of wrath, like the rest of mankind. But God, being rich in mercy, because the great love with which he loved us, even when we were dead in our trespasses...[31]

God took this initiative not because he had to or because he saw anything worthy in us,[32] but only because of his own decision.[33] The Bible expresses this in three ways:

→ *God set his **love** on sinners in spite of their rebellion.[34] In the Bible God's love is an act of his will to save.[35] God's justice is not the opposite of his love. Rather, God's just wrath is the backdrop to his love.[36] If the dark and bleak backdrop of God's wrath is removed, the brilliant glory and warmth of his love is dimmed. The teaching of the Bible is that "God so loved the world that he gave his only Son that whoever believes in him will not perish...[37]" Remove the backdrop (the "perish" of God's wrath), and the love doesn't make any sense.*

→ *To those who deserve condemnation and eternal punishment in satisfaction of his justice, God shows **mercy**.[38] Mercy does not give a person what he or she deserves. Mercy spares justice due. The Bible says, "But when the goodness and loving kindness of God our Savior appeared, he saved us, not because of works done by us in righteousness, but according to his own mercy."[39]*

→ *If mercy does not give us what we do deserve, **grace**[40] gives us what we* *do not deserve. To say that God's salvation (rescue from sin for eternal life) is by grace means that it comes to us as a gift. It is not something we can earn by our efforts at obeying God's law or by trying to make up for the sin we have done in the past. A gift is free, not something we deserve. Salvation does not come by turning over a new leaf or trying harder, but by the grace of God to bestow new life.[41] In fact, the Bible says that "by grace you have been saved through faith. And this is not your own doing; it is the gift of God, not a result of works, so that no one may boast."[42] Faith comes as a gift of new life.*

As sinners we are unlovely and unlovable. Yet, amazingly, God set his love upon sinners such as us to provide salvation and to restore that broken relationship. But that begs the question, how can we as sinners possibly[43] find acceptance and a restored relationship with a holy God who must punish us for our sin?[44]

The only way God could reconcile sinners to himself was...

<hr>

Cause for Pause

Do I suppose God will ignore my sin and accept me because I am basically a good person?

RECONCILIATION
(rek´-ən-sīl, *to bring into harmony; to restore relationship*)

> *God sent his Son to accomplish that restored relationship.*

Everything that was needed for salvation and a restored relationship with God, which was impossible for us, God himself did through the work of his Son, Jesus Christ. The whole Old Testament speaks of God's promise of salvation and presents previews to help us understand what God would do on sinners' behalf. Then in God's perfect timing:

> **But when the fullness of time had come, God sent forth his Son, born of woman, born under the law, to redeem those under the law, so that we might receive adoption as sons.**[45]

What exactly did Jesus do to reconcile sinners to God?

→ Jesus, the eternal Son of God,[46] also became a real human being[47] so that he could stand in the place of sinful human beings as their sinless representative.[48] This is what we celebrate at **Christmas**.[49] As God incarnate (God in full humanity), Jesus came to live a perfect sinless life of flawless obedience[50] that we could not, and to pay the penalty of the lawbreaker that we deserved.[51]

→ In order to satisfy the justice of a holy God, Jesus gave his life as a sacrifice by dying on the cross as a sinless substitute.[52] This is what we celebrate at **Good Friday**. Jesus arrived at the cross with no sin of his own, and so was able to serve as a substitute for sinners. On the cross: (1) Jesus atoned for[53] (paid the price for, removing the guilt) the sins of those he came to save; (2) he suffered the full wrath of God to satisfy the justice[54] of God's holiness; and (3) he made those who were the objects of his wrath[55] acceptable and pleasing to him.[56]

→ And in approval of Jesus' sacrifice[57] and declaration of His victory,[58] God raised Jesus from the dead. This is what we celebrate at **Easter**. His resurrection means that Jesus' mission to redeem (pay the price for) a people for God was a success.[59] God had provided the way for forgiveness of sins, newness of life and reconciliation of sinners with himself, all without compromising his character. In fact, God has provided no *other way. As Jesus says, "I am the way, and the truth and the life. No one comes to the Father except through me."*[60] *The Bible's message of life has to do with Jesus.*

In answer to the question, "Who crucified Christ?" the ultimate answer of the Bible is: "For God so loved the world that he gave his only Son;"[61] "It was the will of the Lord to crush him."[62] God himself accomplished salvation and so all the credit goes to him.

So we see that God did not just ignore the sin of those he decided to save. Nor did he simply issue a pardon. No, God paid for the sins of his people by sending his Son to give his life a ransom[63] for them and to provide the righteousness (perfect obedience) required by his law so that they could be acceptable to Him.[64]

The question now is, how can you be reconciled to God?

Cause for Pause

Have I ever really thought about those Christian holidays in terms of Jesus and what he did that relates to me?

OBLIGATION

(äb´l ə -gāt, *to bind or constrain; to impose a demand or responsibility*)

God calls us to return to him on his terms.

God's good news is that he has accomplished the salvation of sinners through the work of his Son, Jesus Christ. That which we could never do nor would we ever deserve, God did in Christ. He reconciled people to himself, not counting their sins against them.[65] Not that those sins were ignored; quite the contrary, they were met head on in all their ugliness and violence by the Son of God. God has made Jesus Lord and Christ.[66] Our response is to humble ourselves before Jesus as the risen Lord he is.[67] As the Bible says:

> **If you confess with your mouth that Jesus is Lord and believe in your heart that God raised him from the dead, you will be saved. For with the heart one believes and is justified, and with the mouth one confesses and is saved. For the Scripture says, "Everyone who believes in him will not be put to shame."[68]**

God's gracious invitation is to turn to his Son, Jesus Christ, and follow him. What is involved in following Christ? The Bible describes three proper reactions to this Jesus who is Savior of sinners and Lord of life.

→ *We are to* **repent**.*[69] Repentance is not merely being sorry for something. It is turning from our sinful rebellion against God, out of a deep awareness of our sin and sorrow[70] over that sin because it dishonors and displeases God.[71] Repentance (1) turns from any effort to be our own savior, trying to do something to earn salvation; and (2) turns from being our own lord, living our lives independent of God.*

→ *Not only are we to turn from, we are to turn to.[72] We are to turn from self to Jesus Christ.[73] We are to repent and believe on the Lord Jesus Christ. This is what the Bible calls* **"faith."** *Such faith (1) knows the facts (about sin and where salvation is found), (2) admits they are true, and (3) places sole trust and confidence in God's provision for sinners — Jesus Christ.[74] Faith is not wishful thinking, but complete trust in an unseen (that is, spiritual) reality.[75] We are justified (declared 'not guilty') in God's sight not by our efforts at obedience to his law, but by faith in Jesus and his perfect obedience for us.[76]*

→ *Since Jesus is Lord, we are now to live our lives in submission to him.[77] We are to **follow** Jesus as his disciples.[78] We commit our way to him, seeking him and serving him in all our ways[79] because we are his[80]—not that we either earn our acceptance by God or add to the work of Christ. But if God has given us new life to hear the voice of the Shepherd,[81] that new life will result in a new orientation to God.[82] A true change of heart by the Spirit of God will manifest itself in a change of life in new relationship to God.[83]*

God's command is to repent[84] and believe.[85] All of this is God's handiwork of love and power in our lives as he is the one to restore us to relationship with himself, both for this life and the life to come.[86] Perhaps the most amazing thing is this: the relationship to which God brings us is not just as reconciled sinners but as his own adopted children,[87] heirs of eternal life.[88] While God commands that we turn to Christ, his promise is that all who acknowledge Jesus as the one he claimed to be and believe on (completely put my confidence, trust, reliance and expectation in; not just believe in his existence but put personal trust in) him are given the right to become children of God.[89]

Now what?

Cause for Pause

Do I have confidence before God in what I do or could do, or totally in what Jesus did?

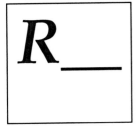

God lays before us one of two responses to his mercy and love.

There you have it, God's good news, the wonderful account of what God did in reconciling sinners to himself. Does this make sense to you? Has the Spirit of God convicted you of your sin, convinced you of your need and of what God has done in his Son to meet that need? Has he brought you to a point where you want to repent of your sin and place your trust in Christ? If so, review what you have read above, and express to God in prayer your understanding, your repentance and your trust in his Son.

Tell God in your own words that you...
   ...admit you are a sinner in rebellion against him
   ...rightfully deserve only his justice and condemnation for your sins
   ...understand what he has done through the perfect life, the sacrificial death and the victorious resurrection of his Son, Jesus Christ
   ...see the beauty of his incredible mercy, amazing grace and glorious love
   ...turn from your sinful rebellion out of a genuine sorrow for your sin because it dishonors and displeases God
   ...place your complete trust, not in who you are or what you did, could do or could ever do, but entirely and exclusively in Jesus Christ and what he did in the place of sinners
   ...desire from this day forward by God's grace to follow Jesus as his disciple — loving, serving, and obeying him in all of your life

How do you complete the "R" in the box above? as "repent"? or, as "rebel"? Those are the only two options.[90] Either we bow our hearts before Jesus, repenting of our rebellion against him, or we remain in our rebellion.[91] The question that confronts us, though, is: "How could we refuse such a great salvation and turn our back on such a loving God?"

Cause for Pause

What happens next?

If you do profess faith in Jesus Christ to save you from your sins and reconcile you to God, remember that it is all of God. And it is in dependence upon God that you will grow and mature as his child. God gives you several ways by which you can grow in your new relationship with him.

- ✓ *Gather with God's people for **worship**[92] and **fellowship**.[93]*
- ✓ *Read the **Bible**[94] to learn of God and his will for your life.*
- ✓ *Approach God continually in **prayer**.[95]*
- ✓ ***Commit**[96] your ways to the Lord.*
- ✓ ***Engage others**[97] for Christ.*

If you are not at the point of turning to Jesus Christ in faith and repentance, continue to study God's Word, the Bible, asking him for his wisdom and help for you to understand this most wonderful and urgent of messages that you might know the joy of your sins forgiven and the peace of a personal relationship with the living God as your Father in heaven.

The Gospel of John is a great book of the Bible to learn about this life that God offers in Jesus. You might read a chapter a day, asking God to show you the beauty of his gift of life. Listen to God's promise from John's Gospel:

> *Now Jesus did many other signs in the presence of the disciples, which are not written in this book; but these are written so that you may believe that Jesus is the Christ, the Son of God, and that by believing you may have life in his name.[98]*

The FAQs about sin

Q: What exactly is sin?
A: Sin is breaking the law of God in thought, word or deed, not doing what God commands or doing what he forbids. Jesus explained that lusting in our hearts was a violation of God's command not to commit adultery, or hating another person breaks God's command not to murder.

Q: But am I a sinner?
A: The Bible says that everyone is a sinner. We sin because we are born sinners. Sin involves not only our acts of disobedience, but includes our hearts that are full of sin and in rebellion against God.

Q: But I know plenty of people worse than I am.
A: God's standard is not other people. His standard is his own perfect holiness. God gives us his moral law to compare ourselves to, not other sinners. Jesus' point in saying that even our thought life breaks God's law makes it clear that every one of us is a sinner and that we cannot be good enough to measure up to God's standard of perfection.

Q: Won't God give me a break if I try to be good and to obey his commandments?
A: Often we think of sin as those big crimes like murder, but the Bible says if we do any wrong we fall short of God's standard of perfection necessary for salvation and so are guilty before him. And God must and will punish eternally all who are guilty.

Q: Isn't that awfully severe? It doesn't seem fair.
A: We don't grasp just how serious sin is because we don't understand just how holy God is. God's judgment on sin is fair and just. Not to punish sin would be to make God unjust.

Q: Can't I just try harder to obey God's commandments?
A: The Bible says even our very best efforts are contaminated by our sinful hearts. Also, God must exact the justice his holiness demands for the sins we have committed. If it was just a matter of trying harder Jesus would not have had to die.

Q: But won't God forgive my sins if I confess them?
A: Yes, but not just because you confess them. God forgives sins only through his provision for sin that meets the demands of his justice and provides what is necessary to be right with Him. Forgiveness of sin comes only from the saving work of Jesus and our resting in that work by faith. (see 1 John 1:8-2:2)

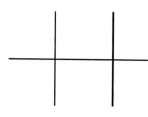

"GOD'S good news" can be a useful tool in your effort to bring the Bible's message of life in Christ to others. It gives you a systematic presentation of the gospel that you can share in part or in whole in relationship with another.

The front depicts six images that correspond to those that follow in unfolding a presentation of the gospel. These six images are to be read in a clockwise fashion, beginning with creation, turning at God's work in the cross and taking a person back to a restored relationship with God through repentance and faith.

These images are useful for a visual point of reference in sketching out the gospel as you sit down with a person. Once you gain their ear, take a piece of paper and sketch the gospel visually and verbally, through diagram and dialog. Start by drawing a horizontal line, intersected by two vertical lines.

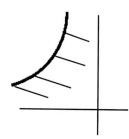

Beginning with the upper left section, draw a sun as representative of creation. Above it, write the **key concept**, "Created," while stating "God created us for relationship with himself."

Genesis 1:27

Ability
Identity
Meaning

CREATED

Explain what it means for us to be made in God's image. Write **focus words** for each point:: first 'ability,' then 'identity' and lastly 'meaning.' At some point, write the reference to a **key Bible text** at the top. Work your way through the diagram to the extent of the person's interest and attention. Try to invite interaction.

On the next page you'll find a completed diagram. Your study of the booklet and the knowledge you've gained over the years in your study of the Bible will help you in what to say.

Be sure to cover all aspects in prayer, knowing it is the Holy Spirit who makes your efforts effective.

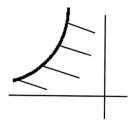

Genesis 1:27	Romans 3:23	Romans 5:8
Ability	*Hollow*	*Love*
Identity	*Helpless*	*Mercy*
Meaning	*Hopeless*	*Grace*
CREATED	*BROKEN*	*INITIATIVE*

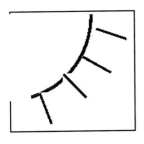 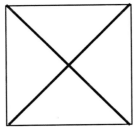 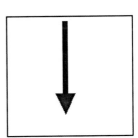

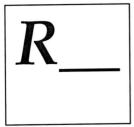  

RESPONSE	*LORD*	*JESUS*
(they fill in 1 of 2 options)	*Repent*	*Christmas*
Repent	*Believe*	*Good Friday*
Rebel	*Follow*	*Easter*
Matthew 12:30	*Romans 10:9-11*	*Galatians 4:4-5*

Endnotes

[1] Genesis 1:27
[2] Psalm 65:2
[3] James 3:9
[4] Psalm 8:1-9
[5] Genesis 1:28; Colossians 3:23-24
[6] Acts 17:29
[7] Psalm 100:3
[8] Psalm 42:1-2
[9] Genesis 2:15-17; Genesis 3:1-12
[10] Romans 5:12-21.
[11] Romans 3:23
[12] Isaiah 59:2
[13] Isaiah 55:1-2
[14] Psalm 99:9
[15] Psalm 5:4-6
[16] Psalm 51:5; Matthew 15:18-19
[17] 1 John 3:4
[18] James 4:17
[19] Matthew 12:36; Romans 13:9
[20] Matthew 5:21-22, 27-28
[21] James 2:10; Isaiah 64:6-7; Romans 3:19-20
[22] John 3:17-18,36; Hebrews 10:31; Isaiah 6:3-5
[23] Ephesians 2:12
[24] Hebrews 9:27
[25] 2 Thessalonians 1:8-10
[26] Ecclesiastes 2:10-11
[27] Romans 3:9,19
[28] Romans 6:16
[29] Genesis 3:14-15
[30] Romans 5:8
[31] Ephesians 2:3-4
[32] Deuteronomy 7:7-8
[33] Ephesians 1:4-5
[34] Romans 9:10-13
[35] Romans 8:28-29
[36] Romans 5:8-9
[37] John 3:16
[38] Romans 9:15-18
[39] Titus 3:4-5
[40] Romans 11:6

41 John 3:3; 1 Corinthians 15:50; Ezekiel 36:26-27
42 Ephesians 2:8-9
43 Luke 18:26-27
44 Romans 3:26
45 Galatians 4:4-5
46 John 1:1; Mark 2:7; John 8:58
47 John 1:14
48 Hebrews 2:14-17
49 Matthew 1:21
50 Hebrews 4:15; Hebrews 5:8-9; Romans 5:19
51 Philippians 2:6-8; Isaiah 53:3-5; Galatians 3:10-13
52 Colossians 1:19-20; Colossians 2:13-14
53 Ephesians 1:7; Hebrews 9:24-28
54 Romans 3:23-26; 1 John 4:9-10
55 Ephesians 2:3-5; Romans 9:22-24
56 Ephesians 1:4-7
57 1 Timothy 3:16
58 1 Corinthians 15:12-20
59 1 Thessalonians 1:9-10
60 John 14:6
61 John 3:16
62 Isaiah 53:10
63 Mark 10:45; John 10:14-15,27
64 Romans 3:19-26; Romans 8:1,31-34
65 2 Corinthians 5:19
66 Acts 2:36
67 Philippians 2:5-11
68 Romans 10:9-11
69 Luke 24:45-47
70 Joel 2:12-13
71 2 Corinthians 7:8-10
72 1 Thessalonians 1:9-10
73 Galatians 2:16
74 Romans 1:16-17; Romans 4:23-25; Romans 10:9-10
75 Hebrews 11:1; 1 Peter 1:3-9
76 Galatians 2:16, 21
77 Luke 9:23-26
78 Luke 9:23-26
79 Proverbs 3:5-7
80 1 Corinthians 6:19-20
81 John 10:25-28

[82] Acts 26:20; James 2:17-18; 1 John 2:3
[83] Titus 2:11-14; Ephesians 2:10
[84] Acts 17:29-30
[85] 1 John 3:23
[86] John 10:10
[87] 1 John 3:1
[88] Romans 8:16-17; Titus 3:3-7
[89] John 1:12-13; John 20:31; Galatians 4:4-5
[90] Matthew 12:30
[91] John 3:36
[92] John 4:23
[93] Hebrews 10:23-25
[94] 2 Timothy 3:14-16
[95] Colossians 4:2
[96] Colossians 2:6-8; 1 Peter 1:14-15; Proverbs 3:5-8
[97] 1 Peter 2:11-12; 1 Peter 3:15
[98] John 20:30-31

To order additional copies of the *Community Houses of Prayer Ministry Manual,* or to get a catalog of other books we publish, contact Deo Volente Publishing.

Phone: (731)824-2919
FAX: (731)-824-2526
Web: www.deovolente.net
email: books@deovolente.net

Printed in the United States
111660LV00005B/14/A